WORLD ECONOMY IN TRANSITION

KENNIKAT PRESS SCHOLARLY REPRINTS
Dr. Ralph Adams Brown, Senior Editor

Series on
ECONOMIC THOUGHT, HISTORY AND CHALLENGE
Under the General Editorial Supervision of
Dr. Sanford D. Gordon
Professor of Economics, State University of New York

WORLD ECONOMY IN TRANSITION

Technology vs. Politics
Laissez Faire vs. Planning
Power vs. Welfare

BY

EUGENE STALEY

KENNIKAT PRESS
Port Washington, N. Y./London

WORLD ECONOMY IN TRANSITION

First published in 1939
Reissued in 1971 by Kennikat Press
Library of Congress Catalog Card No: 76-137961
ISBN 0-8046-1463-6

Manufactured by Taylor Publishing Company Dallas, Texas

KENNIKAT SERIES ON ECONOMIC THOUGHT,
HISTORY AND CHALLENGE

To

Alvah H. and Helen T. Staley

FOREWORD

This report has been prepared under the auspices of the American Coördinating Committee for International Studies for submission to the Twelfth Session of the International Studies Conference to be held at Bergen, Norway, August 27–September 2, 1939. The members of the American Coördinating Committee are:

Henry M. Wriston (Chairman), Francis P. Miller (Secretary), Vera Micheles Dean, Calvin B. Hoover, Halford L. Hoskins, W. W. Lockwood, Jr., Harold S. Quigley, Carl F. Remer, James T. Shotwell and Jacob Viner.

The American Coördinating Committee is the American representative of the International Studies Conference.

The cost of research and publication has been met by a generous grant from the Rockefeller Foundation. The collection of the material and the writing of the report were entrusted to Professor Eugene Staley who is solely responsible for the presentation of facts, arguments, and conclusions. Professor Jacob Viner and Dean Halford L. Hoskins have served as Professor Staley's advisers at the request of the American Coördinating Committee.

AUTHOR'S PREFACE

The general plan of this book is as follows:

Part I ("Technology versus Politics") shows that fundamental technological changes are pushing mankind in the direction of world-wide economic integration and interdependence, but that political tendencies, at least in recent years, have strongly resisted that trend.

Part II ("The Best Use of World Resources") inquires into the meaning for human welfare of the two conflicting tendencies of technology and politics. Modern technology, by lessening the handicaps of distance and by utilizing large markets and wide supply areas, has put into man's hands a powerful instrument for improving his living standards. It would be unfortunate if inability to solve the political problems connected with a world-wide economy should snatch away the productive advantages thus offered by our technicians. The tendency of politics today towards nationalistic exclusiveness in economic life imperils living standards by making production less efficient. It also lays the basis for endless conflicts and wars by making economic opportunity depend on the amount of territory that a particular state controls.

Part III ("Laissez Faire and Planning") explores the consequences for international economic relations and international economic policy that flow from recent changes in the structure of economic organization, particularly from the increased rôle of governments in economic life and from the rise of "totalitarian" economies. It attempts to state the conditions on which a "mixed" system—partly free enterprise, partly control—can operate successfully. This is a relatively untouched field of investigation, but a very important one today.

Part IV ("The Challenge of War") issues a warning. In an era of totalitarian war, preparedness to fight is no longer just a matter of having an army and a navy in readiness. War preparation has a vital effect on general economic policy, and on all of economic life. The economic policies that must be followed where it is necessary to build up military power are often in direct conflict with those that would be best from the point of view of economic welfare. Unless ways can be found to make it unnecessary for nations to rely on their own armed power for security the world economy will be shaped more and more by the economics of power, less and less by the economics of welfare. Chronic waste and recurring crises will make it futile to hope for a long-continued rise in living standards anywhere in the world.

Part V ("Problems of Policy in a Mixed System") seeks to make constructive application of the general principles developed earlier in the book. The last chapter discusses the relation of the United States, in particular, to the world economy.

In the preparation of this study I have incurred obligations of gratitude to so many persons for aid in getting information, for advice, for criticism of preliminary drafts of the manuscript, and for help in other ways, that it seems better to thank them collectively here rather than to try to list them all by name. Special mention should be made, however, of Ralph Hocker and Dr. Karl W. Kapp for aid in research, of Miss Adele Haley for help with the manuscript, and of the Geneva Research Center for coöperation in securing certain information not available here.

EUGENE STALEY

Fletcher School of Law and Diplomacy
April 10, 1939

CONTENTS

PART ONE

TECHNOLOGY VERSUS POLITICS

CHAPTER ONE

THE TREND OF TECHNOLOGY: PLANETARY ECONOMY

IN THE lives of human beings a mile or a kilometer is not just an abstract unit of physical measure. It is a space to be overcome—by travel, by messages, by transporting goods. As man's techniques for overcoming distance improve, the significance to him of a mile or a kilometer changes profoundly. Distances, measured in terms of their meaning for economic life, have been shrinking at an unprecedented rate. Political boundaries, on the other hand, have remained relatively fixed and rigid in terms of physical dimensions—so many miles north and south, so many miles east and west. The result is that boundaries have become more and more narrow from the standpoint of economic activity, and from the standpoint of human living in general.

The Technology of Distance

All economic relations between people in different localities, from the simplest exchange of glass beads against coconuts to the management of branch factories or intricate transactions in finance, rest ultimately on three means of overcoming distance: travel technology, transport technology, and the technology of communication. In a primitive society the ability to travel, to transport, and to communicate depends on the use of human muscles and the unaided human senses. The range of economic contact is therefore narrowly limited. Historically, horses and camels on land, galleys and sailing vessels on the sea, extended the area over which economic relations could fruitfully take place, but once these means of overcoming distance had been invented further progress was slow. For hundreds, in some respects even thousands, of years before the beginning of the nineteenth century there had been little improvement. Julius Cæsar could send a letter practically as fast as Napoleon.[1] Then came advances in the technology of distance that revolutionized all three of the components upon which economic contacts depend. Travel, transport, and communication are still undergoing revolutionary changes today.

Just as we often divide the history of man's early culture into stages according to the tools at his disposal—old stone or paleolithic age, new stone or neolithic age, age of bronze, and the like—so it has been suggested that modern civilization has experienced three technological phases which may be labeled, respectively, "eotechnics," "paleotechnics," and "neotechnics."[2] Eotechnics, or the dawn age of modern technics, stretched roughly from the year 1000 to the latter part of the eighteenth century, and in some respects into the mid-nineteenth century. It was a water-wind-and-wood complex. The express mail coach on land and the perfected sailing vessel on the sea were its highest achievements in the field of travel and transport. Paleotechnics dominated the nineteenth and early twentieth centuries. It was a coal-and-iron complex, and produced the steam railway and

[1] As late as 1834, Sir Robert Peel, called back post-haste from Rome to London by a cabinet crisis, took 13 days for the journey—"just the time allowed to a Roman official seventeen hundred years ago." (Astley J. H. Goodwin, *Communication Has Been Established,* London: Methuen, 1937, p. 214.)

[2] Lewis Mumford, *Technics and Civilization* (New York: Harcourt, Brace, 1934), p. 109 ff. Mumford has enlarged on a classification suggested by Professor Patrick Geddes.

the steamship. Neotechnics, of which we have been experiencing the beginnings since the late nineteenth century, is an electricity-and-alloy complex. It has produced radio communication, the modern automobile, the Diesel-electric streamlined train, and the airplane.

Chart I compares the size of the world, ***measured in travel-time,*** under each of these three technological epochs, supposing that the best methods available to each epoch were applied over the whole surface of the earth. Within each of the three maps in Chart I the land areas have been proportioned to the travel-time on land for the epoch in question, while the space around the continents represents the sea area of the earth, proportioned to travel-time by sea.

A word is needed on the speeds used in this chart to represent the best consistent performance of each of the three technological epochs. The land speed of 10 miles an hour for eotechnics is that of the best mail-coach routes in England in the 1830's.[3] Travel speeds on the Continent, even in the more progressive countries and on the main roads, were only about half as fast.[4] In the United States about 1800 it took four days in the best season to go by stage from Boston to New York, not much over 200 miles. On the sea, the full possibilities of eotechnics were not attained until the 1840's and 1850's, when the famous American clipper ships were still holding their own against the competition of early steam navigation. From a list of "Best Passages across the Atlantic" [5] it appears that fast runs of 13 to 14 days eastward

[3] James Wilson Hyde, *The Royal Mail, Its Curiosities and Romance* (New York: Harper and Bros., 1885), p. 51.

[4] About 1812 twenty-four hours of travel without rest at night but with allowance for reharnessing time would cover some 150 kilometers (90 miles) according to studies made by Hossinger for his isochrone map referred to later in this chapter (Chart IV).

[5] Basil Lubbock, *The Western Ocean Packets* (Glasgow: James Brown and Son, 1925), Appendix V.

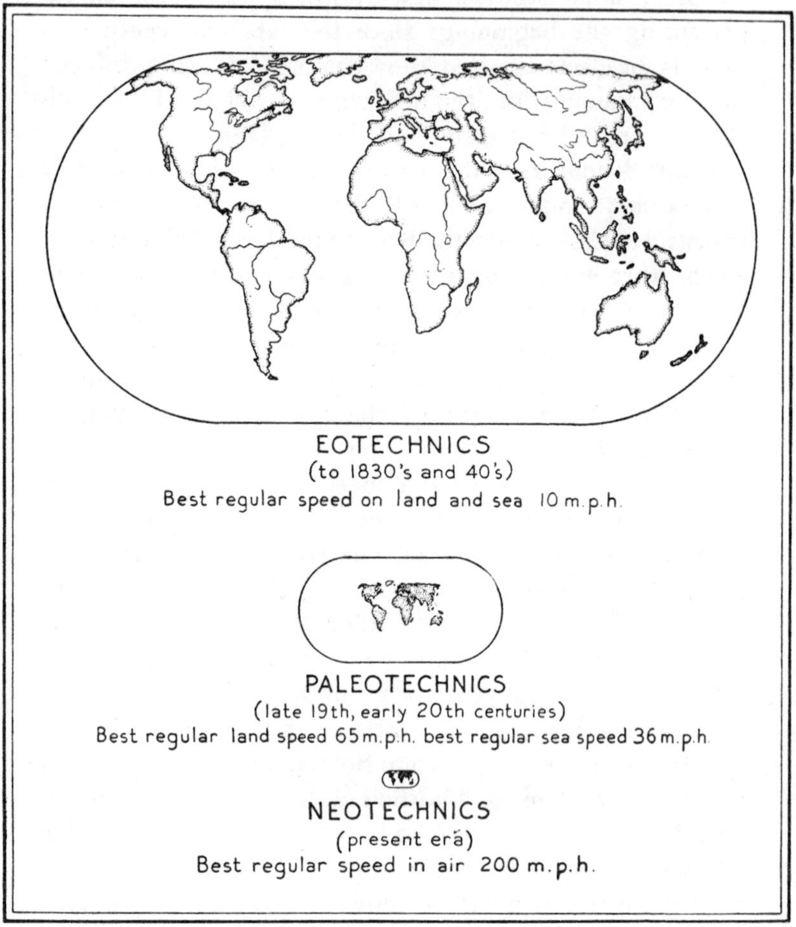

CHART I
TECHNICAL PROGRESS IN TRAVEL TIME

Size of the world, supposing best travel technology in each epoch were applied over the whole surface of the earth and 17 to 19 days westward were common enough to be recorded every year or two, or even several times in some years. If we take 15 days as an average over the distance from New York to Liverpool the speed works out at almost exactly 240 miles a day or 10 miles an hour. The land speed of 65 miles an hour, used to represent the achievements of paleotechnics, is based on what is believed to be the fastest scheduled run for a steam train over a long distance: that of the London and North Eastern Railway "Coronation" over the 392 miles between London and Edinburgh.[6] The steamship speed of 36 miles (land miles) an hour is the average of the best eastward passage and the best westward passage made by the "Queen Mary."[7] It is a puzzle what speed to accept for the neotechnic era. The possibilities of present known methods in aviation have obviously not yet been exploited to the full. A conservative figure of 200 miles an hour—nearly attained already in scheduled passenger flights and clearly attainable—has been used for the chart. According to newspaper reports, experiments are now under way with passenger planes designed to fly at 300 miles an hour in the sub-stratosphere.

Chart I really *understates* the shrinkage of the world brought about by travel technology in the last century and a quarter. It takes no account, for example, of the growth of a network of roads and railroads and airplane routes that is nearly world-wide, so that the best methods of travel in our age are available over much more of the earth's surface than were the best methods of previous

[6] The "Hiawatha" of the Chicago, Milwaukee, St. Paul and Pacific averages 63 miles an hour between Chicago and St. Paul; the "Detroit Arrow" of the Pennsylvania Railroad runs on a 62-mile-an-hour schedule between Chicago and Detroit; the "Coronation Scot" makes 62 miles an hour between London and Glasgow. These are all on the basis of over-all time. (Information supplied by Associated British and Irish Railways, Inc., and by *Railway Age*.)

[7] Information supplied by the Cunard White Star Line.

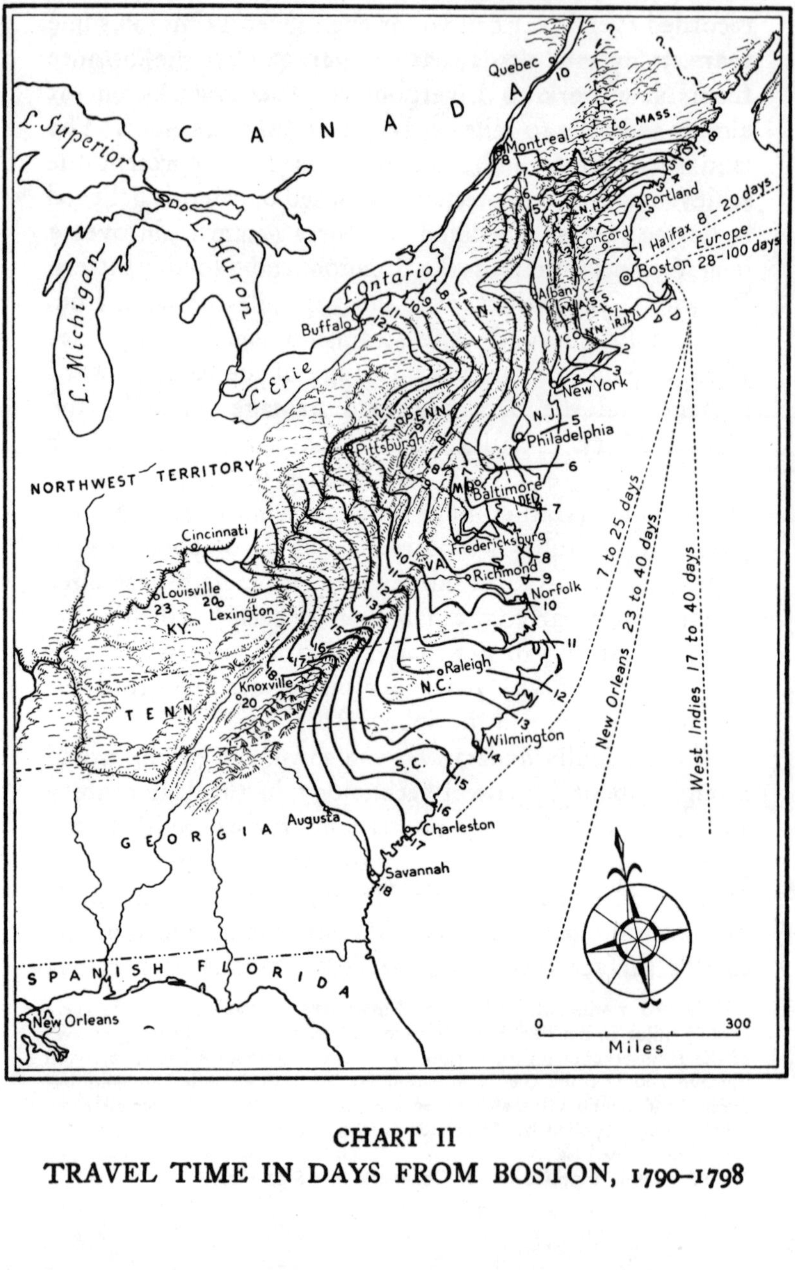

CHART II

TRAVEL TIME IN DAYS FROM BOSTON, 1790–1798

ages. Only in England, for example, could one expect to average 10 miles an hour overland in the 1830's, and then on only a few roads. Today the latest improvements in air travel quickly affect schedules around the globe, and for special purposes an airplane can be detached from its regular route to reach ordinarily inaccessible places—something impossible for a stage coach or a railroad train.

Let us turn to more concrete comparisons. Chart II is an isochrone (equal-time) map centered on Boston.[8] It shows the number of days of travel required in the 1790's to reach various points by the fastest regularly scheduled means of public transportation (where available). It is based on authentic data gathered from the stage-coach advertisements in contemporary newspapers and from specifications published by the young United States Post Office when calling for bids on the transport of mails. For travel conditions in the more remote regions memoirs and travel books had to be relied upon. The lines on the map connect points that could be reached in one day, two days, three days, and so on, under the best conditions, assuming perfect connections.[9] Thus, the time from Boston to New York is shown as four days, but this was possible only in good weather. In winter, or over the

[8] Both Charts II and III are based on the work of Mr. Huntington Damon, formerly a student in my seminar at the Fletcher School of Law and Diplomacy, now on the staff of International House, New York. I am grateful to him for permission to use the charts in this book. Besides the original research done by Mr. Damon, valuable technical aid has been supplied by Dr. Erwin Raisz, Instructor in Cartography at the Institute of Geographical Exploration, Harvard University.

[9] For the time required to reach backwoods points the isochrone lines are not reliable. In particular, they probably make too little allowance for mountain barriers and other topographic features that slowed travel in certain directions more than others. It would be necessary to have elaborate curves and kinks in the lines to show such conditions accurately, but the information available is not detailed enough for that purpose. The map is fairly reliable as regards the main centers of population.

muddy roads of spring, the same journey took a week or longer.

Chart III shows travel-time from the same starting point in the spring of 1938, again by the fastest regularly scheduled means of public transportation under the best conditions, assuming perfect connections.[10] It is based on the published time-tables of air and steamship and railway services. The time-distances on this chart, therefore, are not those of a Howard Hughes, but those available to any citizen able to travel and to pay the fare by scheduled, public transportation. In fact, anyone wishing to go to the farthest cities on the chart (Melbourne and Wellington) in the 15 days indicated has a choice of routes—either westward over the Pacific with Pan-American Airways (one flight a week at present), or eastward by steamship and then on to the East Indies and beyond by either Imperial Airways or Royal Dutch Airways (a total of six departures a week). It should be added that this chart will be out of date soon, perhaps before it is published. The travel-times shown allow 5 days to cross the North Atlantic by steamship, but that ocean will shortly be spanned by passenger airways, as is the Pacific already. Furthermore, when night flying becomes economically feasible (it is technically feasible, but raises costs of operation by necessitating changes of crew en route) most of the present long-distance air schedules can be cut in half.

In the 1790's Pittsburgh and Raleigh were 11 days distant from Boston, the same as Mandalay and Irkutsk now. Hong Kong, Moscow, Port Said, and Istanbul are as close today as Baltimore and Utica used to be—that is, 7 days of travel. It formerly took at least 18 days of strenuous journeying by stage to reach Savannah (7 to

[10] A comment similar to that in the preceding note applies to this chart as well. It should be read only for the principal centers of population.

CHART III

TRAVEL TIME IN DAYS
FROM BOSTON
1938

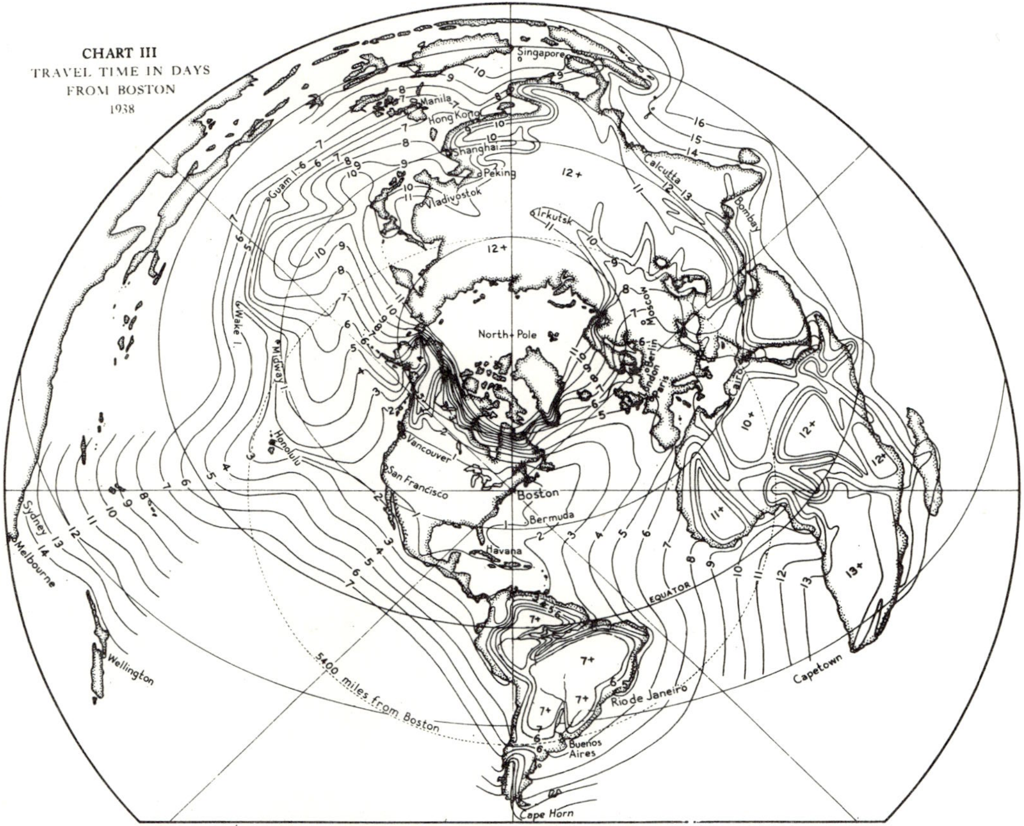

25 days by sea, depending on the winds, if there happened to be a sailing). Today any important city on the globe can be reached within 15 days, and that by means far more comfortable than the old stagecoach. The world is now actually smaller, measured in travel-time, than were the thirteen original states that united to inaugurate George Washington as president in 1789—just 150 years ago.

As it was impracticable to show many place names on the maps, some other comparisons of Charts II and III may be interesting, and they are given in the following table.

TRAVEL TIME-DISTANCE FROM BOSTON

1790's		*1938*
Worcester, Providence, Portsmouth	1 day	Bermuda, Haiti, Mexico City, San Francisco, Vancouver
Portland, Brattleboro, Vt., Hartford	2 days	Panama, Caracas, Honolulu
New York, Albany, Burlington, Vt.	4 days	Pernambuco, Wake Island
Philadelphia, Atlantic City, Schenectady, St. Albans, Bar Harbor, Me.	5 days	London, Paris, Rio de Janeiro, Santiago, Guam
Reading, Wilmington, Lake Champlain	6 days	Manila, Berlin, Riga, Rome, Bucharest, Buenos Aires, Valdivia, Behring Straits
Baltimore, Bangor, Me., Harrisburg, Utica	7 days	Hong Kong, Moscow, Port Said, Istanbul
Richmond, Altoona, Syracuse	9 days	Cape Horn, Peking, Gondo Koro (Uganda)
Raleigh, Lynchburg, Pittsburgh, Rochester	11 days	Mandalay, Irkutsk, Zanzibar, Singapore

1790's		*1938*
	13 days	Cape Town, Lake Baikal
	15 days	Melbourne, Wellington
Charleston	17 days	
Savannah	18 days	
Cincinnati	19 days	
Knoxville, Lexington, Ky.	20 days	
(by sea) West Indies	17-40 days	
(by sea) New Orleans	23-40 days	
(by sea) Europe	28-100 days	

The special properties of the base-map used in Chart III make clear some very interesting results that are likely to come from future developments in travel technology. The projection used is one that shows accurately the direction and the air-line distance from the central point (Cambridge, metropolitan Boston) to any point on the map.[11] Suppose that it becomes possible to fly long distances in the stratosphere or sub-stratosphere, above storm clouds, so that air-line routes can regularly be taken over seas and over the Polar regions. The circle passing near Buenos Aires on the map encloses those points within a radius of 5,400 miles from the northeastern United States. Note that Irkutsk in Siberia is not much

[11] This projection, technically known as the "oblique azimuthal equidistant," is so drawn that the straight-line distance from the center point is exact to any point on the map. However, as one moves towards the circumference circular distortion becomes great, with the result that distances in any direction except straight out from the center are highly deceiving. This distortion occurs because the map is constructed around a central point (in this case Boston), and the method of construction represents the antipodal point (a point in the South Pacific) as a circle which is the circumference of the map. The projection was prepared at the Harvard Institute of Geographical Exploration and is kindly made available by Dr. Erwin Raisz.

farther than Buenos Aires. All of Europe is closer. The circle passes through the Caspian Sea, runs near Palestine, crosses Africa from Cairo to the mouth of the Niger. A similar circle centered on San Francisco, as can be verified on a globe, would include Tokyo, most of Manchuria, and one end of Lake Baikal. Now, 5,400 miles is 18 hours' flying time at 300 miles an hour. That is, passengers could embark at 6 P.M. and arrive the next morning before noon. Is 300 miles an hour an improbable passenger transport speed within twenty-five years? Racing planes and warplanes easily exceed that speed now, while "huge, sleek, streamlined air-liners, carrying from 10 to 21 passengers . . . today fly faster, stay in the air longer, and support greater loads than the racing and record-breaking airplanes developed right after the World War." [12] Under the conditions that the technology of distance will establish in the future, to what area will the Good Neighbor policy apply, and what will happen to "regional understandings" like the Monroe Doctrine?

Finally, Chart IV shows time-distances for personal travel in Europe at about 1812.[13] Strenuous journeying from Berlin would bring the traveler in 5 days to Vienna, in 10 days to northern Italy, in 15 days to the frontier of Spain. Twenty days were sufficient to reach northern Africa, but not parts of Russia or Spain, and it took 30 days to get to the Caspian Sea. Just as the whole world

[12] The world record for airplane speed began at 30 miles an hour with Orville Wright's flight in 1903, stood at 126 miles an hour in 1913, 162 miles an hour in 1919, 222 miles an hour in 1922, and 440 miles an hour from 1934 to 1938. (*The Gulf Aviation Atlas,* fifth edition, published by the Gulf Oil Corporation, Pittsburgh.)

[13] Drawn from Professor Theodor Hossinger's 1812 isochrone map of the world. He also made a 1912 isochrone map of the world. See *Karl Andree's Geographie des Welthandels* (Vienna: L. W. Seidel and Son, 1921 edition), edited by Fr. Heiderich and R. Sieger, Vol. IV, pp. 419-454, and two maps bound in the back cover. Only the 1921 edition contains this material. Used by permission of the publishers, L. W. Seidel and Son, Vienna.

today is smaller in time-size than George Washington's United States, it is also smaller than Napoleon's Europe.

Travel-time is a very important factor in making it economical or uneconomical to carry on many sorts of industrial and trading operations at a distance. A busi-

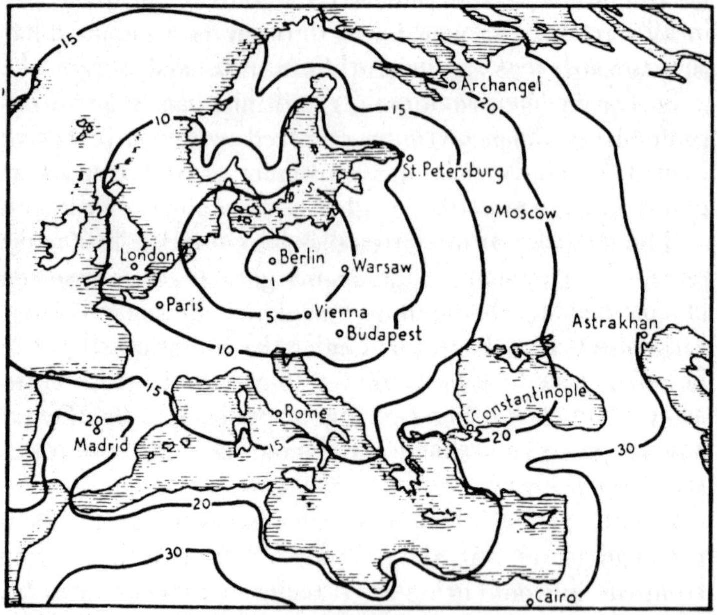

CHART IV
TRAVEL TIME IN DAYS FROM BERLIN
ABOUT 1812

ness corporation in New York can afford to send a highly paid executive to Rio de Janeiro to establish a branch office or to negotiate for materials if he can be back in a few days; but if the trip means months of lost time, the cost becomes prohibitive. A number of branch factories can be opened near to the largest markets, or plants can be set up to do the first processing near to the source of raw materials, regardless of distance in miles, if distance ceases to be a great obstacle to periodic inspection from the home office and if blueprints and reports can flow rapidly back and forth. Rapid circulation of written and printed matter, which goes with rapid travel, makes for greater knowledge of industrial resources and demands in all parts of the world and thus exerts a steady pressure towards making the world one industrial whole.

So far we have dealt mainly with just one of the three components that determine effective economic distance: human travel. Now let us look briefly at the transport of goods and the exchange of messages.

The tendency of modern technology to make the world more of an economic unit shows itself through changes in cost-distance between points formerly remote from each other as well as through changes in time-distance. Shipping cost is a basic factor in determining how far away from each other two places can be and still find it advantageous to exchange products. As improvements in technology lower transport charges, the radius within which any particular factory or mine, or any given farming region, can market its output grows larger. The economic fortunes of ever broader areas are knit together by thousands of ties that could not exist before. The wider market encourages production in larger quantities, the use of specialized machinery, and the splitting up of processes. Modern automatic tools and mass-production methods have become economical not only because population and capital have increased and because engineers have improved the techniques of factory operation, but also because of shrinking transport costs.

There can be no doubt that the effects of advancing technology on the costs of shipping goods have been among the most powerful forces shaping the world's recent economic development. Consider, for example, the transport of bananas from Central America to interior markets in the United States or Europe. Until a few years before 1900 the cost was prohibitive, because spoilage of the fruit was so great. Then refrigerated ships and refrigerated railway cars were introduced. Bananas ceased to be a sailor's curiosity and became an important article of food in the temperate zone. In the tropics they soon formed the basis of a large industry. A whole new network of interdependence was set up between the consuming and the producing areas, involving long-term investments, new shipping lines, new labor and social problems, and international political problems as well. Similarly, the great revolution in transport costs which came with the opening of railways into the central plains region of the United States suddenly made it possible to grow wheat there and to market it economically in Europe—a change which upset the economies of some European countries but, once the transition adjustment had been made, raised their standard of living. At the same time it forged the economic link which now makes the rise of war-scare "autarchy" movements in Europe drive down the price of grain and hogs in Kansas.

Changes in cost-distance are more complex and harder to measure than changes in travel-time.[14] In general, it seems likely that the cost of transporting freight over long distances has not been affected quite so drastically by modern technology as has the speed of personal travel. Nonetheless, the changes have been very important.

[14] The writer has planned some studies designed to measure cost-distance at different epochs. They proceed along lines somewhat similar to those on time-distance for which some results have been given above. The hope is to build up a comprehensive picture of changing world conditions based on careful studies of distance technology—travel, transport, and communication—and to explore some of the social effects of changes that have come about, especially as they affect international relations. This is a project requiring more time and funds for gathering scattered data than have yet been available.

Here are some fragments of information bearing on the way in which transport technology has prepared the way for economic interdependence over large areas.

In 1785 the price of tobacco at various points in Virginia and in Philadelphia varied from 20 to 95 per cent, although each of these places was "the same distance from its ultimate market," so seriously did want of transportation affect commerce.[15] In England at the end of the eighteenth century, the means of communication between London and a market town such as Horsham, less than 50 miles away, were so bad that meat selling at 1¼*d.* per pound in Horsham sold for 8*d.* in London.[16]

In the 1790's, freight in wagons over the bad roads from Philadelphia to Pittsburgh cost from $5 to $10 a hundred pounds (30 to 60 cents per ton-mile), with the result that salt sold at $5 a bushel in Pittsburgh and iron and steel from 15 to 20 cents a pound. Around 1800–1825 long land movements of bulky freight in the United States were said to cost, on the average, about 33½ cents per ton-mile, but were rarely attempted.[17]

In 1837 the following freight rates were reported on various railroads in the United States, in cents per ton-mile: Baltimore and Ohio, 4½; Portsmouth and Roanoke, 8; Boston and Providence, 10; Boston and Lowell, 7; Mohawk and Hudson, 8.[18] The average freight revenue per ton-mile on the principal American railways in 1852 was 3½ cents. This had fallen to 1½ cents by 1880 and

[15] Albert J. Beveridge, *The Life of John Marshall* (Boston and New York: Houghton Mifflin, 1916), Vol. I, Ch. VII, citing contemporary writings.

[16] N. F. Hall, *Measures of a National or International Character for Raising the Standard of Living,* memorandum prepared for the Economic Committee, League of Nations (1938, II.B.4), pp. 54-5.

[17] J. L. Ringwalt, *The Development of Transportation Systems in the United States* (Philadelphia: Railway World Office, 1888), pp. 15, 27.

[18] C. M. Depew, ed., *1795–1895, One Hundred Years of American Commerce* (New York: D. O. Haynes and Co., 1895), I, 28.

reached a low of less than 1 cent in the decade 1900–1910. In the last few decades, the costs of transporting goods by rail or water have ceased to fall.[19]

When the railroad was introduced into Germany, just before the middle of the nineteenth century, it provided transport eight times faster than the existing transportation by wagons, at a cost one-fourth as much.[20]

The greatest revolution in the social significance of miles and kilometers has undoubtedly come in the field of communication. The exchange of messages and transmission of news over long distances used to depend on facilities for personal travel. Charts II and IV show the time required for messages as well as passengers to reach their destinations in former days—except that a dispatch-bearer on horseback might make better time when matters were urgent. Costs were correspondingly high. The electric telegraph, the undersea cable, and the telephone revolutionized all this. More recently the radio has brought a second revolution. Millions of people in the United States have had the experience of hearing words spoken by Chancellor Hitler before they were heard by some of the party-comrades in Hitler's immediate audience—since electric signals travel across oceans before sound waves can reach the back of a large auditorium. Electrical transmission of pictures, handwriting, or any written records has reached the stage where it has almost ceased to be a novelty. Anyone with a telephone may get a rapid connection to nearly any city on the globe, and the rates, while still high, are coming down. To show graphically the shrinkage in the size of the world as measured by speed of communication, using the same system as in Chart I, we should have to draw the latest

[19] Edgar M. Hoover, Jr., *Location Theory and the Shoe and Leather Industries* (Cambridge: Harvard University Press, 1937), pp. 71-3.

[20] Adolf Weber, *Weltwirtschaft* (Munich: Bruckmann, 1932), p. 6.

section of the chart on a microscopic scale and magnify it several hundred-fold to make it large enough to read!

The significance of new communication techniques for world-wide economic relations is clear. Daily arrangements concerning trade and investment and coördination of production plans at points remote from each other can go forward across oceans or continental barriers with a convenience hardly possible as far as the next county not many decades ago, and the cost is not great. The famous banking houses of old used to hire special couriers to bring them the political, financial, and economic information that can be had more fully and more rapidly today in the morning newspapers. Not only speed, but intensity of communication has changed. The tons of personal and business messages carried by the international postal service, which we now take for granted, is something new and revolutionary in the world's history. News, pictures, sounds (to say nothing of sights that will soon be transmitted by television radio) flow constantly to and from far places at the speed of electricity. From the point of view of communication, one may almost speak of the annihilation of distance.

Thus, all three components of economic distance have been shrinking at an astounding rate since the early nineteenth century. Communication has been most affected, long-distance transport costs for heavy goods relatively least. Improvements in personal travel have been intermediate between these two, so that in this sense the charts in this chapter can be regarded as a rough, average index of the extent to which the trite remark that "the world is a small place after all" has become literal truth in modern times. As distances shrink, the area of economic interdependence tends to expand, and today, so far as the technology of distance is concerned, we are well into the era of planetary economy. Still, the ultimate in the technology of travel, transport and communication has certainly not been reached.

Technology and the Wide Market

If it were not for import taxes and quotas, or horsepower and fuel taxes that penalize more powerful cars, or government subsidies to domestic motor industries, American automobiles would outsell all competitors in every country in the world. The reason is that American-made automobiles, quality for quality, *cost less to produce* than do any others, and can be sold to the consumer for less. This fact, vouched for by an executive whose international connections in the motor industry give him accurate knowledge of production costs all over the world,[21] cannot be explained by differences in wage rates, for the American automobile industry pays by far the highest wages. It is only partly due to greater efficiency on the part of American labor and management. The most important factor is the large mass market in the United States. Because American automobile makers have a larger market for their product, they have been able to take more complete advantage of all that modern technology can devise in the way of automatic machinery and highly specialized equipment. Huge machines to stamp out whole sections of a car body in one operation are very expensive, but they bring costs down if the costs of the machines themselves can be spread over a sufficient number of units. A $4,000,000 investment in new dies and tools might be quite impracticable for an output of

21 The Automobile Manufacturers Association of the United States states in its brochure, *The World Buys a Motor Car* (New York, 1938), that the cost (in ounces of gold per pound of vehicle) of manufacturing an automobile of superior quality is 44 per cent less in the United States than in the country with the next lowest cost. That is, what costs the equivalent of $100 to manufacture in the next most economical country costs $56 in the United States.

20,000 units (it would cost $200 a car), but not at all unreasonable for an output of 2,000,000 units (only $2 for each car).

Everyone is familiar with the economies of large-scale or mass production bound up with modern methods of production involving large fixed capital investment. Perhaps the actual extent of the economy resulting from great producing units is somewhat exaggerated in the public mind. Certainly not all of the growth of "big business" has been based on superior technical efficiency. The worship of bigness, and the quest for financial advantages and monopoly power through mergers, have carried some modern business units beyond the point of greatest efficiency. Nevertheless, it seems clear that the "optimum" size of plants and of management units (firms) under the technology of today is considerably larger in most industries than the "optimum" of a century or a half-century ago. This means that wide markets are more necessary today than formerly if the best methods of production known to the age are to be applied.

Compare the number of customers needed to justify the methods of the modern automobile factory or the highly organized electric light bulb factory with the clientele of the wagon-maker and the candle-maker a few decades ago. More specialized machinery, fundamental inventions like interchangeable parts, greater use of scientific technical control in expensive laboratories, revolutionary improvements in methods of accounting, billing, and statistical control of operations—all these things and more have tended towards larger individual plants and larger units of management. A smooth flow of materials, thousands of processes delicately articulated with each other, a high degree of specialization in skills and machinery—these are the characteristics of modern production on which its efficiency rests, and they require a market large enough to take great quantities with great regularity.

It is worth noting, furthermore, that a market wide enough to absorb the output of one or two or several big firms in an industry where the "optimum" size of firm is large may not be wide enough to avoid serious problems of monopoly. Not national markets but world markets are necessary today if there is to be effective competition in some lines where the technology of production gives an advantage in costs to large firms.

The specialized nature of many products of industry in this age also enlarges the market area required for efficient operation. For some industries every person may be a potential customer, for others not one person in a hundred thousand. In general, industries making durable goods and highly specialized producers' goods require a wider market area in order to maintain a steady output at large volume than do those making non-durable consumers' goods. A tomato cannery may reach maximum output for efficient operation by supplying the needs of one small country, or one section of a large country, but for ten-ton automobile trucks with automatic dumping mechanisms the case is different. Or consider the difference between the market area needed to keep an automatic loom busy at making cotton cloth, and the market area needed to justify mass production of automatic looms. It is not so much in the final stages of production as in the earlier stages—making machines to make machines to turn out goods—that modern technology particularly needs world-wide distribution. The United States is a large enough market to put passenger automobiles on a mass production basis, but not electric locomotives. Only a world market will make it possible to produce in quantity rather than to "build" such items as large power-station dynamos and freight ships, or to take maximum advantage of specialized machinery to get lowest per-unit cost for gyroscopic compasses, tabulators and other business machines, automatic color-printing presses, and the more specialized sorts of machine tools.

Technology and the Raw Material Supply Area

In yet another way the technological developments of modern times are pushing towards wider economic interdependence. The raw material needs of modern industry, under the impact of new methods of production and the demands created by new ways of living and working, have increased enormously in variety and volume. For example, more of the world's mineral resources have been used in the last quarter of a century than in all preceding history.[22] The tremendous growth in raw material use has encouraged the development of specialized sources of supply scattered all over the earth, has called forth trade and investment, and in general has widened the area of everyday economic contact.

The real importance of a wide raw material supply area to modern technology is not adequately shown by the values of materials imported and exported, although these total to considerable sums. Many "key" materials that do not bulk large in the trade returns are vital to the efficient working of present-day industry and are also extremely important for further technical progress. Some of these materials, especially many of the minerals, can be had at only a few places on the earth in sufficient quantities and at low enough costs to make them available for industrial uses. Relative freedom of movement for the key materials themselves (governments often recognize

[22] See Eugene Staley, *Raw Materials in Peace and War* (New York: Council on Foreign Relations, 1937), p. 4.

their importance by admitting them at low duty, or with no duty at all) is not enough to meet the needs of modern technology for a wide supply area. The raw material needs of industrial peoples today are among the most insistent forces urging us towards a workable international system, in order that trade in *other* goods may move freely enough to pay for raw material imports, in order that capital may go abroad in reasonable security and carry with it the newest techniques for developing mines and plantations, and in order that established commodity flows may be less imperiled by gluts and scarcities and war panics than they often are nowadays.

To illustrate concretely the key importance of raw materials from widely scattered sources consider the electrical communications industry. There is no industry more "modern," more closely geared to the advances of scientific technology, and no industry, therefore, more likely to be prophetic of what the future trends in use of materials will be if technology is allowed to exert its full influence (unhampered, that is, by political restrictions and needs for wartime self-sufficiency). The raw material needs of a modern telephone system—which may be taken as representative of even further needs created by radio broadcasting, telegraphy, and television—have been described by the world's largest makers of telephone equipment in a booklet that bears a significant title: "From the Far Corners of the Earth." Chart V is reproduced from that booklet.[23] The nice adaptation of materials to function which helps to make the telephone of today, for all its far-flung connections, so much more dependable than the squeaky instrument of the 1890's,

[23] "From the Far Corners of the Earth," published by the Western Electric Company. A 1939 edition is soon to appear, and Chart V is from the revised map prepared for that edition, kindly made available by the Western Electric Company. The description of telephone materials in the text, however, is based on the previous edition, revised in 1935.

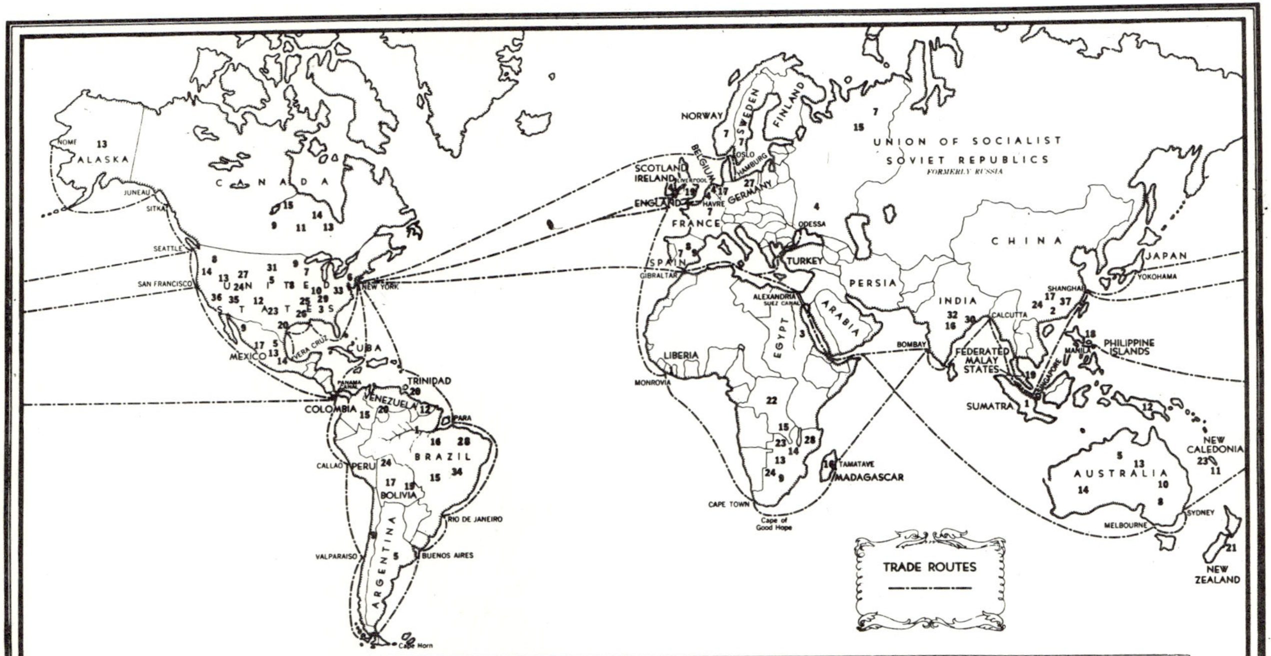

1 Rubber
2 Silk
3 Cotton
4 Flax (linen)
5 Wool
6 Coal
7 Iron
8 Lead
9 Copper
10 Zinc
11 Nickel
12 Aluminum
13 Gold
14 Silver
15 Platinum
16 Mica
17 Antimony
18 Hemp
19 Tin
20 Asphalt
21 Kauri Gum
22 Cobalt
23 Chromium
24 Tungsten
25 Cellulose Acetate
26 Stearin Pitch
27 Magnesium
28 Wax
29 Silicon
30 Shellac
31 Leather
32 Jute
33 Phenol Plastic & Fibre
34 Carnauba wax
35 Gilsonite
36 Clay and Talc
37 Chinawood Oil

CHART V

THE MORE IMPORTANT AND VARIED SOURCES OF SUPPLY OF MATERIALS WHICH MAKE UP A TELEPHONE

would have been impossible had there been no world-wide supply area. Telephones would be either less efficient, or more costly, or both. Here are some of the reasons:

Permanent magnets in receivers are now made of a steel alloy containing *chromium* (Rhodesia, the Soviet Union, South Africa, and Turkey are the principal producers at present) and *cobalt* (from the Belgian Congo and elsewhere), because this special alloy makes the most efficient magnets, smaller and lighter than was possible with former materials.

Iron is alloyed with *nickel* (85 per cent of the world supply comes from the Sudbury district of Canada) to make "permalloy," used in the loading coils on long telephone lines because of its extremely high permeability in weak magnetic fields. The result is a great saving in space and cost. By wrapping a thin tape of this alloy around the *copper* wire beneath the *gutta-percha* insulation on Atlantic telegraph cables, the speed of sending messages has been increased eight-fold. A similar alloy known as "perminvar," in which some of the *nickel* is replaced by *cobalt,* has made submarine telephone cables feasible. They were "only impracticable dreams prior to the discovery of this remarkable alloy."

Antimony, which ordinarily comes half-way round the globe from Hunan, China, though some comes from Belgium and Mexico, is used as an alloy with *lead* to harden the sheath around telephone cables carrying hundreds of wires. The quantity required is only one part antimony to 99 parts lead, but it is very important.

Tin, from Malaya and the East Indies, is used in solder wherever wires are spliced, and in the terminal rooms of central offices where thousands of wires have to be soldered to connectors.

Rubber, also from Malaya and the East Indies, insulates thousands of wires in every telephone exchange, as in electrical apparatus everywhere. *Silk* (Japan) insulates miles of wire in telephone switchboard apparatus and all the connecting wires attached to the telephone instrument in the home, and is used on fine wires for small coils because it fits smoothly and takes up little space. *Cotton, wood-pulp, linen (flax)* provide insulating materials for other purposes.

A varnish-like enamel made from the gum of the *kauri* tree, which grows only in New Zealand, is used on wire for relay coils and similar apparatus because it retains its flexibility and insulating qualities for a very long time. It is mixed with *tung oil* (China), as in the making of fine furniture varnishes.

Manila hemp, grown only in the Philippine Islands, makes a strong, tough paper which is wrapped around the bundles of wire inside a telephone cable. *Jute,* a vegetable fiber grown in India (familiar in the form of burlap bags), serves as an inner wrapping in telephone cables.

Carnauba wax, from the leaves of a palm tree that grows only in northern Brazil, is part of a compound for moisture-proofing certain types of switchboard wires. *Shellac,* given to the world by an insect that drinks the sap of trees in India and Siam, was the answer to a pressing need of the electrical industry for some coating material that would be a non-conductor and an effective bar to dampness. There is scarcely an electrical device, from huge generators to simple switch cabinets, in which it is not used.

The advantage to modern technology of being able to draw upon the largest and most concentrated sources of supply, no matter where located in the world, thereby getting comparatively rare materials at a much lower cost than would otherwise be possible, is well illustrated in *platinum.* Formerly six times the price of gold, platinum could be used in industry only for the most urgent needs—in scientific laboratory apparatus, and the like. Now new supplies from Canada have been added to those from Russia, the price has fallen to about that of gold, and many branches of industry are able to take advantage of platinum's high melting point and high specific gravity, its freedom from oxidation at high temperatures, and its resistance to acids.

> In recent years the electrical industry has greatly increased its purchases of platinum for such purposes as contact points, power switches, thermostats, resistors for high temperatures, electric control apparatus, clocks, etc., and the chemical industries have found it useful for laboratory equipment, for anodes, and as a catalyst in the production of sulphuric, acetic and nitric acid. Rayon firms now use platinum for spinnerets, glass manufacturers use it as a dye, architects employ it as a plating material. The armament industries have developed a considerable demand for platinum and platinum metals for instruments, for reflectors and lamps for search-lights, and for contact points in aeroplane engines . . . The world's absorption of platinum increased from the low level of 75,000 ounces in 1932 to 200,000 ounces in 1934 and to approximately 450,000 ounces in 1937.[24]

Calling a number on a dial telephone may operate as many as 236 relays, each with one or more pairs of contacts that open or close one, two, three or more times. Platinum on these contacts, alloyed with gold and silver, keeps them from wearing out and sticking.

Tungsten is an example of the alloy metals that have become so important to industry in recent years. The best source of supply has been South China, but under the influence of the Far Eastern war other sources are now being tapped more extensively. As always, if smaller or inferior deposits have to be relied upon and the cost of the metal is made greater, industry cannot take quite

[24] *Economist* (London), June 25, 1938.

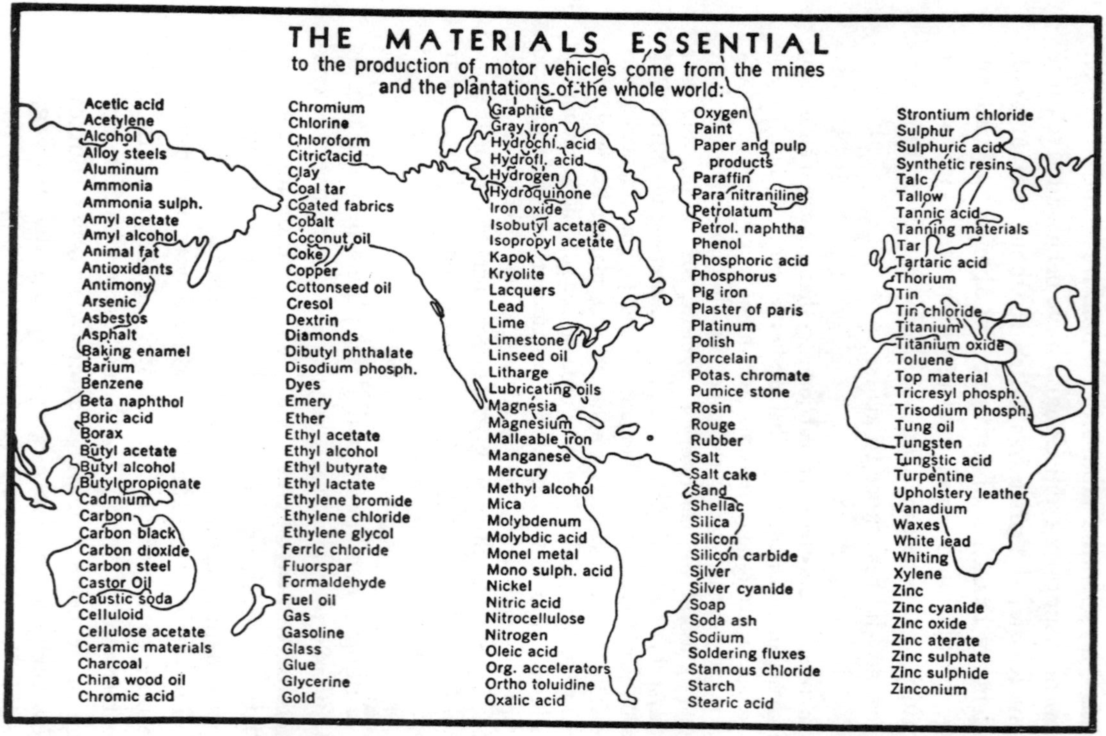

CHART VI

From *The World Buys a Motor Car* (Automobile Manufacturers Association, 1938), by permission.

such full advantage of its special properties. Tungsten is used in making high-speed steel, a steel alloy that retains its cutting edge even when hot and thus makes it possible to run machine tools faster. According to one noted mechanical engineer, high-speed steel allows the production in five days of what would otherwise take six. Thomas A. Edison spent $100,000 and tried more than 6,000 different substances in his search for a more satisfactory filament for the first incandescent electric lamps and finally settled upon the carbonized fiber of a certain kind of Japanese bamboo.[25] Then tungsten superseded carbon filaments, and it has been estimated that if carbon filaments had to be used instead of tungsten in all the electric bulbs of the United States it would cost an additional three billion dollars yearly to maintain the same levels of illumination.[26] Tomorrow a radically new method of electrical illumination may have superseded tungsten in this particular use; but it will continue to be true that the more readily available and the lower the cost of all the varied materials the earth has to offer, the more perfectly can engineers apply the advancing knowledge of science.

Chart VI shows the many raw materials that go into the making of a modern automobile. *Rubber* for tires and *tin* for babbitt metal used in bearings come from the East Indies, *asbestos* for brake linings from Canada, the Soviet Union, and southern Africa, *manganese* (the third indispensable ingredient with coal and iron for most steels) from the Soviet Union, Brazil, and India. New technology in the building industry, substituting metals for wood and stone, has added many of these scattered materials to its list of wants. The leather industry,

[25] George S. Bryan, *Edison, the Man and His Work* (London and New York: Knopf, 1926), pp. 127-38.

[26] Letter to the writer from Mr. Zay Jeffries, Incandescent Lamp Department, General Electric Company.

which, in the days when every village had its tannery, used local hides and tanned them with the aid of bark from nearby oak and hemlock trees, now gathers specialized kinds of hides from afar and uses as its principal tanning agent *quebracho* extract, taken from a tree that grows in South American forests. Chemistry has also made available an inorganic tanning agent based on *chromium,* for which Rhodesia in southern Africa is the chief source of supply. The tractor, a scientific substitute for hay-burning horsepower, has put modern agriculture on a world-wide raw material base, for many of the same materials that go into an automobile are also essential for a tractor, especially the metals. The aviation industry—can we expect it to be less exacting in its raw material demands than the automobile?

It is sometimes asserted that the progress of science in the future will reverse these past trends and make industry less dependent on far-flung sources of raw material supply. Talk of *"Ersatz"* is in the air. Laboratories develop synthetic rubber, substitutes for wool, gasoline from coal. We hear of a new "light metal economy" in which aluminum, obtainable from clay (though it is much more economical to get it from bauxite), will release us from dependence on relatively concentrated iron deposits and thereby—judging from some expressions that have been used—remove the reason for international trade. "The belief that increasing scientific knowledge makes for closer economic interdependence" has recently been characterized as one of the "dogmas almost universally held by progressive thinkers in the nineteenth century" on which "our own perspective should be different."

We need only recall that Chilean saltpeter can now be made out of atmospheric nitrogen, that Cheddar cheese can now be made anywhere, that hospitals are using radio-active sodium prepared from ordinary salt instead of having to import the rare radio-active minerals, that the Channel Islands are no longer regarded as a sufficient guaranty of the genetic credentials of cattle, that we may soon be making most of our machinery of aluminum from the clay of our soils, that we are already beginning to feed our pigs on the disintegration products of wood pulp, to grow several crops of tomatoes a year by tank gardening, and to produce sugar by the agency of bacteria from vegetable waste matter.[27]

Of course, improvements constantly being made in hundreds of branches of technology do not all run one way. In the paragraph quoted above a number of examples, some of them quite valid, have been cited to show how scientific discoveries may bring a shift away from materials that are concentrated in a few places to materials that are widely diffused.[28] On the other hand, many

[27] Lancelot Hogben, "The Creed of a Scientific Humanist," *Nation* (New York), November 12, 1938, p. 508.

[28] It should be pointed out that even "synthetic" products have to be made out of something, and the important question from the point of view of wise resource utilization is what resources, material or human, are thus made to substitute for the ones formerly used. The fixation process for atmospheric nitrogen really substitutes other materials, electric power, and large amounts of fixed capital equipment (not just air) for Chilean saltpeter. This may or may not be good social economy, depending on the relative costs—and, of course, the extent to which the fear of war makes people willing to disregard costs for the sake of having an important munitions industry close at hand. Synthetic rubber is now produced in Germany and elsewhere at a cost said to be about four times the market price of natural rubber. Perhaps the process can be cheapened in the future, but the same amount of effort devoted to improving the rubber tree—using nature's chemical factory instead of starting from scratch—would also yield amazing results. In fact, it is reported that by applying the latest discoveries in scientific bud-grafting and tree selection it is now possible to *quadruple* the output from a well-run plantation in the East Indies within a few years. (See Harold Butler, *Problems of Industry in the East,* I.L.O., Studies and Reports, Series B, No. 29, 1938, pp. 2, 52-3.)

Extracting aluminum from clay would likewise mean substituting larger amounts of electric power and more labor and equipment for a gift of nature—natural bauxite, an ore with a higher aluminum content than clay, but not present in many countries. It will be a long time before aluminum *from clay* will be cheap enough to make it feasible to have "most of our machinery" made from aluminum, unless we use much less machinery or some revolutionary process not now in sight is invented. Cheap aluminum *from bauxite* may well make possible lighter construction of many machines, but the idea that it will reduce the amount of iron used is far-

other discoveries and inventions and the new consumer demands made possible by higher productive power are constantly adding to the need for relatively rare or concentrated materials. If the electric lamp may be regarded as a synthetic candle, the tractor as a synthetic horse, the steamship as a synthetic canoe, and the refrigeration machine as a synthetic ice-house, then it is hard to imagine that the increased raw material demands resulting from similar "synthetics" in the future will be outbalanced by discoveries tending to reduce the need for far-flung raw material sources.

No one doubts that science is finding ways by which a country, under duress, may increase its capacity to resist a siege. But science is also developing new industries and finding new ways to take maximum advantage of special resources that exist in only a few places in the world and which must, for most countries, be imported. If we are interested primarily in the best ways of using resources for human welfare, not in military strategy, the net effect of scientific advance on raw material needs has been to make nations decidedly less self-contained, and there is no reason to expect an early reversal of this trend. After weighing arguments on these points with care, the author sees no reason now to withdraw an earlier statement that "modern industrial civilization rests upon a raw material base that is unavoidably international." [29]

Let us sum up certain general principles that have been illustrated above by concrete instances. (1) New and more powerful techniques made possible by modern

---

fetched, in view of the tremendous advance in the metallurgy of alloys, including steel alloys, which some engineers consider the chief characteristic of the present age in technology. Iron "replaced" wood; but the world uses more wood than ever before. In the future we shall use more aluminum, *and* more iron, *and* more alloy metals.

[29] The first sentence in a report to the International Studies Conference two years ago. *Raw Materials in Peace and War,* p. 3.

science do not simply replace older techniques. They create new ways of life, new needs as well as new means of meeting needs. Nitrogen fixation replacing Chilean saltpeter is not altogether typical of the effect of science on industry. More typical are motor trucks replacing the wagon, electric air-conditioning apparatus replacing the stove in winter and the palm-leaf fan in summer, modern hospitals with intricate apparatus and crowded store-rooms replacing treatment based on home-grown herbs. All these products of scientific technology make us more dependent on raw materials from afar, not less. (2) A striking characteristic of "neotechnic" advance, illustrated by Edison's search for an electric light filament and by the specifications for a modern telephone or motor car, is the more exact fitting of materials to function. This has greatly increased the variety of materials demanded by industry. (3) The most striking examples of world-wide raw material needs are to be found in the newest industries, those most typical of modern scientific technology: electricity, automobiles, aviation. (4) This has been called "the age of alloys." [80] It is certainly an age

[80] "The present science of metallurgy might be described as a process of breaking down complex ores into their constituent elements and then re-combining them into even more complex and elaborate products. In both these processes the relatively minor or so-called "rare metals" are sometimes the most important constituents. Take steel for example. It is not one product but a seemingly infinite series of varieties; metal markets recognize over eight thousand individual types of steel and new varieties are being evolved almost daily. Each of these is specifically intended for a particular purpose, from light alloys for aeroplane engines to powerful, tough steel for armour plate. All these varieties are produced by gradations in the amount or kind of rare metal employed in their manufacture; the inclusion of one-fifth of one per cent of vanadium increases the tensile strength of steel by approximately 50 per cent.

"Because of the small amount of these metals necessary for alloy production and the complexity of the processes in which they are employed, such metals as vanadium, manganese, chromium, titanium, cobalt and molybdenum receive little general attention. But their value in metallurgy makes them of vital importance to all industrial nations." (The Royal Bank of Canada, News Letter of December, 1938.)

of minerals. Yet minerals have to be taken out of the earth's crust where nature has placed them, and no region has a full assortment of minerals, especially of the rarer alloy metals. (5) The mere growth in *size* of industry under modern ways of living has set such huge demands for all sorts of materials that only by concentrating on the best sources can these demands be met at reasonable cost, or even met at all. Nickel, for instance, occurs at various places on the globe, and if it were used only for jewelry it could be had from any of the minor deposits. But only in one region of Canada is it feasible to mine nickel in the huge industrial quantities used today.

The conclusion that a world economic system is the natural and necessary consequence if modern technology is to be given free rein has been strongly stated by Lewis Mumford in *Technics and Civilization.*[31] After observing that some of the characteristic materials of "neotechnic" life, such as glass, copper, and aluminum, exist in great quantities at many places over the earth, he adds that others are exceedingly rare, or are concentrated in a few places. Their availability depends upon world commodity flows.

Both eotechnic and paleotechnic industry could be carried on within the framework of European society: England, Germany, France, the leading countries, had a sufficient supply of wind, wood, water, limestone, coal, iron ore; so did the United States. Under the neotechnic regime their independence and their self-sufficiency are gone. *They must either organize and safeguard and conserve a world-wide basis of supply, or run the risk of going destitute and relapse into a lower and cruder technology.*[32] The basis of the material elements in the new industry is neither national nor continental but planetary: this is equally true, of course, of its technological and scientific heritage. A laboratory in Tokio

[31] Pp. 232-3.
[32] Italics are Mr. Mumford's.

or Calcutta may produce a theory or an invention which will entirely alter the possibilities of life for a fishing community in Norway. Under these conditions, no country and no continent can surround itself with a wall without wrecking the essential, international basis of its technology: so if the neotechnic economy is to survive, it has no other alternative than to organize industry and its polity on a worldwide scale. Isolation and national hostilities are forms of deliberate technological suicide. The geographical distribution of the rare earths and metals by itself almost establishes that fact.

Conclusion

To look back from this point in the twentieth century at the changes in the very foundations of economic (and cultural and political) life wrought by recent advances in the technology of distance leaves one gasping. The world has been shrinking at a rate unprecedented in history, and it continues to shrink. At the same time, new methods of production have been introduced. Large-scale industries and specialized products have put a premium on wide markets. More exact adaptation of materials to function, rising industrial outputs, new inventions creating new wants, have brought a mounting demand for an unimagined variety and volume of raw materials, to be satisfied adequately only by drawing on widely scattered sources. In all these ways our scientists, inventors, and engineers have been pushing us in the direction of a unified, world-wide economic system. The profound consequences of this fact are as yet but dimly seen by citizen and statesman alike.

CHAPTER TWO

THE TREND OF POLITICS: NATIONAL ECONOMY

As TECHNOLOGY advances, the area of economic contact widens. Political boundaries, relatively fixed in terms of miles and kilometers, seem to shrink. This would make no great difference in economic life were all political boundaries like the lines between the different provinces of France, or like state lines and the limits of Congressional districts in the United States. Such boundaries would give rise to no deep-seated economic grievances, no feelings that national life depends on expansion of the political frontier to include raw materials, or markets, or settlement areas for population. Political boundaries do take on economic significance, however, when directly or indirectly they turn the complex flows of production and distribution out of the channels they would otherwise follow en route from primary resources to ultimate consumer—whenever, in other words, political boundaries become economic barriers.

In the Middle Ages the range of each feudal lord's power had economic significance. As goods moved down the most important trade route of Central Europe, the Rhine, toll had to be paid at one "frontier" after another. In the sixteenth century the average appears to have been one customs station every nine miles, and the exactions got to be so high that supplies actually forsook the much more economical highway of the river to go forward by cart over the miserable roads of the time.[1]

The Rhine tolls and the petty regulations of local barons over the movement of traffic have been swept away. But today the national state lays taxes on commerce and forces the flow of production and distribution to conform, not to the pattern that technological conditions might make most economical, but to political wishes. A multitude of measures, enforced at frontiers that are not much farther apart in hours of travel than the limits of baronial authority in the old days, restrict the movements of goods, capital, persons, and knowledge.

Goods and Boundaries

Suppose that we travel over the world with a shipment of ordinary cotton yarn and cotton cloth. In no country could it enter without paying a duty or meeting some kind of restriction at the frontier.[2] In the following places it would find comparatively liberal treatment—that is, a low or moderately high duty levied in a non-discriminatory way on goods from all countries:

British East Africa, Belgian Congo, China, Iraq, Latvia, Morocco, Norway, Siam, Sudan, Sweden, Switzerland, Syria.[3]

In some other countries the cotton yarn and cloth would meet a high protective tariff, but the duties would be non-discriminatory:

1 Eli F. Heckscher, *Mercantilism* (London: Allen and Unwin, 1935), I, 57.

2 The statements in the text were suggested originally by a "Classification of Cotton Yarn and Cloth Markets by Tariff and Monetary Policies in Force, 1935–36" reproduced from a trade journal in *The World Textile Industry, Economic and Social Problems* (I.L.O., 1937, Studies and Reports, Series B, No. 27), pp. 113-14. Serious factual inaccuracies in the "Classification" have been remedied and the data brought more nearly up to date through the helpfulness of the Division of Foreign Tariffs, Henry Chalmers, Chief, U. S. Bureau of Foreign and Domestic Commerce.

3 Note that several of the places on this list are colonial areas held under League of Nations mandates or subject to "open door" treaties (as in the Belgian Congo and Morocco). The absence of tariff discrimination is there a matter of legal obligation rather than liberal trade policy.

Brazil, Colombia, Eire, Japan, Mexico, United Kingdom, Peru, United States, Portugal.

There would be import quotas or import licensing systems, usually combined with a protective tariff, for at least some types of cotton fabric or cotton yarn in:

Belgium, Colombia, France, French West Africa and other French colonies, Greece, Italy, Netherlands, Rumania, Turkey, Venezuela.

Exchange controls, under which payments abroad depend upon government regulations, would hamper imports of cotton yarn and cloth in such countries as:

Argentina, Chile, Denmark, Germany, Greece, Italy, Rumania, Spain, Turkey, Uruguay, Yugoslavia.

Finally, the country of origin would make a difference in the reception encountered in many places. For example, in the Union of South Africa cloth from Japan, China, and the United States would be subject to maximum rates; from the United Kingdom, to minimum rates; from all British Dominions and colonies and most other textile-producing countries, to intermediate rates. There would be more or less complicated preferences for British or British Empire goods in Canada, Australia, New Zealand, Southern Rhodesia, and other parts of the Empire. Colonies, such as Portuguese East Africa, which are not bound by "open door" obligations in treaties or in League mandates, commonly have preferential rates for goods from the mother country. "Gentlemen's agreements" limit Japanese textile shipments to the United States, the Philippine Islands, and Peru, while in India a quota on Japanese cotton piece-goods has been established in exchange for a quota in Japan on Indian raw cotton.[4]

Every state maintains customs officers to levy import

[4] See Chapter VI for further information on restrictions encountered by Japanese goods.

duties on goods entering its territory, and the present height of these duties would amaze protectionists of an older day. The newer quantitative restrictions, however, raise barriers that are even more difficult for goods to scale. Quotas on imports, which limit the quantities of given commodities that may be brought in from abroad or from particular countries, were introduced as emergency measures during the depression. Countries that had not devalued their currencies used them to counteract the effect on their import trade of devaluation elsewhere. The system spread widely and stayed on after the emergency had passed. Quotas have a much more rigid effect on movements of goods than duties alone, for if a great enough differential develops between prices at home and abroad some goods will be imported in spite of high duties, but quotas keep goods out regardless of how much could be saved by buying abroad. Import licensing systems, under which each transaction has to be approved by a department of the government, also spread rapidly during the depression emergency, and remained in many cases after the emergency had passed. Exchange controls, when applied in such a way as to set up government supervision of each separate transaction involving payments abroad, provide the most thoroughgoing check of all on movements of commodities across boundaries.

The newer quantitative forms of restriction and the practice of regulating individual transactions have brought a complexity of administrative details that is itself a barrier to trade with many countries. The difficulties, delays, and costs added to the movement of goods under these conditions can be imagined from the fact that in Germany an entirely new profession has developed and been recognized officially: that of "adviser on exchange control questions." It has also been necessary to create a new bureaucracy to handle the vast mass of detailed permissions that must be given to German enterprises concerned with foreign trade, as well as to take care of the intricate trade negotiations with other governments under the system in force.

Discrimination is a natural tendency under quantitative regulation of trade. Each country bargains with the others for quota allocations and for favorable treatment by the exchange control authorities. Trade negotiations are tied in with the play of political power. Bilateralism tends to develop, reducing not only the total amount of trade but its *quality* as well. Bilateralism may not be an inevitable result of quotas and exchange controls, but the system leans that way. Thus, Yugoslavia in order to sell more grain to Germany has had to take a considerable quantity of relatively unwanted German articles—such as enough aspirin to last ten years—instead of getting money that could be used on the international market for buying, let us say, Australian wool. Under conditions that permit multi-angular trade, Australian wool-growers might complete the circle by buying German manufactured goods. Bilateralism imposes conditions more like primitive barter, as though the watch-maker could sell to the baker only by taking cookies and doughnuts in payment.

There are still other types of restrictions on the movement of goods across national boundaries. These include milling and mixing requirements that specify a certain percentage of domestic-grown grain in flour, excise and other special taxes, import prohibitions and monopolies, administrative regulations of a burdensome kind, including use of alleged sanitary regulations to restrict goods movements, domestic subsidies, currency depreciation, and all sorts of propaganda devices, such as "Buy American," "Buy Italian," and "Buy So-and-So" campaigns. On top of the measures taken by governments and by associations of producers, such factors as monetary uncertainties, the fear of war, and the stagnation of international capital movements also operate to make it more difficult for goods to cross frontiers. The total result is a strong tendency in just the opposite direction from the long-run influence of technology—a tendency to localize trade and production, to confine economic intercourse within the boundaries of nations or empires.

Capital and Boundaries

In the century before the World War large sums of capital moved across national boundaries to speed the development of resources in many countries. The United States, Canada, countries in South America and the Far East, were brought into the world economy in this way. During the 1920's the flow of capital was resumed, along lines that appeared to be continuing the trend that had proved so productive before the War, though later events showed that the foundation of post-war economy was full of cracks and strains which were to endanger the whole structure. The main sources of capital supply during this period were the United States, Great Britain, France and the Netherlands. The flow reached greatest volume in 1927 and 1928, declined in 1929, recovered slightly in 1930, and fell during the depression years to one-tenth [5] of what it had been at the peak. Some of the creditor countries even became net importers of capital as repayments of former loans and sales of securities continued after new issues had practically ceased.

While the decline in the flow of new investment during the depression was mainly the result of purely economic

[5] Measured in gold values. Royal Institute of International Affairs, *The Problem of International Investments* (London: Oxford University Press, 1937), pp. 281-2.

considerations, governments also took measures that worked in the same direction. The British Treasury and the Bank of England, using informal methods of control in the interest of their financial and monetary policy, discouraged new foreign loans—though it is unlikely that there would have been much foreign lending during the depression in any case. In the United States the Johnson Act, approved in April 1934, prohibited the floating of foreign securities in the United States for the benefit of governments of states that had defaulted on war debt payments. Though the Act probably had little immediate effect, since foreign issues had already fallen to negligible amounts, it remains on the statute books as one more barrier to the resumption of capital movements across national boundaries. In every country where exchange control exists, of course, there is an automatic control of outward capital movements. This usually amounts to a prohibition on loans abroad, except for those that sustain a government's program of political or economic "penetration" in some particular area. However, the exchange control countries are not those that would ordinarily have the most capital available for lending abroad; the very fact that they have exchange control usually means that they are financially weak.

On the whole, the indirect rather than the direct effects of political conditions and policies do most to restrain capital flows. Trade barriers, by making repayment of loans or repatriation of earnings on investments more difficult, increase the risk and lessen the amount of international investment. This is especially true of restrictions on trade imposed by countries that are normally creditors.[6] Uncertainty arising from the fear of war is

[6] Some protective barriers, especially when imposed by less-industrialized countries, have the effect of increasing the international flow of investment capital. Branch factories are erected inside the tariff walls by foreign firms, thus substituting a flow of capital for a flow of goods.

a major influence at work to increase the risk of new ventures abroad and also to lessen the amount of investible funds in potential lending countries (by absorbing them for rearmament). "Hot money" flowing from countries with higher interest rates to countries where the earnings on investments are lower demonstrates anew in each recurring crisis how extensively capital nowadays seeks places of safety rather than places where the most productive economic work is to be done. The wariness of investors has been increased by currency instabilities and by experiences with devaluation. Defaults and repudiations and the taking of foreign-owned property without compensation have added to the riskiness of foreign investment, though investment losses in recent years have not by any means been confined to international dealings. Fear that foreign capital will be the mask for foreign political and economic domination has made some of the industrially undeveloped countries, on their side, less receptive to capital from abroad.

The net result of all these restraints, direct and indirect, is that savings and investible funds, though much more plentiful on one side of a political boundary than on the other, move across only sluggishly, or do not move at all, or actually move in the wrong direction.

Persons and Boundaries

Private persons are no longer free to roam at will over the surface of the earth and to settle where they please. New lands made available for European settlement by the Age of Discoveries and by improvements in technology of transport and communication were peopled by the first part of the twentieth century to the point where their inhabitants began to watch immigration carefully, to make crude efforts at selecting those most fit, and to put drastic limitations on the total number to be admitted. The United States, greatest of all destinations for migrants during the past hundred years, enacted its first federal immigration law in 1882, prohibiting the entry of convicts and paupers and mental defectives. This did not limit the volume of immigration, however, and in some years before the War new arrivals numbered more than one million. In 1917 a literacy test was enacted, designed to be restrictive as well as selective, and in 1921 the quota principle appeared for the first time as an emergency measure to stem the tide of migrants that seemed likely to flow in from war-torn Europe. Modified and made permanent by subsequent legislation, the quotas now applied in the United States admit annually a limited number of persons of each nationality, the total for each group being based on the number of inhabitants in the United States in 1920 having that national origin. All the quotas together add up to slightly more than 150,000, but those of some nationalities go unfilled. Persons not eligible for citizenship under United States law (this includes Chinese, Japanese, and other Asiatics) are not admitted as immigrants even under the quotas.[7]

The United States is not alone in its new attitude towards persons wishing to settle within its borders. A similar evolution has recently taken place in the policies of practically all countries that have in the past received considerable numbers of migrants. The depression, with its accompaniment of poverty and unemployment in the principal immigration countries, everywhere served to crystallize and strengthen the demand for barriers against the inflow of new workers.

[7] Marian Schibsby, "Memorandum on the Immigration Policy of the United States," submitted to the International Studies Conference, 10th Session, Paris, June 28–July 3, 1937, by the American Coördinating Committee for International Studies. United States Memorandum No. 6.

Various methods were employed to achieve the one aim of rapidly reducing, if not entirely suppressing, immigration: the control formalities of the general immigration legislation were applied in a more restrictive manner (in the United States from 1930 onwards), or regulations were passed concerning the admission of foreign workers (in France after 1932); the fees for visas were raised (the Argentine in 1931 and 1934); immigrants were required to have a contract of employment or a permit from the authorities (Belgium in 1930, 1931 and 1935; Australia and the Argentine in 1932; Brazil in 1934); legislation for the protection of the labor market fixed (at least in principle) a maximum percentage of foreign workers to be employed (Brazil in 1930, France on August 11th, 1932, Cuba, Rumania and Belgium in 1934, etc.); systems of quotas were introduced as in the United States (South Africa in 1930, Brazil in 1934); in some cases, countries were more or less completely closed to foreign workers (Australia and Canada in 1930, New Zealand in 1931, Germany on February 11th, 1932, Mexico in 1934, etc.). At the same time, a number of legislative and other measures were applied to facilitate or organize the repatriation or expulsion of certain groups of immigrants (United States and France from 1931 or 1932 onwards, Australia in 1933, etc.).[8]

Lately the emigration countries as well have helped to make national boundaries less passable for persons who wish to move their homes. Exchange controls that prohibit taking funds out of the country or put a heavy tax on the property of emigrants, requirements for permits to leave, restrictions on granting of passports, have made it very difficult, if not impossible, for the ordinary citizen of the Soviet Union, Germany, Italy, and some other countries to settle abroad. At the same time, political and economic persecution and terrorism have created a large new tide of involuntary migrants—refugees, forced to seek homes elsewhere despite all barriers.

[8] League of Nations, "Migration Problems," a memorandum from the International Labour Office communicated to the Assembly, the Council, and Members of the League. Geneva, Sept. 9, 1937 (official No. A. 22, 1937. II. B.), p. 5.

Even tourist movements are subjected to strict regulations, some merely inconvenient, others seriously restrictive. Tourist traffic has become an instrument of national policy, to be directed hither and yon in accordance with the economic or political interest of the rulers of the political state. German tourists have found themselves restricted largely to those countries with which Germany had blocked balances in her clearing agreements, because funds could not be obtained for travel elsewhere. In 1935–36 there was an unsuccessful experiment with Switzerland in offsetting German consumption of Swiss scenery against Swiss consumption of German coal. When Italy bought an excess of German goods, the account was partly balanced by directing more tourists towards Italy.[9]

All this is a far cry from the pre-war days when migration was still relatively free and the traveler did not even need a passport for journeys to most "civilized" countries.[10]

Knowledge and Boundaries

Among the most important resources upon which modern economy relies for its productivity are scientific knowledge and industrial techniques. There is not much

[9] League of Nations, *World Economic Survey*, 1935–36, p. 212.

[10] "The present wide-spread use of passports is essentially a post-War development. Except in Russia and Turkey, all Western Europe had eliminated the passport by 1867. France utilized it in 1870, but only for a brief period."

Since the War the passport and visa nuisance has been so notorious that the League of Nations has held two conferences to try to mitigate it, but without astounding success. "According to figures issued by the United States Passport Bureau in 1933 before the United States depreciated the dollar, an American planning to visit Europe and the Near East, stopping in Great Britain, France, Poland, Austria, Hungary, Belgium, Greece, Rumania, Spain, Portugal, Egypt, and Turkey would have to expend $10 for his passport and about $60 for visas." (Graham H. Stuart, *American Diplomatic and Consular Practice,* New York: Appleton-Century, 1936, pp. 407, 416.)

direct restriction on the transfer of knowledge and techniques across boundaries at the present time, though the growth of political tension and military preparations holds alarming prospects for such restrictions in an age of industrialized warfare. Secret processes and "industrial espionage" are likely to become more and more characteristic of such an age, and more and more matters of state concern. Already certain aspects of geology, geography, chemistry, and other sciences have become dangerous political subjects, which it is not everywhere safe to discuss in frankness with a foreigner. An eminent professor of physics at Harvard University has announced that his laboratory will henceforth be closed to visits from citizens of "totalitarian" states. Let present trends continue a little longer, and it will not be hard to envision the day when scientific periodicals will have to be censored before they can be sent across national frontiers, and when delegates to international technical congresses will have to be as tight-lipped as diplomats, for fear of revealing national secrets.

The spread of knowledge and techniques is restricted indirectly by barriers which national boundaries offer to trade, to investment, and to persons. In the long run, these may be much more important than the direct restrictions. The following view, expressed a few years ago, would seem to give too little weight to the connection between the exchange of ideas and general economic exchange:

> Ideas, knowledge, science, hospitality, travel—these are things which should of their nature be international. But let goods be homespun whenever it is reasonably and conveniently possible, and, above all, let finance be primarily national.[11]

Does not this criticism come nearer to the truth?:

[11] J. M. Keynes, "National Self-Sufficiency," *Yale Review,* June, 1933, p. 758.

Since the days of the Phoenicians, economic exchange has always blazed the trail for cultural exchange. When commercial interchange dries up, the exchange of products of the intellect, of science, of art, is bound to be reduced.

Organized exchange of students selected according to political principles, and the swamping of foreign countries with propaganda material, are no substitute for this free and spontaneous intercourse of science and arts that was the pride of bygone days. If goods and finance are homespun, ideas and culture too become homespun. [12]

Exchange not only spreads, but increases, human knowledge. Even in the old days, before the world had become such a small place, fundamental progress in science and the industrial arts generally had an international history. The story of mathematics, that indispensable tool of emerging science, has lately been retold, and the account reads almost like a chronicle of international trade:

The technique of measurement and counting has followed the caravans and galleys of the great trade routes . . . The beginnings of a size language are to be found in the priestly civilizations of Egypt and Sumeria. From these ancient civilizations we see the first-fruits of secular knowledge radiated along the inland trade routes to China and pushing out into and beyond the Mediterranean, where the Semitic peoples are sending forth ships to trade in tin and dyes . . . The scene shifts to Alexandria, the greatest centre of shipping and the mechanical arts in the ancient world . . . Along the trade routes this new arithmetic is brought into Europe by Jewish scholars from the Moorish universities of Spain and by Gentile merchants trading with the Levant . . .[13]

[12] Leo Grebler, "Self-Sufficiency and Imperialism," *Annals of the American Academy of Political and Social Science,* Vol. 198 (July, 1938), p. 7.

[13] Lancelot Hogben, *Mathematics for the Million* (New York: W. W. Norton, 1937), pp. 32-4.

Professor J. B. Condliffe quotes this same passage and adds: "Mediæval trade enabled the Arabs to bring to Europe three revolutionary inventions —the mariner's compass which made exploration possible, gunpowder which destroyed feudalism, and paper which is the basis of universal education. Can we, in this age of aerial navigation, of wireless telegraphy and chemical progress, believe that these processes of scientific advance on an international front have reached their end?

Or take the development of the art and the materials of printing—the basis of modern universal education:

Of all the world's great inventions that of printing is the most cosmopolitan and international. China invented paper and first experimented with block printing and moveable type. Japan produced the earliest block prints that are now extant. Korea first printed with type of metal, cast from a mould. India furnished the language and religion of the earliest block prints. People of Turkish race were among the most important agents in carrying block printing across Asia, and the earliest extant type are in a Turkish tongue. Persia and Egypt are the two lands of the Near East where block printing is known to have been done before it began in Europe. The Arabs were the agents who prepared the way by carrying the making of paper from China to Europe . . . France and Italy were the first countries in Christendom to manufacture paper. As for block printing, and its advent into Europe, Russia's claim to have been the channel rests on the oldest authority, though Italy's claim is equally strong. Germany, Italy, and the Netherlands were the earliest centers of the block printing art. Holland and France, as well as Germany, claim to have experimented with typography. Germany perfected the invention, and from Germany it spread to all the world. Great Britain and the United States, the two countries that to-day do the bulk of the world's printing, are the two great nations of the world that lay no claim to having had a part in the invention, at least in its early stages, and have contented themselves with such later developments as the power press and linotype.[14]

"The human race has made progress towards the good life as long as thought and economic activity were left free to cross national boundaries and creeds. Wherever they were confined by the intolerance of priestcraft or nationalism, progress languished. But now we face a new and more formidable superstition than the world has ever known, the myth of the nation-state, whose priests are as intolerant as those of the Inquisition. The struggle for the rights of the individual against the all-powerful and intolerant nation-state is the most difficult and crucial issue of our generation. It is a struggle that must be waged on many fronts, and the international front is not the least of these. The struggle is not new, but is the modern form of a fight that has been waged over many centuries—the fight for intellectual freedom against intolerant superstition." ("The Value of International Trade," *Economica,* May, 1938, pp. 136-7.)

[14] Thomas F. Carter, *The Invention of Printing in China and Its Spread Westward* (New York: Columbia University Press, 1925), p. 185, quoted in Lewis Mumford, *Technics and Civilization.*

Compare the slow, century-long migration of the basic ideas back of the printing art with the rapid, almost instantaneous spread of new discoveries in science, new ideas in industry, new means of combating disease, in the modern world. Is not the pace at which science and the arts move forward today due in considerable part to the fact that a wider interchange than ever before takes place among laboratories and investigators and inventors and industrial managers all over the world? Yet the most recent developments in world politics raise a serious question as to how long this fruitful interchange can continue on its present scale.

CHAPTER THREE

THE CONFLICT OF TECHNOLOGY AND POLITICS

TECHNOLOGY makes for easier and larger movements of goods, capital, persons and knowledge across boundaries. Politics in recent years has erected walls that restrict all these movements. This reaction of politics can be viewed in part as a defense against a too rapid pace of readjustment called for by a whole succession of startling technological changes. In part, it arises out of immediate causes like the World War, the continued fear of imminent war, and the tendency for economic planning to develop ahead of international government. Whatever the explanation, the result has been to put people to working at cross-purposes in a way that would be comic if it were not fraught with such serious consequences. One set of men build tunnels through mountains, span oceans with steamships and planes, develop better engines for transport, erect industrial enterprises designed to use the products of far places and to distribute goods in far places. Another set of men erect barriers to increase the cost of transporting goods from one place to another, devise new means of keeping capital within national boundaries, restrict the movements of persons, and slow down the interchange of ideas. A conflict rages between technology and politics. Economics, so closely linked to both, has become the major battlefield. Stability and peace will reign in the world economy only when, somehow, the forces on the side of technology and the forces on the side of politics have once more been accommodated to each other.

Probably the first impulse of those who have been brought up in the climate of modern thought would be to predict that in such a struggle technology must win out, at least in the long run. Politics must ultimately adapt itself to the more fundamental forces—though its failure to do so quickly and smoothly enough may cause trouble in the meantime. The economic determinist, who holds that man's methods of production shape his social system, would doubtless support such a view. So might those sociologists who emphasize the role of invention in social change and speak of the "cultural lag" with which social adaptation follows technical innovation. But is there any necessary adjustment of politics to technology? Adjustment there must be, but may it not take place the other way round? In the "Dark Ages" following the collapse of the Roman Empire, technology adjusted itself to politics. The magnificent Roman roads fell into disrepair, the baths and aqueducts and amphitheatres and villas into ruins. Society lapsed back to localism in production and distribution, forgot much of the learning and the technology and the governmental systems of earlier days. Classical knowledge survived in the manuscripts of the monasteries and at length came to a rebirth, but for long it was dormant. There are those who suggest that we are now entering another such period.

We should not underestimate, however, the strength of the forces making for adaptation of politics to modern technology, or the extent of the ground already won by them. The political adjustments over the last few centuries, and particularly in the last century, have been very great indeed. We have already mentioned the abolition of the Rhine tolls and the disappearance of feudalism. In the national unification movements of the mid-nineteenth century one can see the same forces at work. Wider areas of economic and social contact needed wider areas of political organization, and the creation of national states out of the dozens of little principalities that had survived so long in such places as Germany and Italy was a response to that need. Recall the crusade of men like Friedrich List:

> Thirty-eight customs boundaries in Germany cripple commerce . . . as if each limb of a man's body were bound so that the blood could not flow over into another. To trade from Hamburg to Austria or from Berlin to Switzerland you must go through ten states, . . . pay ten transit duties.

The feeling of cramped quarters within the tiny German states a century ago was expressed by a writer of comic verse who composed "A Travel Adventure in Germany"—about a man out for a walk whose hat was carried away by the wind, over the boundary "of course." By the time he had gone for his passport the hat was in a third state, and it led him through a dozen more.[1] In those days nationalism was a movement for unity, though it has since become in large part a movement for disunity, as technology and economics have widened out far beyond national limits.

The surge of imperialism in the late nineteenth and early twentieth centuries may also be regarded as a type of political adjustment to technological and economic changes. It was unsatisfactory, because it led to conflict between rival imperialisms and to injustice for subject peoples, but it was adjustment of a sort. It is strange that technological factors have been so little emphasized in explanations of imperialism. They are more fundamental than factors supposed to derive from the inner soul of "capitalism." To be sure, nineteenth century imperialism

[1] The quotation from List and the lines from the verse by Chr. Fr. Hebbel are in Adolf Weber, *Weltwirtschaft* (Munich: Bruckmann, 1932), pp. 286-7.

was capitalistic, because everything in the nineteenth century was capitalistic. But a socialist or any other kind of society would have developed an outward thrust under the same technical conditions. The new machines for covering distance, the technical superiority of European culture over the cultures of Africa and other continents, which gave both military and economic power, the new techniques in industry which made for efficient use of widespread sources of supply and for large-scale production and distribution—these things would have produced a socialist imperialism if they had suddenly come into being in a socialist rather than a capitalist Europe (supposing that the socialist society would have evolved the same technical devices).

Another of the political adjustments to technological change that surged forward in the nineteenth and twentieth centuries was the rise of internationalism in many forms. The very word "international" was unknown in the English language until 1780, when Jeremy Bentham used it and apologized for introducing a strange term. Even then it was confined to legal studies for years. There was not enough "internationalism" to make that word appear in print until 1877.[2] Today popular usage includes such expressions as "World Court" and "World Bank"—instead of the official names of the institutions referred to—and "world records" are common. Thus language betrays an evolution in habits of thought that has started to go even beyond the "inter-national" stage.[3]

[2] *A New English Dictionary on Historical Principles,* James A. H. Murray, ed. (Oxford: Clarendon Press, 1933).

[3] "Mondial," borrowed from the French, also appears in the great Oxford dictionary cited above, dating from 1919 when English and American journalists were covering the Peace Conference at Paris. A few years ago the writer urged that this adjective form of the French noun for "world" should be used in English to distinguish between "inter-national" in the literal sense of "between or among nations" and world-wide, or cosmopolitan, or planetary.

As for the institutional growth of internationalism, here, with their dates of origin, are some of the thousands of comparatively new organizations that testify to adjustments being made in many fields to the new technology of distance and the new world economy.[4]

Institute of International Law (1873)
International Federation of Journalists (1926)
International Accountants' Association (1910)
International Aeronautic Federation (1905)
International Astronomic Union (1919)
International Bureau of the Universal Postal Union (1875)
International Bureau of Weights and Measures (1875)
International Chamber of Commerce (1920)
International Co-operative Alliance (1895)
International Dental Federation (1900)
International Federation for Town- and Garden-Planning and Garden Cities (1913)
International Federation of Trades Unions (1919)
International Hydrographic Bureau (1921)
International Institute of Agriculture (1905)
International Labour Organization (1919)
International Metaphysical Institute (1919)
International Institute of Refrigeration (1920)
International Red Cross Committee (1863)
International Time Bureau (1919)
International Union Against Tuberculosis (1920)
Inter-Parliamentary Union (1888)
League of Nations (1920)
Permanent Court of Arbitration (1899)
Permanent Court of International Justice (1921)
Permanent Health Organisation of the League of Nations (1923)
World Association for Adult Education (1918)

Thus, the *long-run* trend from the Middle Ages to the twentieth century has been, on the whole, towards social and political and economic adjustments in line with the

[4] League of Nations, *Handbook of International Organizations* (1937. XII. B. 1).

long-run pressure of technology. But in the last few years a sharp reversal of that trend has seemed to be dominant. No one can yet tell whether the march towards world integration will be resumed—the Hull trade agreements program shows that what we have called the trend of "politics" is not unresisted—or whether the course of the world is really set, and has been since 1914, towards a new localism. A clear view of the situation cannot give hope that a permanent reversal towards localism will be a successful adjustment, unless it succeeds by destroying or severely limiting a technology that still presses in the opposite direction. The conflict between technology and politics is already producing symptoms of strain that are only too evident to all.

PART TWO

THE BEST USE OF WORLD RESOURCES

CHAPTER FOUR

ECONOMIC WELFARE AND WORLD ECONOMY

INTELLIGENT economic policy should be based on reasoning that begins with human needs and desires, moves on to the resources available to meet them, and ends with decisions on the best ways of organizing and using the resources. The primary object should be to meet human needs and desires more effectively. Trade or self-sufficiency, private business profits or the growth of state enterprise, are all to be judged by what they contribute to that end; they are not ends themselves. It is from this point of view—the increase of human welfare insofar as economics can contribute to that result—that we now want to examine the conflicting trends revealed in Part I.

The tendency of technology, we have seen, is to make it easier to move resources and goods from place to place over the earth's surface, to increase the economic connections between different regions, and to create a planetary economy. The tendency of politics in recent years has been, by and large, to increase the economic significance of political boundaries, to confine the movements of resources and goods within national or imperial frontiers, and so to counteract the tendency of technology towards world-wide economic integration. For the welfare of the mass of human beings on this earth, which of these trends ought to be encouraged and which resisted? Is it better to foster world economic unity or national economic unity or some compromise between the two?

In what ways would an intelligent social policy seek to guide and shape the forces at work?

In the following chapters of Part II one particular problem will be the center of attention: *How is human welfare affected by greater ease of movement of goods, capital, persons, and knowledge from country to country, and by restrictions on such movements?* For the time being, the discussion concerns basic principles of economic relations between different regions and countries, *regardless of the economic system by which those relations are conducted.* What follows is applicable to the particular method of carrying on exchange by private enterprise and market economy called "capitalism," but it is just as applicable to a socialist or any other conceivable kind of economic environment. That is to say, Part II should not be construed as an argument either for or against free competition, government control, or any particular combination of "laissez faire" and "planning." These questions will be treated later. In the meantime, we are interested in fundamental problems having to do with the exchange of resources between regions under *any* system.

Economic Welfare

Let us start with a definition: Economic welfare is increased when human beings get the goods and services that they need or want [1] in greater abundance, or with less toil and less damage to life values, or with greater regularity and security.

The total production of goods and services can be

[1] It would serve no purpose here to go into questions raised by the fact that people sometimes "need," in the opinion of experts such as nutritionists, things that they are ignorant or stubborn enough not to want, and sometimes want things that they do not need (*e.g.*, under the influence of advertising). For practical purposes in analysis of welfare there are plenty of things that are both needed and wanted.

vastly increased over present levels without going beyond what is reasonably needed in the interest of human welfare. That is true of the world as a whole and of every country in the world. The point is one that no thoughtful person is likely to dispute, and yet there is a strong subconscious tendency among many people to react on international economic issues as though the main problem were to find ways of producing less, or of using more labor to produce the same—to defend ourselves against "over-production" and a "flood of goods." Because such attitudes exist, it is important to see clearly what a great gap there is today between the amounts of various economic goods that people have and the amounts that they "need" as judged by modern standards.

For the first time, under the influence of work being done by the Economic and Financial Organisation of the League of Nations and the International Labour Office, we are getting a picture of actual levels of consumption in the world. These actual levels are being compared with norms agreed upon by experts as essential for healthful and humane living, or, where it is hard to fix objective norms, with customary standards of decency and comfort expressed in the wants of people in different countries. The work has progressed farthest in the field of nutrition, where the Health Organisation of the League, with the collaboration of an international technical committee of eminent physiologists, has provided carefully-worked-out norms for the food required to keep human beings healthy under various conditions.[2] Efforts are now

[2] The so-called London standards, originally established by a committee which met in London in 1935, run in these terms: (1) A minimum of 2,400 net calories are essential for the maintenance of health of the average person not engaged in manual labor in countries of temperate climate. (2) Additional calories must be supplied for various kinds of labor, ranging from 50 calories per hour for light work to 200 or more calories for very heavy work. (3) This number of calories must be supplied by a

being made to extend similar methods into such fields as housing, medical care, clothing, and opportunities for education. So far the results are all in the nature of preliminary surveys—fragmentary and very tentative.

With many reservations and qualifications the International Labour Office has just published some of these preliminary findings on consumption levels in relation to tentative norms. The data come from the United States (a large and highly developed industrial country), from Poland (Eastern European, predominantly agricultural), from India (a large non-industrialized area with 360 million inhabitants and special problems), and from Japan (a modern industrial country of the Far East). More accurate information will be available later, but meanwhile here are a few straws in the wind: [3]

Food

United States. Surveys have been made of diet adequacy at various income levels. Combining the results of these surveys with other surveys of income distribution, it has been found that the following percentages of *native-white, non-relief* families fall within the income groups for which the statistical probability is less than

variety of foodstuffs, including not less than 1 gram of protein a day for each kilogram of body weight. A part of the protein should be of animal origin. (4) A sufficient quantity of minerals and vitamins must be contained in the diet. This requirement is met by the consumption of the so-called protective foods—milk and milk products, eggs and glandular tissues, green-leaf vegetables, fruit, fish, and lean meat.

Deficiencies of modern diets are usually in the protective foods. *Malnutrition* is present even where a person is getting "enough to eat" in the sense of enough energy foods to keep him from "starving." Food budgets must be large enough to allow for the somewhat more expensive products that insure minerals and vitamins. See *Report on the Physiological Bases of Nutrition* (League of Nations, 1936, II.B.4); *Workers' Nutrition and Social Policy* (I.L.O., 1936, Studies and Reports, Series B, No. 23); *Nutrition: Final Report of the Mixed Committee of the League of Nations on the Relation of Nutrition to Health, Agriculture and Economic Policy* (League of Nations, 1937, II.A.13). The last-mentioned report is the most comprehensive.

[3] Compiled from *The Worker's Standard of Living* (I.L.O., 1938, Studies and Reports, Series B, No. 30), Ch. 3.

one chance in two that they had an adequate diet in 1936–37: New York City, 19 per cent of the families, including 29 per cent of the children; Portland (Oregon), 50 per cent of the families, including 61 per cent of the children; Atlanta (Georgia), 17 per cent of the families, including 27 per cent of the children; share-croppers in the Southeast, 83 per cent of the families, including 90 per cent of the children.

Poland. If a very rough estimate be made that food expenditures may constitute half of total expenditures, then about 71 per cent of the families and 79 per cent of the "consumption units" in representative working-class districts of Warsaw in 1935 had incomes insufficient to buy an adequate diet. Cutting the estimate of food costs in half and allowing 65 per cent of family expenditure to go for food, the figures would still be 29 per cent of the families and 38 per cent of the consumption units. (Consumption unit: a technical device used in family budget studies to allow for the fact that children's consumption needs are not equivalent to those of a full-grown person.)

India. Diet surveys in South Indian villages in 1936 showed that practically all the families were below minimum standards except for a few in the higher income groups. From one-third to one-half of the families did not consume *enough* food, let alone a well-balanced diet of protective foods.

Japan. Of a group of employed urban, wage-earning families in 1931–32, so selected as to be above the average of urban families in income, probably 25 per cent, including 32 per cent of the children, had a diet which in the long run would not guarantee either normal working efficiency or health.

Housing

United States. An appraisal of housing in the United States on the basis of four simple tests, which it is generally considered that housing in this era ought to meet (pure supply of running water, indoor flush toilet, bathtub or shower, sewer connection if in built-up area) gives the following estimate: six million non-farm homes and five million farm homes, or over one-third of all the homes of the nation, are definitely sub-standard.

Poland. Taking more than two persons per room as the definition of overcrowding, 45 per cent of all urban dwellings were overcrowded in 1931. Only 10 per cent of all urban dwellings had the following combination of facilities: sewer connections, running water, gas or electricity. Rural housing was worse. Half of the rural dwellings had only one room.

India. In Bombay City 33 per cent of the population live in rooms occupied by more than 5 persons at a time (1931 census).

Japan. A rough estimate is that perhaps 30 per cent of wage earners' households fall below standards considered by a Japanese slum-clearance association to be "minimum."

Education

India. Literacy is the most elementary test of opportunity to "consume" modern knowledge. Among the one-fifth of the human race that inhabits India, over 90 per cent are illiterate—that is, unable to read and write an intelligible letter in any language. In 1936, of the boys of school-going age (6 to 11) who should have been in primary schools, 51 per cent were enrolled, while the percentage among the girls was only 17. Only 27 per cent of the boys and 14 per cent of the girls that were enrolled finished the primary course.

Poland. Illiteracy figures have dropped sharply in Poland since 1921—from 33 per cent in 1921 to 23 per cent in 1931. Of children aged 7 to 13 inclusive, 75 per cent are enrolled in primary schools in eastern Poland (1934–35), over 90 per cent in central and southern districts, and 99 per cent in western districts.

Japan. The problem of illiteracy is said to be practically nonexistent in Japan. As a result of enforcement of compulsory education, school attendance is almost 100 per cent (reported as 99.58 per cent in 1935) among children 6 to 14.

United States. In the United States, likewise, the problem of raising living standards in the field of educational opportunity has passed beyond the elementary levels of literacy and primary education for the great majority of the people. Inequalities still remain, even at the elementary level. The 1930 census showed an illiteracy rate of 16.3 among negroes, against 4.3 per cent for the country as a whole. The President of the National Education Association recently said that 800,000 children between the ages of 7 and 13 are not going to school because schools are not available, or are so located that attendance is practically impossible; that 760,000 children are attending school daily in buildings which have been declared unfit for use; that approximately 3,500,000 youths of high school age are not enrolled in high school; and that more than one-fourth of the teachers of America are receiving a salary less than the wage worked out by a Federal commission as a minimum for unskilled labor.[4]

While there are, of course, serious problems of "economic balance," it seems safe to say that few industries are over-expanded in the absolute sense of being able to produce, at full capacity, more of their products than even a well-housed, well-clothed, and well-nourished group of customers would use. Most industries now suffering from "over-production" and "over-capacity," with resulting unemployment of men and capital, would find their problems disappearing in a world where *other* lines were expanding and where purchasing power of consumers was increasing.

For example, consider the textile industry and the cotton-grower. Data presented to the I.L.O. Conference on the World Textile Industry (1937) showed that if cotton textile consumption all over the world equaled the average per capita consumption of the present population of Western Europe, 40 million bales of cotton a year would have to be supplied *for piece-goods alone.* The present world consumption of cotton for all uses (including large industrial uses) is about 26 million bales. The average inhabitant of the United States in 1929 was using four times more cotton, personally and industrially, than the average inhabitant of the world. He was using ten times more silk, three times more jute, five times more rayon, and an equal amount of wool. Budgetary studies show that small incomes, not lack of needs and wants, limit clothing consumption at present. For instance, in Shanghai in 1929–30 families with a spending power of $796 a year spent four times as much on clothing as families with a spending power of $337—

[4] Address to New England Association of School Superintendents, reported in *Christian Science Monitor,* Nov. 21, 1938.

that is, $84 as over against $21. In Czechoslovakia clothing purchases were three times as high in families with a spending power of about 7,000 crowns per "consumption unit" as in families with a spending power of just under 5,000 crowns. "If ways and means could be found to bring textile commodities within the effective reach of wage workers, salary earners and agricultural workers of the lowest income status, the demand for textile manufactures would swell out far beyond the highest levels attained in 1927–1929." [5]

Now, the author does not intend to suggest that human welfare can be measured by the consumption of goods and services, nor that the purpose of an economic system is to pile up an ever-mounting accumulation of "things." Industry is no social benefit unless it makes possible better human living. Our civilization of the last hundred years has suffered from too little attention to that fact.[6] One of the "goods" of which the production needs to be greatly increased is a by-product: the health and happiness that come from conditions of daily work sanely adjusted to the physiological and psychological make-up of human beings, and from daily surroundings in which individual personality and family life may flourish. To get more of this by-product it would be worth while to sacrifice some of the stream of "things" that flows from the close-packed industrial quarters of our great cities and from bleak mining towns. But the new technical bases of industry ought to make this unnecessary. The advantages of electric power over coal-steam power for decentralized installations, combined with sane city and town and regional planning and the greater pro-

[5] *The World Textile Industry, Economic and Social Problems* (I.L.O., 1937, Studies and Reports, Series B, No. 27), Vol. II, p. 246, and Vol. I, p. 172.

[6] Lewis Mumford's *Technics and Civilization* (New York: Harcourt, Brace, 1934) is worth reading on this point.

ductivity of modern industry based on new techniques and wider access by modern transport to all the varied resources of the world—all these advances should now give us the chance to create much better conditions for good living with little or no sacrifice of efficiency in producing "things."

Another "good" that has a vital place in the standard of living which it ought to be the object of economic policy to raise is carefree time—leisure. This is something quite different, of course, from the forced and anxious idleness of unemployment. It will be convenient in all the discussion that follows to speak as though leisure were a commodity that people might choose to "buy" and consume in larger quantities as growing economic efficiency gives them larger real incomes—and in a very real sense this is true. Leisure is an alternative that may be chosen instead of more goods. In a society where economics serves human welfare carefree time must surely be made available in much larger quantities to the masses of people than in any of our industrial countries today. Along with leisure, there must be a great increase in the services of adult education: training and equipment for the wise use of leisure. To the extent that economics is successful in solving its problems the purely economic side of life can become less and less important to the ordinary man, leaving more place for camaraderie and the pursuit of hobbies, art and religion, and family life. In the words of Mr. Frank H. Knight, "It ought to be the first aim of economic policy to reduce the importance of economic policy in life as a whole." [7] Perhaps

[7] "Social Economic Organization," in the *Syllabus and Selected Readings for the Second-Year Course in the Study of Contemporary Society,* University of Chicago, 1935 edition, p. 127. "It is an exaggeration which may be useful to say that economic goods as a class are predominantly 'necessary' rather than truly valuable. The importance of economic provision is chiefly that of a prerequisite to the enjoyment of the free goods of the world, the beauty of the natural scene, the intercourse of friends in 'aim-

we can even look far ahead with Mr. J. M. Keynes to the day when the age-old "economic problem" of getting a subsistence has ceased to worry the citizen and occupies only the economists, who will then be thought of as "humble, competent people like dentists." [8]

"If wishes were horses, beggars might ride." The economic millennium sketched above will not be brought by hoping for it. In fact, our first problem is to fill deficiencies between actual levels of economic welfare and what enlightened people would accept as reasonable *minimum* standards for good living under modern conditions. That in itself, not to speak of farther goals on beyond, calls for organizing production and distribution so as to make the best use of the world's resources that is possible with existing knowledge.

World Resources

A fundamental fact about world resources is that they are distributed unevenly over the earth. The result is not a mere difference between "haves" and "have-nots." Even as between regions equally rich or equally poor there always exists a difference in the exact make-up of their resources: different *kinds* of resources exist in different relative proportions in any two places on the earth's surface.

The older economists used to classify all resources into three "factors of production": land, labor, and capital. By "land" as a factor of production they meant every-

less' camaraderie, the appreciation and creation of art, discovery of truth and communion with one's own inner being and the Nature of Things. Civilization should look forward to a day when the material product of industrial activity shall become rather its by-product, and its primary significance shall be that of a sphere for creative self-expression and the development of a higher type of individual and of human fellowship."

[8] "Economic Possibilities for Our Grandchildren," in *Essays in Persuasion* (New York: Harcourt, Brace, 1932), p. 373.

thing that we call natural resources. There are thousands of specific kinds of natural resources, "sub-factors" of the general factor "land." There are sunny climates of the kind where grapes grow best, warm wet climates preferred by banana plants, broad plains suitable for machine cultivation of wheat; land favored by location for airfields, for tourist resorts, for market gardening; natural resources in the form of sheltered harbors and navigable rivers or habitats of animals or fish. It is inconceivable that any two regions should have all of these resources in the same relative abundance or scarcity. These are facts of nature to which man must adapt his economic arrangements if he wants to make the best use of resources for human welfare.

Next consider the pattern of distribution of capital equipment and capital funds over the earth. This, unlike the pattern of natural resources, can be changed by man's own actions, given time. But when the problem is to find what manner of using the world's resources will give the greatest economic welfare within the fairly near future, the present arrangement of equipment and the present capacity to accumulate additional surpluses for investment is a fact that must have a large place in our calculations.

The following comparisons of the amount of machinery in use per inhabitant in different countries are extremely revealing as to the variations in equipment that exist in the world. Lacking later figures, 1925 estimates are used. This understates the present position of Japan and the Soviet Union, and other countries that have made rapid industrial progress in recent years, but it does not affect the main point, which is the existence of enormous differences in capital equipment. Taking the amount of machinery per inhabitant in the industrial countries of northwestern Europe as 100, the corresponding index for the United States would be 403. For all of Asia except the Soviet Union and Japan, it would be 1.6 —showing, that is, less than 1/200th as much machinery per person as in the United States. In more detail:

INDEX OF AMOUNT OF MACHINERY IN USE, PER CAPITA, 1925 [9]

(Average for industrial countries of northwestern Europe = 100)

Countries, listed in order of height of index:	
United States	403
Canada	296
United Kingdom, Switzerland, Australia, Germany, New Zealand	200-100
Belgium-Luxembourg, Netherlands, Sweden, Denmark	100-50
Austria, Argentina, France, Norway, Czechoslovakia, Union of South Africa, Chile, Italy, Finland, Hungary, Latvia, Irish Free State	50-25
Japan, Peru, Mexico, Estonia, Uruguay, Spain, Poland, U.S.S.R.	25-10
Egypt, Brazil, Algiers, Colombia, Portugal, Lithuania, Bulgaria, Greece, Yugoslavia, Bolivia, Tunis, Roumania	10-5
French Morocco, Netherlands Indies, Turkey, British India, Siam	5-1
China	1-0

A further fact is that the existing capital equipment of the world is in highly specialized forms, suited to turning out particular products in particular places. What we have to deal with in making the best use of the world's real-capital resources is not some abstraction, easy to manipulate on paper, but a vast accumulation of

[9] Calculated from a table of values of machinery per capita given by Ernst Wagemann, *Struktur und Rhythmus der Weltwirtschaft* (Berlin: Reimar Hobbing, 1931), pp. 406-8. Wagemann's figures are based on a report of the Association of German Machine Building Establishments on the machine industry of the world and relate mainly to 1925.

printing presses, railway tracks, steam engines and electric turbines already installed, mine shafts, fields that have been cleared of stones, irrigation ditches, automatic looms, machines for stamping out rear axles of particular kinds of trucks, specialized warehouses and storage bins, tank cars and refrigerator ships. Even two regions where approximately equal amounts of capital have been invested never contain exactly the same kinds of capital equipment in the same proportions.

To a certain extent (with more or less waste) some kinds of capital equipment can be converted into others. Factories designed to make phonographs might be remodeled to make radio receivers. Railway tracks can be melted up to make ships. But most of the flexibility in capital equipment comes through re-directing the flow of new capital—investing new funds in radio factories, and perhaps failing to repair or replace the phonograph factory as it wears out. Fluid capital, then, in the form of individual or social savings which can be invested in new equipment of almost any desired sort, is a most important resource in a progressive society. The distribution of this resource is also very uneven over the earth. In some areas, like China or India, the people live so near the margin of subsistence that rapid capital accumulation could take place only at a great cost in human deprivation.

Before the World War, the great providers of capital for international investment had been the people of Great Britain, France, Germany, the United States, Holland, Switzerland, and Belgium—in order of total gross foreign investments outstanding in 1914. The United States became the greatest source of capital during and after the War. In the boom years of the 1920's the national income of the country reached 80 billion dollars, and it is estimated that more than a tenth of that income was put into new capital investment—well over 9 billion dollars in some years. Of course, most of this was invested at home, but the net amount of new long-term capital sent abroad in 1926–28 was over one billion dollars a year.[10] This exceeded the rate at which Great Britain had been lending when it was placing half its national savings abroad in the years just before the War,[11] and was considerably larger than the annual amount of new overseas capital supplied in London during the 1920's.[12]

Turning now to human resources, the relative abundance of crude labor power in proportion to other factors of production such as machinery and skilled management and natural resources is obviously much greater in countries like India and China than in countries like England and the United States. But human resources are far from homogeneous. Skilled machinists are much more abundant in the United States than in India. The knack for making fine linens is a special kind of labor resource more plentiful in Belfast than in Detroit or Rio de Janeiro. Managerial skills of certain specialized kinds (*e.g.*, in marine insurance) can be found in London and not in Chicago; others, demanding knowledge of meat packing or farm machinery, are more common in Chicago. The specialized skills connected with laboratory control of production tend to concentrate.

Like capital equipment, special sorts of human abilities can be "produced" by education, training, and ex-

[10] Simon Kuznets, *National Income and Capital Formation, 1919–1935* (New York: National Bureau of Economic Research, 1937), p. 53; National Industrial Conference Board, *The International Financial Position of the United States* (New York, 1929), p. 56.

[11] British foreign investment increased, according to the estimates of Herbert Feis, at a rate of about $900,000,000 a year in 1909–13. (*Europe: The World's Banker, 1870–1914,* New Haven, Yale University Press, for the Council on Foreign Relations, 1930, pp. x, 15.)

[12] *Economist,* November 20, 1937, p. 362, and July 4, 1931, p. 34.

perience. But, also as in the case of capital equipment, the process costs something and takes time. Large fixed investments are represented in the special skills of the expert shoemaker, the designers of women's fashions, the mining engineer, the industrial chemist, the expert farmer, the marine navigator, the bone surgeon, the maker of optical goods, the jewel cutter, the horticulturalist, the architect of bridges, the irrigation engineer. Some of these skills are passed on from father to son or are picked up "naturally" by the young people in a certain community; others require long and expensive training in elaborate institutions of learning. That different regions of the earth will usually have human resources of these types in different degrees of abundance or scarcity is clear.

Finally, there is a human resource not entirely bound to any particular persons, but socially carried, and institutionally preserved and fostered: knowledge, especially the systematic knowledge of science, and industrial techniques based upon it. This resource exists in libraries, in laboratories, in universities and public school systems, in the practices of office and shop and mill, in the traditions of science and the scientific spirit. Important parts of it are in the "atmosphere" of a particular culture. Knowledge of different kinds, techniques of different kinds, are unevenly distributed over the earth today and probably always will be, despite rapid communication, because knowledge is highly specialized.

The whole point of these last few pages has been to make clear that the different sorts of resources which must be combined to make the commonest things are distributed over the earth in such a way that any particular resource is relatively abundant in some places and relatively scarce in others. What is the bearing of this fact on wise use of resources?

The Principle of Social Economy[13]

For the sake of greater economic welfare, the world's human and material resources must be used efficiently, not wastefully. Is efficiency, in the broad social sense of the maximum contribution to welfare, promoted by easier movement of goods, capital, persons, and knowledge from place to place, or is it better to restrict such movements? What is the nature of the social gains and losses, the advantages and difficulties, that may be associated with a lively economic interchange among the different countries of the earth? These are questions to which answers will now be sought on the basis of certain broad principles of efficiency that apply to the use of resources in any society. Details and qualifications concerning the conclusions reached here will, of course, be added throughout the book.

The basic principle of good social housekeeping, of "economizing" in the broadest sense (which means making the most of given resources) is simple enough, and it applies universally, regardless of the type of economic system. *Every good should be produced with that combination of resources which, when withdrawn from other uses, subtracts the least from the total social product. In other words, good social economy calls for meeting each demand with the cheapest possible combination of resources—"cheap" meaning low cost, and cost being measured by the social value*[14] *of the alternative use to*

[13] Readers versed in economic theory will recognize that the analysis in these pages owes much to Pigou's *Economics of Welfare,* and that the exposition of international economic relations in terms of abundant and scarce resources builds on Ohlin's *Interregional and International Trade.*

[14] "Social value" is used here to mean the value to society as measured by whatever method is accepted in the society concerned. In a free-enterprise or market economy the price as determined in a competitive market is accepted in practice as such a measure, except in special cases, where state intervention through bounties, taxes, and the like indicates that market

which each resource might otherwise be put. This rule amounts to the plain common sense of not filling a less urgent want by making a more urgent want go begging. The householder's need for kindling-wood should not be met by chopping up fine walnut veneers when old pine boards will do as well. Society's need for sugar should not be met by using toilsome hand labor or the socially wasteful labor of children on beetfields if improved varieties of cane in tropical islands can meet the same needs at less cost.

It is, of course, just another way of looking at this same principle to say that every resource—each unit of each factor or "sub-factor" of production—so far as it can be turned to a number of different uses, should always be directed towards that use in which it performs the greatest service to society—satisfies, that is, the most urgent or important human wants. Consider, for instance, an acre of very fertile land located near a great city. Even if its soil were better suited for wheat-growing than any other soil in the world it would be wasteful to plant wheat there, for the land would be better used in growing fresh vegetables, while broad acres far removed from centers of population could provide the wheat. A skilled surgeon who happens also to be an excellent carpenter would add less to the community welfare if he pursued carpentry, except as a hobby, than if he used his rarer skill for the relief of human suffering and left house-building to the many other people who can do that. A country which is quite capable of making all its own textile products might find that its labor skills and mechanical ingenuity and capital supply would be

price is not accepted by the governing authorities as a perfect measure of value to society. In a non-market economy, other methods, ranging from the estimates of a military high-command or the whims of a dictator to parliamentary decisions or a price system adjusted to consumer demands, might conceivably be the means used in practice to decide relative values.

better employed if partly diverted into making machine tools, or other articles that require somewhat rarer industrial abilities, now that textiles can be made efficiently in many countries that have a lower level of skills.

It is a familiar economic principle, and one that applies to a capitalist or a socialist or any other kind of society, that any single unit of a commodity is less valued when the commodity is abundant than when it is scarce relative to the demand for it. If water flows freely into the farmer's well or through the city man's pipes, any particular quart of water is not even worth the trouble of saving overnight. But if the well threatens to go dry, or if we live in a desert land or are cast adrift on the ocean, then the scarcity of water makes every quart valuable. The same principle holds for wheat, or wheat land, or labor skills of various kinds, or capital funds—indeed, for any commodity, and for any resource used in production. In technical language, the marginal social value of a good is small where the good is abundant—"marginal" being used to emphasize that we are not talking about the social usefulness of that good in general, but about the loss that would be felt if one unit of it were taken away.[15] Where a particular resource is abundant, then, any one unit of it has less value for production than where it is scarce (other things, especially the intensity of demand for the product, being equal). It follows that if additional amounts of that particular resource are needed for meeting some social demand the demand can be met with least damage to the total social product of

[15] Fundamentally, the reason for this is twofold: (1) The physical facts of production make for certain "optimum" proportions in which resources can best be combined for getting a particular product, and once a given resource is available in amounts that permit its use in at least the optimum proportion, additional amounts of it will add less and less to the total product. (2) Human wants for any particular product are satiable, so that as more and more of any commodity becomes available the desire for an additional unit (at least after a certain point) becomes less intense.

other things (alternative uses of the same resource) by drawing upon the resource where it is relatively most abundant.

A more refined statement of the principle of social economy can now be given. This statement has the virtue of describing the ideally efficient use of resources with greater exactness, and also of giving us a test which can be applied in concrete situations to see how the actual use of resources measures up against the ideal efficiency. *Each particular type of resource (factor or "sub-factor" of production) should be directed towards the various uses to which it can be put in such amounts that the last unit of it in any one use yields a product of the same social value as the last unit of it in any other use.* In technical language, the marginal social return from each particular type of resource should be made equal in all industries and all places.

The truth of this way of stating the principle of social economy is seen most clearly by supposing for a moment that the principle is not followed and that the same type of resource, say the labor of skilled electricians of exactly the same ability, produces twice as much per man-day in Toronto as it does in Buffalo, or twice as much in the refrigerator industry as it does in the telephone industry. Plainly, taking some men off the job in Buffalo where they add less to the social product and putting them on in Toronto where they add more, or taking some out of the telephone industry and adding them to the refrigerator industry, would increase the total income of society. And so long as there exists any inequality in the marginal yield of the same resource in different places or occupations, there is a possibility of increasing the total social income in a similar way by transferring some units of the resource from a point where it yields less than average to a point where it yields more than average.

So far as this principle is concerned (disregarding any other considerations for the moment) transfers should continue until the return per extra unit added to the above-average point has fallen enough, and the loss per unit taken away from the below-average point has risen enough, so that marginal returns are made equal. *When marginal social returns from interchangeable units of resources are everywhere equal, the social product will be a maximum.*[16]

An important qualification is necessary to make this conclusion strictly accurate. The transfer of resources from low-yield to high-yield points usually costs something. For instance, there is a cost to the men and their families and to the community in shifting electricians from Buffalo to Toronto. Strictly speaking, then, transfers should not be made, even where there is some inequality in marginal yield of interchangeable resources, unless the promised social gain from the shift is enough to represent a return on the transfer cost (regarded as an investment) at least as large as the return on other investments that might be made.

On the basis of the principle of social economy, which is the very core of all welfare reasoning in economics, one must *prima facie* condemn the tendency of politics to

[16] Certain other considerations that are disregarded here for the sake of clarity in stating the general principle must be taken into account later when appraising policies. For example, if controlled birth-rates in one area keep the population relatively small in relation to resources and thus help to maintain high living standards, while another area lacks voluntary birth control and experiences population growth up to the limits of subsistence, then transfer of resources and shifts of population that might temporarily raise the *average* well-being of the two places would simply be absorbed in population growth in the long run.

The "maximum social product" for one institutional set-up and for one distribution of income would not necessarily be the same as for another. But, however the particular society determines what is socially desirable, the principle of social economy given above states the condition under which its resources are being used most effectively, as measured by its own scale of values.

make national boundaries into economic walls. When boundaries become economic barriers they impede the transfer of movable resources from points of lower social yield to points of higher social yield. This restricts economic welfare. Certain qualifications of this general principle, such as have been alluded to in a footnote above, will be introduced later.

Of course, no one expects individuals and groups to contribute *gratis* their capital, or technical knowledge, or raw materials, or other kinds of resources that they have in abundance, in order that the level of productivity may be raised in some other region, even if it can be proved that the givers would sacrifice less than the receivers would gain. The practical application of the principle of social economy is that in an *exchange* by which one region gives up some of its most abundant resources and gets in return resources that are scarce for it, but abundant from the point of view of the other region, both regions become more productive than before. On each half of the swap, resources are being moved from points of lower social yield to points of higher social yield.

The Social Economy of Trade

But not all resources are mobile. Some, like a sunny climate or ore deposits, cannot be moved at all. Other resources, like savings that can be used for investment in new capital equipment, or human labor, are tied to one locality more or less strongly by habit, friendship, lack of information, or the expense of moving, even in the absence of political restrictions. *The exchange of goods, however, is a partial substitute for the direct exchange of resources.* If the electricians of Buffalo cannot go to Toronto, they can make electrical products and ship them from Buffalo to Toronto.

Every commodity is a "bundle" of primary resources in some special combination. The economic "recipe" for an automobile tire includes rubber, which is made from hot climate, a special tree, plantation management, special labor skills and special capital equipment. Then some other materials such as sulphur and cotton have to be added, and the tire is finished with the aid of a host of very specialized ingredients in a complicated process of manufacture. The primary resources for growing the rubber are abundant and therefore cheap in Sumatra; the primary resources for the manufacturing process are abundant and therefore cheap (per unit of output, though wages per day are high) in Akron, Ohio, where years of operation have located skilled rubber workers, equipment, and experienced management, and where transportation costs for the finished product to the principal market are small. Thus Sumatra supplies Akron with rubber; Akron supplies a large part of the world with tires. This is as it should be in accordance with the principle of social economy.

Similarly, the shipment of hand-made rugs from China to the United States and of radio apparatus from the United States to China is to the advantage of both regions. Unskilled labor is abundant in China in relation to other resources and therefore cheap—that is, in all the alternative uses open to unskilled labor in China the yield is small. In the United States, on the other hand, because capital, equipment, skills, and natural resources are abundant, common labor is a "scarce factor," relatively speaking. Even in its least productive uses in, let us say, sweeping the floor of a radio factory, it works at a higher margin, produces more (and is paid more) than Chinese labor of the same quality. On the other hand, goods embodying large proportions of capital, technical labor, organizing ability (radio apparatus) should be produced in the United States, for these are its "abundant factors." When China makes rugs for the United States and the United States makes radios for China the relatively abundant factors of production in both countries are more productively employed than if there were no such exchange. Restrictions on the exchange of goods, on the other hand, direct the American worker out of the radio factory into the rug factory, the Chinese worker out of the rug factory back to his overcrowded farm patch. Then China cannot afford radios, and Americans have to revise their household budgets to find more money for rugs. Welfare suffers on both sides.

Sometimes it is said that as outlying areas of the world become industrialized the social productivity of international trade will pass, or at least the volume needed will be much less than before. This is a false analysis, usually based on the over-simplified view of trade as an exchange between classes of goods—manufactures against raw materials and foodstuffs—instead of what is really the case: an exchange of particular commodities, highly specialized in themselves, dependent on specialized resources, and becoming more specialized every day. The industrialization of the United States did not lessen the intensity or the importance of trade between the United States and England. Quite the contrary. There is no reason to think that the industrialization of South America or of China will have a different effect on the trade of these regions with the United States and Europe, in so far as the economic welfare of all the peoples concerned is allowed to influence the matter. The busiest railway traffic is between highly industrialized districts—New York and Chicago, Chicago and Detroit—and the busiest steamship lanes are those of the North Atlantic between industrial countries. Industrialization tends to increase trade, though it often changes the items traded in.

The spread of modern techniques throughout the world will not decrease the social economy of trade (though local trade may rise faster in some places than inter-regional trade as local living standards improve, thus causing a decline in the *relative* amount of inter-regional trade). Thoughtful analysis cannot sustain a statement like this one: ". . . the machine has long since ironed out regional productive differentiation; except in the case of labor differentials, it is cheaper to produce manufactured goods at home than it is to import them." [17] This not only grossly misstates the facts as they exist today (one wonders why manufacturers ever bother to lobby for protective tariffs, why American automobiles have a cost-advantage over all the world), but it also leaves out of account the following important effects of "the machine" on the future course of industrial life: (1) The machine lowers costs of overcoming distance, which is equally important with cost-differentials between regions in determining whether or not trade can be socially productive. (2) The machine increases the volume and variety of raw materials that are needed, and these cannot be had in one region. Industrialization in the present "raw material countries" will make them *importers* of many specialized materials that they do not produce, while they will continue to export their own specialties. (The United States imports tin, rubber, manganese, but exports cotton, tobacco, wheat.) (3) As industrialism arrives in less-developed areas they may import less of some consumers' goods (making textiles, shoes, etc. at home) but their purchases of capital goods (business machines, trucks, electrical equipment) will increase

[17] John Chamberlain, in the *New Republic* (New York), June 29, 1938. Mr. Chamberlain credits this proposition to Professor Charles A. Beard, who has written a book on economic policy in which the argument rests on a number of assertions of this general character. See *The Open Door at Home* (New York: Macmillan, 1934).

enormously, and their rising living standards will increase the demand for specialized consumers' goods (tennis rackets, perfumes, photographic supplies) from abroad. (4) Finally, the advantages of large-scale production introduced by machine methods, and the advantages of specialized resources like technical labor and specialized scientific laboratories, increase the production cost-differential between a large industry able to supply an international market and a local home industry. If economic welfare is consulted, there will eventually be some large-scale industries in every country, but they will be *different* in different countries, all exchanging their products and all getting the economies of a large market. (Detroit and two or three other places will build the world's automobiles, Leipzig and a few other places the world's optical instruments, Buenos Aires will eventually take the lead in some industry-of-the-future.)

To summarize: Economic walls at national frontiers violate the principle of social economy on two counts. They prevent a socially productive transfer of primary resources from place to place, and they prevent the achievement of similar results through trade in goods. There is thus a strong presumption that technology, in increasing the mobility and the range of economic activity, favors economic welfare, while nationalistic politics, restricting movements of resources and goods, works against economic welfare. But this can be no more than a presumption until the analysis is carried further along certain lines.

CHAPTER FIVE

PROBLEMS OF PROGRESS

Costs of Transition

ALTHOUGH labor-saving machines make possible a larger social product (including greater leisure) and thus create the basis for a higher level of economic welfare, they also raise difficult problems. They may create technological unemployment when they are first introduced, and they may alter established ways of life. In a similar way, the more efficient use of resources made possible by the conquest of distance and the world-wide division of labor opens up the possibility of new and higher levels of economic welfare, but it also creates problems of adjustment during a transition period.

Some thinkers, contemplating certain baneful effects of the machine upon human life and civilization, or appalled by the complex problems the machine sets for society, have advocated scrapping our improved instruments of production and returning to more primitive ways. Aside from the fact that this could hardly be done without a cataclysm (given the fact that there are three times as many people to be fed and clothed and housed in the world today as in the days of handicraft, and that they demand more things), the argument ignores a most important point. *Transition costs and difficulties, once we have reached an advanced stage of development on a new basis, are just as great or greater for returning in the reverse direction as for moving ahead.* To be sure, machine weaving played havoc with the earnings of hand-loom weavers, electric refrigerators created unemployment among ice-men, factory machinery increased the hazards of workmen until safety codes were worked out to match the new developments, and the urban environment produced by the machine has caused social and political problems without end. But close the textile factories, shut off the orders for electrical equipment, put workmen back at their hand tools, and enforce a decree that all the people who have come to the city in the last fifty years must return to the farm—does anyone imagine that this would bring back "the good old days," or bring anything but chaos?

The problem of world economic relations is a close parallel to the problem of the machine in modern civilization (it is, of course, one part of the problem of the machine). The coming of the world economy has decade after decade brought troubles to established industries—such as the wheat industry in Europe at the time the American Middle West was opened up—and it has created very complex problems. At the same time it has been making possible a more efficient use of resources and a higher level of consumption. There will be transition costs in the future, as in the past, if the world economy is permitted to develop further. But, just as in the case of the machine, *we have come a long way already, many adjustments have been made, and to abandon the world economy will cost at least as much in social upsets and political frictions as to develop it.*

In the United States, where the difficulty of getting along in economic isolation would be less than in many other countries, the Secretary of Agriculture has estimated that to make the transition to a self-sufficient economy it would be necessary to retire 40 million acres of good land or 100 million acres of poor land from the cultivation of crops normally exported.

> If the national will is completely bent in this direction we can arrive together at a self-contained life, but the process of transition to this self-contained Utopia is certain to be extremely difficult. It may require a great amount of governmental aid to take care of people formerly engaged in import and export businesses. It will mean the shifting of millions of people from the farms of the South. But these are minor considerations in comparison with the extraordinarily complete control of all the agencies of public opinion which is generally necessary to keep the national will at a tensity necessary to carry through a program of isolated prosperity.[1]

Even greater costs than these might ultimately have to be charged up to the abandonment of the world economy, for the pressures that affect the prospects for war or peace all over the world would be greatly increased by the repercussions abroad of measures of economic isolation adopted in the United States or other important countries.[2]

The point of view adopted in this book is that the best course is to follow a positive, forward policy of increasing rather than decreasing the use of the machine (including all the devices of modern technology, chemical and biological as well as mechanical), at the same time matching material technology with social technology that will help to mold the machine environment more to man's needs. Similarly, the increased economic efficiency made possible by world-wide economic relations should not be sacrificed to blind resistance inspired by some of the very real difficulties that world economic relations

[1] Henry A. Wallace, *America Must Choose: The Advantages and Disadvantages of Nationalism, of World Trade, and of a Planned Middle Course* (World Affairs Pamphlet No. 3, Foreign Policy Association and World Peace Foundation, 1934), pp. 10, 17.

[2] See Chapter VI.

create. It would be at least as costly and dangerous to go backward towards less efficient division of labor between regions, less rational use of world resources, and lower living standards, as to go forward in a direction that offers more efficient tools to use in the struggle to abolish poverty.

Intelligent policy ought to accept the presumption, on grounds of economic welfare, in favor of world-wide mobility of resources and trade in goods. It ought to work to perfect the world economy. At the same time it ought to be on watch for danger of sudden economic upsets in one country brought about by the introduction of new methods and hitherto untapped resources in another country thousands of miles away, or for social disorganization that might be caused by bringing new industrial methods to an undeveloped country from outside. Conscious efforts should be made to anticipate problems like these, and to meet them, not by a negative attitude that places obstructions in the path of economic progress, but by minimizing costs of transition to a more productive adjustment.

On occasion it may be good social economy, from this standpoint, to interfere with some trend that represents, fundamentally, an improvement in the use of resources. It may be well to slow down the transition to prevent too great a shock in other parts of the world economic system.[3] Some kinds of movements of goods, or capital, or

[3] "Contemporary economic theory is coming to the view that the waste of short-time maladjustment, or 'instability' may be more important than the exact optimum long-run adjustment, since the latter is never realized anyhow. It may be sound policy to depart from the canons of long-run equilibrium in order to avoid sudden shocks . . . Logical extension of the principle would imply putting the brakes on too rapid interregional migrations of industry, so as to allow for an easier, and from a broad point of view a cheaper adjustment of the productive factors. The real problems are the definitions of too rapid migration and the broad point of view . . ." (Edgar M. Hoover, Jr. *Location Theory and the Shoe and Leather Industries,* Cambridge: Harvard University Press, 1937, p. 296.)

persons, or new techniques may need to be held in check, perhaps even stopped altogether, pending other adjustments. However, the most important part of a policy of minimizing transition costs should be the deliberate stimulation of compensating adjustments. If new mines in a more favored location threaten the livelihood of established mining villages, there ought to be a policy of finding new products for the region affected, or, if this is impossible, the people ought to be assisted to move elsewhere and to retrain for better positions. To the extent that positive adjustments of this sort are encouraged it will not be necessary, and there will be less pressure, to set up merely defensive measures of "protection" to shield the obsolete industry at the expense of consumers and the better producers.

We should give more attention than in the past to costs of transition, both narrowly economic and broadly social, in reaching more productive adjustments of international economic relations. But this is not by any means to justify any and every type of restriction on mobility of resources and goods. Least of all does the argument justify most of the existing nationalistic restrictions. Indeed, one of the chief effects of the economic walls erected around national boundaries has been to create new maladjustments, new irrationalities in the use of the world's resources, and thus to pile on society a double burden of transition costs—one as the irrational situation is brought into being, another if it is ever to be remedied in the future. Barriers at national boundaries are *not* among the most useful tools for minimizing transition costs in the world economy, and they are among the most dangerous. Most important in avoiding excessive transition costs is international concerted action, especially in the fields of monetary policy and investment and encouragement of trade, so that transitions can take place in an atmosphere of progressive economic expansion rather than in one of economic contraction or depression. For this purpose and for others, as will be argued later, high barriers at national boundaries are not good instruments of constructive economic planning.

General Welfare versus Welfare of Particular Groups

Improved means of production and more efficient use of resources, despite the difficulties of transition, increase the means of meeting fundamental human needs and make possible higher levels of economic welfare. It often happens, however, that the welfare of particular persons or groups may be adversely affected by the very improvements that benefit society as a whole. Those who gain their livelihood by methods made obsolete, whose specialized property in capital equipment or going business enterprises cannot be turned to other uses without loss, those whose specialized labor skills are superseded by better methods or whose employment in a particular industry becomes less secure by reason of a more economical combination of resources discovered somewhere else —these people will render minority reports on the gains in welfare from better use of resources.

"Turnpike companies profiting by tolls, and owners of stagecoaches were among the most active opponents of railroads. They were supported by tavern-keepers along the route of the roads, and by farmers who felt that the introduction of the railroad would deprive them of markets for horses and for hay."[4] Similar opposition is

[4] "Propaganda of vested interest groups was potent. It was easy to arouse opposition of farmers along the right-of-way, on the grounds that the roaring locomotives would startle the cattle and prevent them from grazing in safety, that hens would not lay, that the poisoned air from the locomotives would kill the wild birds and destroy vegetation, that farmhouses would be ignited by sparks, and property would deteriorate."

In England the landlord, country-gentleman class arrayed itself against

aroused when technical improvements in the use of the world's resources, made possible through the conquest of distance and the world-wide division of labor, happen to run against established interests—as they often do. The textile industry of Lancashire sees to it that barriers are erected to keep the inhabitants of British colonies from benefiting by bargains in cotton cloth from the new Japanese looms. The war-born American dye industry supplies money for propaganda on "America self-contained," thus buttressing protective tariff sentiment that may be useful in keeping American consumers from the temptation of looking for cheaper or better dyes and chemicals abroad.[5] Workers' organizations and manufacturers and mayors of cities in New England are roused to (mostly short-sighted) opposition against Secretary Hull's reciprocal trade agreements program by fear that the local shoe or textile industries might have to meet stiffer competition. Sugar-producing interests in the United States have their economic welfare promoted by tariff and quota protection and subsidies for the relatively wasteful production of an industry little suited to the country, but this costs consumers nearly $300,000,000 a year.[6] To "help

---

the aggressive industrialists. Said a Member of Parliament for Cheltenham: "Nothing is more distasteful to me than to hear the echoes of our hills reverberating with the noise of hissing railroad engines running through the heart of our hunting country, and destroying that noble sport [fox hunting] to which I have been accustomed from my childhood." (*Technological Trends and National Policies, Including the Social Implications of New Inventions,* Report of the Sub-committee on Technology to the National Resources Committee, Washington: U. S. Government Printing Office, 1937, pp. 40-41.)

[5] The propaganda is carried on by the Chemical Foundation, Inc. It has flooded the desks of persons on its mailing list (*e.g.,* members of the American Economic Association) with dozens of books and booklets, divided between the wonders of chemistry and the menace of foreign goods. The "scientific" arguments on this latter subject are usually presented between patriotic red-white-and-blue covers.

[6] "During the years 1931–33 the protective tariff (on sugar) represented an annual net cost to consumers of approximately $180 million a year, and since the quota system has been in operation this has risen to approximately

silver" the government of the United States has been led, by the influence of sparsely inhabited states where silver is a big force in politics, to follow a policy for a number of years that was not only costly to its own citizens but had a harmful effect on the economy of China through raising the price of its money-metal.

Illustrations of this sort could be multiplied indefinitely. They can be found in all the countries of the world. Nor is the problem of conflict between the general welfare and the welfare of particular groups peculiar to international economic policy. Small grocers get the legislatures to protect them against the more efficient distribution system of the chain store, and insurance companies fight savings-bank life insurance. Internally as well as internationally, producers form cartels, or trusts, or trade unions, or milk-distributors' associations which may, and often do, carve out specially favored economic niches for themselves at the expense of the public in general.

Now, an intelligent and humane economic policy will certainly give attention to the particular interests of all groups directly affected by better methods of production and distribution. But the danger today is not so much that the particular interests will be forgotten as that the general welfare will be forgotten. In the general scramble to protect each group separately the interests of all together are being overlooked. "Help wheat," "help sugar," "help the chemical industry," "help cotton," "help the small store owner," "help the textile workers," "help the railroad bond-holder"—these are appealing slogans in themselves, but if interpreted to mean policies that maintain the scarcity-values of the particular goods

$290 million a year." This is an estimate based on a thorough study, which applies only through the year 1937. (J. P. Cavin, "The Sugar Quota System of the United States, 1933–37," unpublished dissertation in library of Harvard University, 1938, p. 313.)

controlled by these groups, at the expense of the general economic welfare, then they are ultimately self-defeating. The only alternative to self-defeating restrictionism is a positive, forward-looking program in which the expansion of new economic opportunities and a conscious policy of encouraging rather than hindering readjustments will remove the menace to groups temporarily threatened by economic progress.

World Welfare versus Welfare of Particular Countries

One special type of conflict between the general welfare and the welfare of particular groups deserves separate mention. Frequently there is a clash between at least the short-run economic interest of one country and the economic welfare of the world as a whole (though what is regarded as national economic interest is often the special interest of some favored group, quite possibly contrary to the interest of most of the people of the nation). The use of national raw material monopolies to exploit consumers in the rest of the world is one illustration of conflict between local and world welfare. Sometimes the economic and social costs of transition made necessary by improved use of the world's resources fall unequally on different countries, so that one country may get more of the cost than of the benefit. The British textile industry, for example, has thus far borne the brunt of the transition costs occasioned by the increased efficiency of Japanese textile-making.

Conflicts of this sort cannot be avoided entirely, but they can be minimized by forward-looking international coöperation. Merely defensive action against the rise of new competitive industries elsewhere is mutually self-defeating. Readjustment must be sought in a positive way, through expansion of new lines rather than barriers and restrictions in the old. Also, in order to avoid friction and bitterness, the increase of world economic welfare must be sought in such a way that there will be no impairment of the standard of living in any single country by reason of improvement elsewhere. This is not impossible, given organization and coöperation for the right kind of planning.

"Non-Economic" Aspects of Welfare

We have defined economic welfare very broadly, but even so there may be other human values at times in conflict with it. When that occurs, of course, it is not for the economist to say whether a higher and more regular consumption standard and less toil ought really to be preferred to some other good. This is a question in ultimate values, related to the philosopher's discussion of the highest good and the plain man's notion of how life ought to be lived. Perhaps we shall finally all side with the Chemical Foundation, Inc.,[7] which regularly prints on the back of its red-white-and-blue propaganda for a self-contained economy the following lines from Goldsmith's *Deserted Village:*

> Teach erring man to spurn the rage of gain;
> Teach him that states of native strength possest,
> Tho' very poor, may still be very blest.

Or we may all decide with Premier Mussolini that military glory is much more important than mere economic welfare:

> War alone brings all human energies to their highest tension and sets a seal of nobility on the peoples who have the virtue to face it.[8]

[7] See Footnote 5.

[8] "The Doctrine of Fascism," by Benito Mussolini, from the *Enciclopedia Italiana,* Vol. XIV, official English translation.

It is safe to say that most of humanity rejects this view today. But at the same time, most of humanity feels insecure, and therefore looks on with alarm, but approval, while governments spend countless millions on military equipment and squander resources (from the point of view of peacetime welfare) in frantic efforts to be self-sufficient in foodstuffs and other strategic commodities should war come. More will be said later about the impossibility of reconciling the quest for military power or the necessity for war preparedness with ordinary economic welfare under modern conditions.

Some other ideals may also conflict at times with the desire to improve economic welfare. For example, some extreme types of specialization, even if productive of more goods, may themselves be regarded as evils. This is true both for the daily occupation of people and for the economic structure of regions or countries. We have really included considerations of this sort in our broad definition of economic welfare, but they are worth emphasizing here. The problem of whether to sacrifice some productivity for diversity does not confront a large country like the United States, with its great variety of resources (except that regional diversity needs conscious encouragement in highly specialized areas like the Southern cotton belt). The question is more acute in some of the South American countries. Brazil depends heavily on coffee, Chile on copper and nitrates. An intelligent program, it goes without saying, would first of all seek diversity by encouraging the development of potentialities that have been overlooked, by improving the level of knowledge and introducing new industrial arts, and would be very hesitant about taking measures that would sacrifice the very real advantages to be gained from the trend towards interregional and international division of labor promoted by modern technology.

The argument for diversity will lose or gain in strength depending upon how much success can be attained in concerted efforts to lessen the instability of the world economy and to put a greater measure of rational planning into the guidance of economic change. The matter has been well stated as follows:

> The benefits of international specialization are often very unequally distributed between countries in a period of rapid change. A country cannot commit itself without misgiving to one or two lines of production on which it is almost entirely dependent for its ability to purchase from abroad its necessities and everyday luxuries. An individual who finds that his occupation has become profitless can in many countries fall back on resources from the public authorities or elsewhere to tide him over until he can find a new occupation. There is no unemployment relief or system of economic insurance for states. The desire for a diversified economic structure is part of the attempt to spread risks. A country dependent on one or two commodities may consider it worth while to pay a high price for economic security, and to develop alternative lines of production as an insurance against the uncertainties of economic change. The justifiable criticism that economic nationalism is wasteful and only makes things worse must be tempered by a realization of the not unreasonable desire of certain countries to achieve greater economic security through a diversified economic structure.[9]

At times the people of a country, or its leaders, may be willing to sacrifice some economic welfare in order to preserve a traditional way of life, to avoid concentration in cities, to stimulate industry in a country better fitted for agriculture, or to conserve special virtues thought to go with a large rural population (for example, large families, religion, or a habit of voting against labor parties). These are considerations which should be weighed against their cost in productivity. If, with a knowledge of the

[9] Royal Institute of International Affairs, *The Problem of International Investment* (London, New York and Toronto: Oxford University Press, 1937), p. 33.

costs, people prefer to buy these things rather than a somewhat more abundant supply of goods and services, that is a fair choice. Often, however, interested groups will seek to represent their proposals as means of promoting economic welfare when the effect is quite the opposite; and against that we can protest.

Conclusions

The object of economic policy should be to bring about the best use of world resources for human needs. Certainly human needs are not being adequately met in any country today. Great gaps exist between generally accepted standards for the necessary material basis of good modern living and actual levels of consumption now possible to the common people. These deficiencies are greater than could be made up by full recovery from depression. Even in boom years and in the most advanced countries the production of clothing, of houses, of protective foodstuffs, of medical services and educational services and the equipment to go with them, has not been enough to satisfy the aspirations of the people, or even to cover "necessities" as defined in modern standards. Certainly from the point of view of human needs there is no margin of surplus in the world to justify deliberate waste, or anything but the most careful, rational use of resources.

Good social economy demands that man take full advantage of the fact that particular kinds of resources are more abundant in some places than in others, that each place has its relatively abundant and its relatively scarce resources. There are two means of getting the maximum social advantage out of this uneven distribution of resources. One complements the other. The first is to shift about persons, or capital, or knowledge—transferring the resources themselves, or the persons that use them.

The other is to trade in goods, letting each kind of good flow from the localities where the resources needed in its production are more abundant to the places where those particular resources are more scarce. By both these means resources can be redirected from uses of lower social benefit to uses of higher social benefit, in accord with what we have called the principle of social economy. Human welfare is thereby increased, provided that in the course of improving the efficiency of production economic policy has given wise attention not only to (1) the basic principle of social economy itself, but also to (2) economic and social costs of transition, (3) possible conflicts between the general welfare and the welfare of particular groups, of which an important special case is (4) possible conflicts between world welfare and the welfare of particular countries, and to (5) "non-economic" aspects of welfare.

CHAPTER SIX

WAR OR PEACE

WE HAVE been discussing the best use of resources for economic welfare. But even more important in total human welfare today than the increase or decrease of goods and services is the issue of peace or war. If one way of using the world's resources makes peace more secure while another stokes the fires of conflict, there is no doubt about which the people of today should prefer. Does the tendency of technology towards world-wide economic contacts or the tendency of politics to keep economic activities within national boundaries offer the better prospect for peace?

Sometimes it is implied that merely extending the area of economic contact will itself insure peace. The theory is that when people "get to know each other" they will not fight. This is naïve. Only people who have contact with each other find occasion to fight, and economic contacts, even more than some other kinds, provide possible occasions for conflict. Economic relations do raise political problems, and whether they finally lead to war or to firmer peace depends very much upon the way in which they are conducted.

On the other hand, it is no less foolish, in fact considerably more so, to suppose that the cause of peace will be furthered by blocking economic contacts. There would be more sense in that simple view if we did not already have a world economy. The real question today is whether to restrict and destroy world economic relations to which we are already partly adjusted, or to develop them further and seek a more perfect adjustment. The first course is a tempting alternative for persons who dwell within the borders of the larger and better-endowed countries and who are perplexed or discouraged by the chaos of the world around them. Yet there are several definite ways in which that course, through the very cutting of contacts that is supposed to avoid trouble, would increase the pressure upon other countries to seek military conquest and would promote a ruthless scramble for the very means of existence. There would be no security for anyone in such a world.

Population Pressure

Since 1750 the population of Europe has nearly quadrupled, that of Asia is thought to have more than doubled (though the best estimates are little more than guesses), and in North America the increase has been more than a hundred-fold. Africa has one and one-half and Oceania five times as many people as in 1850. More details are shown in the following table:

ESTIMATES OF WORLD POPULATION, 1650–1933 [1]
(millions)

Continent	*1650*	*1750*	*1800*	*1850*	*1900*	*1933*
Europe	100	140	187	266	401	519
North America	1	1.3	5.7	26	81	137
Central and South America	12	11.1	18.9	33	63	125
Oceania	2	2	2	2	6	10
Africa	100	95	90	95	120	145
Asia	330	479	602	749	937	1,121
World Total	545	728	906	1,171	1,608	2,057

[1] A. M. Carr-Saunders, *World Population: Past Growth and Present Trends* (Oxford: Clarendon Press, 1936), p. 42. The estimates are based on the work of Professor W. F. Willcox, somewhat revised.

At the same time the standard of living has moved up. In Europe and regions settled by Europeans, and in some other places—areas including a population larger than the total world population in 1750—people count as necessities for their way of life an amount of goods that would have amazed the nobles of an earlier day. How is it possible to sustain an enormously larger number of people in a way that actually provides very many of them with undreamed-of comforts and luxuries? The answer is in improved technology, its spread to new continents, and in the better use of the world's resources by means of geographical specialization—getting the world's nickel from the best deposits, the world's wheat from the low-cost wheat areas, the world's machines from those factories and regions that can supply them most efficiently.

The number of inhabitants that a country can have, while keeping its standard of living at a certain height, is not something rigidly fixed. It is a very complex matter, depending upon: (1) the natural resources of the country, (2) the constitution, natural endowment, acquired skill, knowledge, and habits of the people, and (3) the opportunities, internal and external, for economic activity.[2] This latter factor—particularly the *external* opportunities for economic activity—is most significant for our analysis of the effects of national economic barriers. Belgium, with its 700 inhabitants per square mile (against 135 for Greece) can and does have a moderately high standard of living despite its very great population density. So long as Belgians can specialize in highly productive industrial operations, and can trade with the rest of the world for their raw materials, their food supply, and many kinds of finished goods that are made more cheaply elsewhere, their thickly-settled country need not be poverty-stricken. But if trade with the rest of the world were

[2] *Ibid.*, p. 330.

blocked, a highly industrialized and specialized area like Belgium would soon have "too many people." In other words, an unfavorable relation of population to economic opportunity can arise from a decrease in opportunity to work effectively as well as from a growth of population. It is not too much to say that if what we have called "the trend of politics" continues to confine economic activity more and more within national boundaries, thus lessening the chance for productive specialization, then many areas in the world will be "over-populated" in the sense that they will not be able to maintain their present numbers at present levels of comfort. Not only Belgium, but England, the Netherlands, Germany, Italy, and Switzerland may perhaps be mentioned as examples in Europe, and Japan in Asia.

But merely to maintain present levels of economic opportunity and efficiency is not enough to avoid dangers that may arise from "population pressure" in the years ahead. To be sure, the population in northern and western Europe and in Europeanized countries appears to be nearing its peak, and an actual decline in numbers is expected within a few years or decades in these countries. However, this is not true of the rest of the world. In eastern and southern Europe and Japan population is still increasing rapidly, and it must continue to do so for some time (because of greater numbers entering the reproductive ages), even though the same tendencies which have lowered the birth rate in northwestern Europe are now showing themselves in these countries. In India and China serious pressure of population on bare subsistence is still the rule for great masses of people, and in Java, though living standards have so far improved despite a rapid increase in numbers, the Dutch colonial authorities are looking for ways to meet what promises to be one of the most difficult population problems in the world.

What seems to be happening is that all these countries are now in, or are likely soon to enter, the first phase of the population cycle that earlier brought such tremendous expansion in European numbers. That is, stronger governments able to maintain order and security, medical science, and control of epidemics are bringing a fall in the death rate. The birth rate, meanwhile, stays high, or falls only with a considerable lag; even after people have started to limit their families the number of births may increase because of larger numbers coming into the reproductive ages. In countries already crowded, the introduction of modern methods can thus result in serious population pressure, especially since the "safety valve" of vast new continents for settlement which was present when European population increase was most rapid is no longer present today.

There are three ways to relieve the pressure of population, aside from the unwanted "positive checks" of war, pestilence, and famine described by Malthus. One is mass emigration. This offers relatively little hope in the world of today, for reasons that will be given in a later chapter. Another is birth control. This is effective in the long run, but for some time after it has begun to operate the population continues to increase (as in Japan); so it does not solve the immediate problem. The third is improvement of productivity by better industrial and commercial techniques, increased capital equipment, greater specialization and trade. But industrialization, or more productive specialization in agriculture, is possible only within narrow limits for a thickly-populated country with a small range of natural resources unless it can increase its trade with the rest of the world. It must import necessary materials and equipment from abroad and be able to pay for them by selling its own goods abroad. In addition, it must usually borrow temporarily to improve communication facilities and to install capital equipment of all sorts, repaying later with money obtained by selling goods. The actions of other countries in erecting economic barriers to movements of goods and capital and knowledge (or similar action by the country concerned, itself!) may make this process difficult, if not impossible. Thus, the widespread practice of economic nationalism is likely to produce the feeling in a country of rapidly growing population that it is faced with a terrible dilemma: either accept the miserable prospect of decreased living standards (at least, abandon hope of greatly improved living standards), or seek by conquest to seize control of more territory, more resources, larger market and supply areas. Even though the economic barriers of other countries may not really be so high as to bar the path of industrial development completely, and even though it may be mistaken to think that a war of conquest can really solve the economic problem, *psychologically* the result is the same as though the barriers made conquest the only way out. The world's peace is likely to suffer.

The Case of Japan

Japan illustrates the bearing of these considerations on war or peace. Its population has doubled in the last sixty years. During that period, nevertheless, the people have become better off: average real income per capita has risen, perhaps even doubled.[3] For the future, the population prospect is not so startling as it has sometimes been painted,[4] but that it is serious there can be no doubt. Infant mortality, and the death rate in general, have declined sharply in recent years. The birth rate has also

[3] *Ibid.*, p. 265.

[4] See the illuminating discussion in E. F. Penrose, *Population Theories and their Application, with Special Reference to Japan* (Food Research Institute, Stanford University, 1934), Ch. 4.

started down, but the population will go on increasing for some decades yet, even though families are getting smaller under the influence of birth control and later marriage. Already there is a remarkable density of population in Japan. With about 70 million people (over half the population of the United States) in an area less than that of California, the average is over 400 persons per square mile. Owing to the mountainous nature of the country, less than one-fifth of the land can be cultivated. Extraordinary enterprise, skill, and adaptability have been displayed by the Japanese, both in land use and in the building of modern industries.

Attempts of the government to stimulate migration to the outer Empire have been unsuccessful. After thirty years of effort, there are only about a million Japanese living in the Empire outside Japan proper. Sakhalin has an unfavorable climate, Korea and Formosa have dense populations of their own. There were grandiose plans for Manchuria, but not many more than 200,000 Japanese have settled there. Those who have settled in foreign countries, outside Japan and the Empire, number only about half a million, half of these being in the United States and Hawaii.[5] Why has the migratory movement been so small? The answer is that the countries to which the Japanese would willingly go are shut against them. Not only the fact of exclusion in overseas countries, but the manner of it—most especially in the United States, where Congress insisted in 1924 on absolute exclusion, despite the fact that the immigration quota law if applied to Japan just as to other countries would have admitted only 146 Japanese a year—immensely strengthened the hand of the military party that advocated force and conquest as over against those groups that counseled moderation.

[5] Carr-Saunders, *loc. cit.*, pp. 267-9.

With migration practically barred and population growing rapidly, Japanese leaders have sought to hasten the pace of industrial development as a means of meeting the country's problems. But lacking many of the raw materials necessary for industrial civilization, Japan had to be able to import, and to pay for imports it had to be able to sell abroad. Here obstacles were raised by the economic nationalism of other countries and by the economic nationalism of Japan's own policy.[6]

During the World War Japanese industry forged ahead to turn out war materials for the Allies and to supply their abandoned markets. From 1913 to 1919 the number of modern factories increased one-third and output rose five-fold. With the return to peacetime production in Europe and the United States, Japan lost some of its advance in foreign markets and during the 1920's was engaged in consolidating its gains. When the world depression brought a disastrous decline in the American raw-silk market and took away the means of subsistence for thousands of households as well as the chief source of foreign exchange for the purchase of imports, Japan turned to an export drive on other fronts. In 1931 the government devalued the yen by 65 per cent. This gave a great competitive advantage to Japanese exporters in foreign markets—an "artificial" advantage in the view of other sellers. Japanese trade leaped forward. Faced by contracting markets and depressed industries around the world, competitors were in no mood for such a development. Although Japan was supplying less than 4 per cent of total world exports—not an excessive share for a country of 70 million people—its booming trade became a "menace," especially in certain lines.

[6] The paragraphs that follow, detailing measures taken against Japanese trade, are summarized from Ethel B. Dietrich, "Closing Doors against Japan," *Far Eastern Survey,* August 10, 1938.

"One after another doors banged shut." The first was in China. A few years after China had gained its tariff autonomy in 1928 it began to use high import tariffs to encourage its own industrial program, and the practically free market of the 1920's, which had taken one-sixth of Japan's total exports, was no longer the same. The depression, and anti-Japanese feeling generated by the conquest of Manchuria in 1931–32, subtracted from Japanese sales in China.

Cheap Japanese textiles and manufactured products are eminently suited to the needs of native populations in colonial areas and are desired by the natives themselves. This no one disputes. "But colonial markets are also valuable outlets for the surplus products of the suzerain. In every instance the selfish interests of the latter have triumphed over considerations of native welfare. In every empire, be it the British, French, Dutch, American or Italian, the story has repeated itself. In every empire the doors have been openly or subtly barred against the Japanese upstart, the only competitor who needed drastic treatment." In 1928 Indo-China was "assimilated" under the French tariff system, which means French goods pay no duties while others have to pay the same as if they were entering France. After Japanese devaluation France applied quotas in Indo-China (August 1932) and added a 25 per cent exchange compensation tax. Dutch colonial quotas were a greater blow. A Crisis Import Ordinance passed in 1933 brought 40 per cent of the imports of the rich Netherlands colonies in the East Indies under a quota system within the next two years. Base periods for the quotas were shrewdly chosen to discriminate against Japan, and native industries were encouraged which competed with Japanese goods. British colonies were next. In 1934 Mr. Runciman announced in the House of Commons the government's decision to introduce an import quota system for the Crown Colonies. Based on average imports for the period 1927–31, before the rapid rise of Japanese trade, these quotas "with one stroke of the pen reduced Japanese imports of cotton textiles from 51 million yards in the first quarter of 1934 to 10 million yards in the first quarter of 1935. Colonial protests were overruled by the Colonial Office." The colonies held under League of Nations mandates and those subject to the Congo Basin treaties escaped the new restrictions, but only because of "open door" treaty obligations. The next year the United States stopped the rapid growth of Japanese textile business in the Philippine Islands by a "voluntary" gentlemen's agreement which established Japanese export quotas in return for a pledge not to increase textile tariffs.

In the Latin American countries and the less industrialized countries of Europe and the Near East, Japan has run up against a barrage of difficulties. Its characteristic exports are directly competitive with the new consumption goods industries which these countries find it easiest to encourage in their own industrialization programs. As an importer of raw materials, Japan must buy where the necessary materials are produced, although often these are not the natural markets for her exports. Therefore, the decline of triangular trade and the rise of bilateralism have been especially hard on Japan. High protective tariffs, quotas and license systems designed to protect infant industries at all costs, tariff preferences such as those incorporated in the Ottawa Agreements, exchange controls and restrictions, special duties directed against countries with devalued currencies—all these obstacles met Japan's new trade effort in the younger industrial countries.

The older industrial countries were also, for the most part, well barricaded against intruders. After the disastrous decline of the raw-silk market between 1929 and

1934, Japan began to increase textile shipments to the United States. American textile interests were panic-stricken, for it was evident that they could not meet the price competition, especially as the depression made people prefer cheaper products. By agreement between the Japanese and American governments, quotas were established on American imports of cotton rugs in 1934. Understandings between business men of the two countries, negotiated with the blessings of their governments, set import quotas for cotton textiles, velveteens, and corduroys and seamless cotton hosiery for 1937–39. In addition, the Tariff Commission has used its power under the flexible section of the tariff laws to recommend increases up to 50 per cent on such items as canned fish, rubber footwear, frozen swordfish, wool knit gloves, cordage and cotton cloth. In negotiating reciprocal trade agreements with other countries narrow definitions have been used so that concessions made would not give an opening to Japanese products. (For example, Japanese matches have colored stems, and in the treaty with Sweden the reduction of duty on matches in small boxes was limited to those with uncolored stems.)

Now it would be wrong to suggest that this history justifies or even adequately explains Japanese military aggression in China.[7] The aggressive designs of certain elements in Japan had been evident long before the events just recounted took place. This was shown most clearly in the "twenty-one demands" made on China during the World War. Furthermore, the first step in the present attack on China—the conquest of Manchuria—began in 1931, before any of the latest trade restrictions. Nor does the author want the argument he has given to be inter-

[7] E. F. Penrose, *loc. cit.*, has an excellent discussion of the interrelation of economic and political factors in Japan's expansionist policy. See especially Chapters 9, 10 and 11.

preted as a plea against boycotts, trade embargoes, capital embargoes or other measures that might be taken to halt the supply of foreign materials without which Japan would be unable to carry on its aggression in China or to consolidate its military conquests. It is one thing to advocate peaceful trade with a country that is faced by pressing economic problems that can be solved only through trade, and quite another to advocate supplying the same country with munitions and materials of war (for trade with Japan means only that today) once it has fallen under the control of a military group that is bent on conquest. Wars of aggression can be stopped only if there is (1) united determination to resist any country that resorts to force on whatever excuse, and (2) united determination to coöperate with any country that shows a disposition to solve its problems by industrialization and improved efficiency and increased trade, even if that coöperation involves some temporary transition costs for the coöperators. The world has done little by either method to keep Japan off the warpath.

It would be untrue to say that the disposition of the world to make national boundaries into economic walls *forced* Japan into its present line of conduct. After all, Japan had been able to enlarge its trade enough to keep its living standards rising despite a rapidly increasing population. Trade has continued, even under the new restrictions. During the depression years of the 1930's the Japanese were relatively better off than most peoples, for the early, drastic devaluation of the yen brought an industrial boom while other countries were in the depths of the slump. But it must be said that the world did little to offer the Japanese people a positive and attractive economic alternative which they might set over against the blandishments of the military, and instead gave the advocates of force excellent pretexts and slogans that had a substantial basis in fact. For this, the tendency of nationalistic politics to erect economic barriers is responsible.

Access to Raw Materials

In 1935 two-thirds of the value of imports into Switzerland was made up of raw materials. Among the chief items were:[8]

Coal	—from Germany, France, Netherlands
Wheat	—from Argentina, Hungary, Canada
Other cereals	—from Argentina, Balkans, Poland
Iron and steel	—from Germany, France, Belgium
Potatoes	—from France, Italy, Netherlands
Raw cotton	—from Egypt, United States
Wood	—from Austria, France, Poland, Germany
Leather	—from Germany, France, Great Britain
Raw wool	—from France, Australia, South America
Gasoline	—from Roumania, Iran, United States
Tobacco	—from United States, Netherlands East Indies, Greece
Copper	—from United States, Chile, Germany
Eggs	—from Denmark, Belgium, Yugoslavia

These imports were paid for by the export of Swiss goods and by "invisible" exports such as sales of tourist services in Switzerland and interest on Swiss capital lent abroad. If export markets were closed to Switzerland, and if tourist traffic and capital movements were stopped, the economic effect would be the same as though an enemy had put a military blockade around the country. Switzerland could get nothing from outside, because it would have no means of paying. An industrialized country like Switzerland under these conditions could not maintain its people at a decent standard of life, perhaps could not even feed them all.

[8] From Swiss Memorandum No. 6, by Professor Charles A. Burky, International Studies Conference, Paris, 1937 (mimeographed).

What is true of Switzerland applies to Sweden, Denmark, Germany, Japan, and a host of other countries around the world. Perhaps it is as well to point out here that the question of access to the world's resources is not by any means exclusively a matter affecting the well-being of industrialized European states which import raw materials. To the extent that trade barriers make it difficult for industrial countries to get raw materials because they cannot pay for them, the same barriers make it difficult for the supplying countries to sell their raw materials profitably. Indeed, during the recent depression, countries that depended on raw material exports for the means of purchasing finished goods and other kinds of raw materials—Chile, Costa Rica, Cuba, the cotton region of the United States, and the like—were in at least as bad a plight as regions that, like Germany, export finished goods. Lack of "access" to the world's resources in manufacturing skills, capital equipment, and other factors that go into finished goods is just as real an injustice for these countries as the more advertised lack of access to raw materials suffered by industrial nations.

The complaint that economic policies of other countries create a problem of "access to raw materials" is heard most often on behalf of Germany or Italy, especially Germany. In so far as a just grievance does exist for these countries it exists also for Switzerland, Denmark, Sweden, or any other fairly small and highly industrialized nation whose standard of living would be threatened by inability to purchase imports of raw materials through selling its own exports abroad. Why, then, does one hear so much more about Germany's vital need for raw materials than about the equally vital needs of these other countries?

There are several reasons. One is that Germany is a Great Power and threatens to resort to military force unless its demands are satisfied. Another is that problems of raw material procurement have been more acute in Germany and Italy of recent years than in other countries because of certain policies within the control of the German and Italian governments. Both governments have been using all their available foreign exchange first and foremost for military raw materials. Naturally, this puts an unusual strain upon the supplies of foreign currency by which raw materials for peaceful industrial needs are ordinarily purchased. In the second place, the system of bilateral trading which these two governments have done much to foster has a tendency to make raw material purchases distinctly more expensive than need be. Thus, bilateral trading has deflected German purchases of raw cotton away from the cheaper world market towards dearer "compensation" markets. In 1935 each ton of raw cotton imported into Germany from Brazil had an average value of RM 1,115, while the somewhat better grades from the United States averaged only RM 805 per ton, and the extremely fine grades imported from Egypt averaged only RM 1,000 per ton. Yet, in pursuit of the barter policy, the percentage of German cotton imports supplied by the United States fell from 72.1 in 1933 to 55.1 in 1934 and 26.7 in 1935, while the imports of the dearer Brazilian cotton, negligible in 1933, rose to 2.1 per cent in 1934 and 20.8 per cent in 1935.[9]

Finally, one hears more of "access to raw materials" from Germany and Italy because the issue can be linked to their demands for territorial expansion, especially to Germany's demand for return of its former colonies. This is almost entirely a propaganda device. Colonies in general are much less important as sources of raw materials or as markets than the public has been led to suppose,

[9] *The World Textile Industry: Economic and Social Problems* (I.L.O., Studies and Reports, Series B, No. 27), Vol. I, pp. 117-18.

and the former German colonies in particular have an extremely minute importance in either respect. The colonial problem is mainly a political issue, a question of national pride and power and group psychology, with very little direct economic importance for either the present or the would-be possessors. The raw materials problem of the world, on the other hand, is mainly a problem of mutual access to the resources of self-governing states, for the sources of the major raw materials are found overwhelmingly in self-governing areas and not in colonies. (The important exceptions are rubber and tin, which come from the Dutch and the British East Indies.)

But when the self-governing states of the world erect barriers that make access to their resources difficult, and when great empires set up preferential rates which discriminate against outside countries, then the possession of an empire where trade policies can be controlled does acquire a greater economic value than it would otherwise have. Even more important, it acquires an immensely greater propaganda value.

Economic Walls and the Psychological Basis of Conflict

Probably the most dangerous of all the so-called "economic causes of war" these days is the effect of economic instability on political psychology. Depression, loss of jobs, failure of investments, create a mental atmosphere of frustration in which irrational political movements seize hold of the public mind and offer relief by projecting the people's troubles upon social enemies, real or imagined. Nations, like individuals, are driven to psychoses when reality becomes too hard to bear.

Economic walls along political boundaries are related to this fruitful source of aggressive tendencies in two ways. In the first place, they intensify the economic maladjustments of a depression. Each country seeks to provide employment at home by stopping imports of foreign goods, with the result, after the others have done the same, that all are worse off than before. Secondly, economic barriers erected abroad put effective slogans into the mouths of those who would turn a psychology of desperation into channels of military aggression.

A large part of the economic problem of peace, on the positive side, is to find what William James called "a moral equivalent of war." Expressed in another way, the problem is to "give people something worth living for rather than something worth fighting for." [10] A co-operative effort directed towards a positive goal of better economic welfare for all nations must be the core of successful peace strategy. Forthright recognition of the exaggerated differences that now exist between the economic possibilities of the world and the living standards actually attained, together with a concerted program of action for lessening these gaps between the real and the ideal, would in itself help to lessen the sharpness of present conflicts. "It is not merely that if the masses of the people are allowed to live in poverty there is danger of social unrest which may lead to conflict between the nations. . . . A social and economic régime which cannot hitch its wagon to the star of justice has no way of developing its energy and of guiding the dynamic impulses of its people. Without a wide and progressive program of social advance the extremely dynamic forces of modern society must either be suppressed or find their outlet in external expansion leading to imperialistic adventure, which means war." [11]

[10] Walter Lippmann, as quoted in the Report of the Director of the I.L.O., 1938, p. 15.

[11] Lewis L. Lorwin, "The I.L.O. and World Economic Policy," *International Labor Review,* Vol. 33 (April, 1936), pp. 457-67.

Economic Walls and Imperialism

To the extent, then, that large, important countries controlling substantial portions of the world's resources refuse to carry on economic relations with the rest of the world, they sow the seeds of unrest and war. In particular, they create a powerful dynamic of imperialism. When economic walls are erected along political boundaries, possession of territory is made to coincide with economic opportunity. Imperialistic ambitions are given both a partial justification and a splendid basis for propaganda. This is the main point of the analysis in this chapter, and it can be well summarized by quoting the following lines from Dr. Leo Grebler:

> Modern wars, we have been told, originate in economic imperialism inherent in a system of intensive world trade. The exploitation of foreign markets by commercial and financial interests, rivalry for exports among big powers, frictions over international investments, and the domestic insecurity resulting from capitalism —all these factors necessarily lead to international tension and to war. We have been asked, therefore, to retreat from economic international entanglements for the sake of peace. We have been asked to retreat into the promised land of self-sufficiency where a new social order secures stability in domestic and harmlessness in international relations.
>
> Economic causes of conflict in a system of capitalistic world trade certainly do exist. . . .
>
> To expect [however] that a system of self-sufficiency . . . will bring about international peace, is absurd. The truth is that if there is any system to which the materialistic interpretation of the origin of wars may properly be applied, it is the system of economic isolation.
>
> If economic resources are not available through international exchange, there is only one way to get access to them—political possession of territories. Since practically no country can make itself entirely self-sufficient, a policy of isolation inevitably breeds lust for resources which happen to be located in more fortunate countries; that is, it fosters international aggression. The desire

for larger economic areas leads to the formation of groups and alliances that make for international insecurity. When commercial relations become political in nature and discrimination is applied, ill will between nations is produced. Domestic strain resulting from a policy of isolation is bound to seek an outlet across the frontiers. All this brings imperialism in its wake. The system of economic isolation, far from being an idyl of self-moderation, develops dynamics of its own—dynamics that pave the way for war.[12]

[12] "Self-Sufficiency and Imperialism," *Annals of the American Academy of Political and Social Science,* Vol. 198 (July, 1938), pp. 7-8.

CHAPTER SEVEN

RESOURCES AND BOUNDARIES

ALL the analysis in Part II has been deliberately put in terms that are fundamental to man's use of resources for economic welfare under *any* system of society. One object has been to untangle some of the confusion that has lately centered around the modern version of the old "free trade" controversy. Whether the productivity of society is raised by the possibility of moving goods and resources over the earth without confinement by political boundaries, and whether the best means of organizing such movements is by leaving the whole matter to private profit-seeking enterprise—these are two separate questions. The defenders of the classical "free trade" position have tended to make them one by arguing, or assuming, that only through private enterprise can we have the abundant international exchange that they hold to be desirable. The critics, or many of them, have granted the point in a backhanded way by attacking or minimizing the benefits of international exchange because they do not like some of the results of private enterprise. For the sake of clear thinking the two questions need to be separated, and we have tried to keep them separate here. The second question is left for later discussion.

The fact that different kinds of resources are distributed over the earth in very different proportions, without much regard for political boundary lines, is a *fact* under capitalism, socialism, totalitarianism, social planning, laissez faire, corporativism, democracy or dictatorship. In so far as any of these systems allows its inhabitants to have an interest in economic welfare (and, of course, they may differ in that, though it is significant that under all of them better economic welfare is asserted, at least part of the time, to be one of the goals of the system), the problem of efficiency in use of resources must arise. And there is no disputing the fact that efficient use of resources for human welfare calls for obtaining each product by that combination of resources that *costs least in terms of the social value of other goods that must be given up to get it.* Translated into the relations between different regions, this means that each particular kind of resource should be drawn upon most heavily in those regions where it is relatively most abundant (therefore least valuable in alternative uses). The moral is: for maximum economic welfare, exchange resources freely, or, if the resources are immobile or moving them involves large costs of transition, trade freely in products that embody the characteristic resources of different regions. By "exchange freely" and "trade freely" we mean merely that, however trade is carried on, political boundary lines should have as little as possible to do with the volume and direction of resource flows. If economic welfare is the object, the world's factories and farms and mines and shops should be located with reference to such factors as consumers' demands, relative abundance and scarcity of needed skills and equipment (or the possibility of providing them), cost-distance from raw material supplies as compared with cost-distance to the chief concentrations of consumers, costs of transition involved in shifting to better locations, social desirability of reasonable diversity within regions, and the like. *The less the movements of resources and goods and the location of industries have to be influenced by political boundary lines, the better for economic welfare.*

It would be naïve to suggest that political boundaries can be disregarded in economic arrangements today. But the unduly large part played by them in deflecting resource flows is a great burden on the world's power to produce and consume. The plea here is that we should recognize the tragic waste involved and then consider what, if anything, should be done about it, or whether there may be offsetting "non-economic" considerations that make it undesirable to do anything at all. Let us be intellectually honest with ourselves and refuse to find rationalizations by which the economic effect of our political misfortunes and incapacities may be presented as not so serious after all, or even as outright contributions to economic welfare!

Should not the reflection that "national self-sufficiency, in short, though it costs something, may be becoming a luxury which we can afford, if we happen to want it,"[1] be rephrased? Stripped of "sour grapes" overtones it would read: National self-sufficiency, though it costs something, may be less of an economic drawback in the future than it is now, if we must choose it under the duress of world political chaos. Even that conclusion cannot be accepted without the most serious reservations, for the course of technology, as explained in Chapter I, appears to be set towards large-scale production and specialized automatic machinery requiring exchange of goods over wider-than-national areas, and towards something almost like absolute dependence on a great volume and variety of key materials from the far corners of the earth. Science may "remedy" this dependence if the failure of world politics makes intercourse among the nations too hazardous, but unhampered science would be

[1] J. M. Keynes, "National Self-Sufficiency," *Yale Review*, June, 1933, p. 760.

much more likely to increase the usefulness of peaceful exchange.

Perhaps it is true that "the tendency of discovery during the past two centuries has been to increase the potential local self-sufficiency consistent with the satisfaction of fundamental human needs." [2] If it is (and one can have serious doubts, based on the great growth of population in the meantime and the large markets and supply areas needed for efficient use of modern industry) all that this carefully phrased statement really says is that with the aid of modern knowledge we can now tie one hand behind our backs and do as well as or better than we used to do with both hands. The slang response suggests itself: "So what?" Should we be happy not only for the great productive power of our one hand but also for having the other tied? Holding in mind the actual levels of consumption in the world (see the first part of Chapter IV), can we reasonably talk today of economic walls towering along every boundary as if these were "a luxury that we can afford" or "consistent with the satisfaction of fundamental human needs"? If the author of the first quotation had put it in his essay on "Economic Possibilities for Our Grandchildren" we might have less reason to quarrel with him.[3]

Of course, if present trends continue very long, we may all have to seek comfort in doctrines that are the politico-economic counterpart of that best-seller for frus-

[2] Lancelot Hogben, "The Creed of a Scientific Humanist," *Nation* (New York), Nov. 12, 1938, p. 508.

[3] Except that our grandchildren, supposing that a "new dark ages" does not result from the conflict of politics with technology, will probably be using types of industrial organization and methods of production that would be even more upset by the necessity of beginning and ending all processes within one tiny part of their world. There would be even more cross-connections to be severed by economic walls at boundaries in a higher state of economic development, just as a less-developed country like China can get along under blockade with fewer readjustments than could any modern country.

trated persons, *Live Alone and Like It.* (The growing interest in South American trade and "continental solidarity" in the United States is an example of such a tendency at work.) But let us not delude ourselves completely with the doctrine that we *like* to be frustrated economically, at least while there is a chance that intelligent action might spare us that necessity.

Sometimes non-economic factors, and especially the urgent desire for security and peace, must take precedence over welfare in narrowly economic terms. Would it not be better then—so runs a common argument—to have higher economic walls between the nations, even at some sacrifice in goods? International loans become a source of ill-feeling. Foreign investments may lead to shameless exploitation, or to pressure on governments to intervene in support of their citizens whose property has been seized. International migrations provide the raw material for racial and religious conflicts and irredentism. International trade leads to irritations over competitive imports, subsidies, dumping, tariffs and tariff retaliation, discrimination, manipulations of exchange rates, monopolies of key products. International tourist travel produces false impressions and disagreeable incidents. Even granting that modern developments of technology make it at least theoretically possible to achieve great gains for economic welfare through a world economy, is it worth while to try to get such gains at the cost of creating new sources of conflict and war? Why not let the nations stay at home and cultivate their own gardens?

This argument has been stated as plausibly as possible, but it arrives by a process of half-truths and confused thinking at a conclusion which is the exact opposite of the truth. It is true that economic contacts between peoples provide the material for conflicts, but so do human contacts of any sort. Whether economic contacts lead to fruitful coöperation or to hostility depends upon how they are handled, and especially upon how society has performed its political task of organizing workable institutions of adjustment. The rapid development of international institutions capable of preserving the useful elements of international economic contacts and reducing frictions to a minimum is the great need of this generation. But nationalistic measures taken singly by separate countries usually hinder rather than help in that task.

Secondly, if we did not already have large economic contacts the argument that we can reduce causes of war by economic isolation would be more reasonable. Today very important going parts of industry in every country are geared to international markets and materials. Population in many areas has risen to a point that demands the most efficient use of resources for its support. The whole chance of many important countries to have an efficient industrial system and higher living standards depends upon access to materials they do not possess within their own boundaries. The dangers in destroying economic contacts, now that we have them, are greater than in building them up.

Finally, it seems too simple, on reflection, to imagine that the mere process of putting up economic fences along more or less accidental political boundaries will really lead men to stay at home and cultivate their own national gardens. Something more would have to happen first, and that something would have to be catastrophic enough to stamp out a large part of modern technical knowledge and to change the whole outlook of modern man. Possessed of airplanes that fly several hundred miles an hour, men are not going to stay within national frontiers a few minutes or a few hours wide. They will cross political boundaries, even when the boundaries are oceans. Knowing that tungsten in steel saves days in labor and millions of dollars in industrial effort, and that it can be had abundantly in a few places on the earth—such as China—they are going to try to get it. Either they will trade for it, or they are likely to fight for it. Tungsten, of course, is only one of a long list of materials that are readily available in some places and not in others. Having erected specialized factories that depend for economical operation upon supplying a larger market than the average national market, men are going to be under pressure to find ways to send goods across boundaries—or enlarge the boundaries. Knowing that a rising living standard within a definitely limited area for an increasing population is only possible by a higher degree of industrialization, those who live in the smaller, more densely populated areas are going to want high industrialization. If their efforts are blocked by the economic walls of larger or more diversified countries that have decided they will cultivate their own gardens exclusively, there will be conflict somewhere.

A policy that restrains modern man from using the knowledge he has acquired, that restrains him from using resources in ways which have become essential to his present modes of existence in some parts of the world, builds up pressures for an explosion. Economic walls at national boundaries, far from preventing conflicts, themselves create a grimly materialistic basis for future wars. One of the first principles for those interested in economic progress and political peace must be: *Lessen the economic significance of political boundaries.*

PART THREE

LAISSEZ FAIRE AND PLANNING

CHAPTER EIGHT

THE TREND TOWARDS CONSCIOUS CONTROL

THE early chapters of this book stressed two things: the strong tendency of technological development to create conditions of world-wide economic integration, and the recent surge of political measures which oppose that trend by raising higher economic walls around national boundaries. In Part II grounds were shown for believing that the increase of exchange between regions, as promoted by technology, is the more favorable of these two contrary tendencies, both from the standpoint of economic welfare and from the standpoint of long-run prospects for peace. The general effect of measures that tend to confine economic activity within national or imperial frontiers, by putting obstacles in the way of movements of goods and resources or in other ways, is to lessen the effectiveness of man's weapons against poverty and to build up pressures that make for war.

Part II expressly postponed all questions about the *means* of organizing economic interchange. This was done in order to show more clearly the fundamental productivity and desirability of the interchange itself, supposing it can be reasonably well organized, under *any* system of carrying on economic activity which has as its object the increase of economic welfare among the people.[1] Now it is time to take up the questions that were

[1] The same conclusions do not follow at all, of course, when the object is military power. This point will be emphasized in Part IV, where some

earlier postponed, for they touch upon some of the most important current problems in the whole field of international economic policy. These questions have received very little systematic treatment from previous writers in this field. Because there is less to build on, the chapters that follow can be offered only as a very tentative statement of issues, bearing on the general problem: What is the consequence for international economic relations and international economic policy of the changes in the structure of economic organization everywhere to be seen in recent times?

Today the manner in which world resources are used is less exclusively determined by competitive decisions of private enterprises responding to the play of market forces than at any time in the last century. Conscious control has spread throughout economic life. The daily conduct of international economic relations, in particular, is more and more subject to the influence of governments on general economic activity, to government-controlled foreign trade systems, and to public or quasi-public authorities controlling particular commodities. This chapter will sketch some of these trends factually. The next two chapters consider their effects upon the character of international economic relations, and upon the problem of using world resources wisely.

Government and Economic Life

The enormous increase in the economic rôle of the state over the last few years has the greatest possible importance for the future of international economic relations. State economic activities have grown from such diverse roots as wartime needs, the fear of war and the

of the problems that it raises for present-day economic policy will be stated.

race for rearmament and military self-sufficiency, the feelings of the man in the street on the subject of poverty in the midst of plenty, innumerable specific pressures from private interests, the idea of scientific management, the philosophy of collectivist socialism, the totalitarian philosophy of the state, the sheer pressure of economic emergency in the depression, and the acceptance of the idea that it is the state's business not only to see that nobody starves but also to ensure efficient running of the economic machine. The myriad forms of state economic activity can be no more than indicated here, with enough mention of concrete instances to show that increasing governmental action is not a movement peculiar to one country but is world-wide.[2]

Governments have taken over industries of key importance, such as munition factories in France, have assumed the management of public utility services, as under the Central Electricity Board in Great Britain, and have set up public enterprises to prepare the way for development of whole regions and to provide "yardsticks" for private industries, as in the case of the Tennessee Valley Authority in the United States. Governments have entered industry to eliminate private monopoly, as in the state purchase of wholesale drug and medicine houses in Sweden. New undertakings have been set up as part of a national program of industrialization in Tur-

[2] Most of the data in this section are taken directly, sometimes almost verbatim, from a study of "The Present Status of Economic Planning: I. An International Survey of Governmental Economic Intervention," by P. W. Martin, *International Labour Review*, Vol. XXXIII (May, 1936), pp. 619-45.

A work by F. E. Lawley, *The Growth of Collective Economy*, in which Volume I deals with "The Growth of National Collective Economy," and Volume II with "The Growth of International Collective Economy" (London: P. S. King, 1938), brings together an imposing mass of concrete factual information. One wishes that the author might have been more discriminating in his enthusiasm for the various kinds of collective economic action.

key, Iran, Iraq and Siam. Some form of standing control over private management affects practically all activities of business undertakings in the countries where "corporative" systems prevail, as in Italy. Industries in special difficulties have elsewhere been put under supervision, as in the case of coal-mining in the United States and Belgium and oil production in the United States. Regulations establishing certain basic conditions which management must accept have multiplied enormously. Those relating to health, safety and the protection of labor generally are of long standing. Wages, hours and other conditions of work are now extensively regulated. There are many measures designed to relieve the unemployment situation by limiting the use of labor-saving machinery. The labor boards set up in the United States and the total prohibition of strikes and lockouts in Italy are divergent examples of state intervention in industrial relations. The banking system and the money market in a number of countries have been brought under stringent rules bordering in some cases (for example, in Germany, Italy and Bulgaria) upon actual state management. Grading and branding of products, ethical codes, rules of fair competition and honest advertising have been promoted by the state. Everywhere governmental regulations have multiplied enormously. "The quasi-independent status of industry, *vis-à-vis* the State, has been replaced by a mixture of partnership and dependence, which, whatever may be thought of it as a system, constitutes a totally new situation . . ." [3]

State adjustment of output by direct governmental control of prices, production, and productive capacity, and by control of producers' organizations, has multiplied rapidly through the depression. Direct control of prices ranges all the way from general price control over

[3] P. W. Martin, *loc. cit.*, p. 631.

practically all products, as in Germany, to government action designed to prevent speculative or seasonal price swings of a particular product, as of wheat in Canada. Price control in the consumer's interest has taken the form of state enforcement of a particular price (*e.g.*, of bread and of milk in a number of Central European countries), government action on the wholesale market with the object of keeping the price low (*e.g.*, for rice at certain times in Japan), the compulsory lowering of monopoly prices, as in France, Yugoslavia and Poland, and the prohibition of unjustifiable price-raising after currency devaluation or imposition of new quotas (for example, in Belgium and Switzerland). But price-fixing in the producer's interest is still more widespread. In Great Britain the government pays wheat producers the difference between the market price and a guaranteed price. In Australia the price of butter is fixed on the home market in order to yield a surplus out of which exports may be subsidized. In the United States loans have been granted to farmers on condition that they hold their stocks of corn, cotton and other agricultural products off the market, and plantings have been restricted, thus strongly affecting the market price. In Denmark pigs without a quota-card fetch 50 per cent less than those whose production has been authorized. To influence prices, over ten million acres of cotton were ploughed under in the United States in 1933, and Brazil burned coffee during the depression to an amount exceeding two good average crops. In many countries there has been compulsory formation of cartels (as in the United States for a time under the NRA.), and restrictions upon the installation of new machinery or the opening of new factories have been common. In Germany, for instance, further investment in some thirty important branches of industry has been forbidden. National governments have joined together in international agreements to control the output and price of rubber, wheat, sugar, silver and other commodities. Encouragement has been given to private associations of producers for similar purposes.

There are many forms of state aid to industry, including some of long standing, such as publication of business statistics, operation of experimental farms and research institutes, assistance to foreign traders through consular representatives, and in some countries state insurance and credit facilities. Newer developments include a Bureau for the Rationalization of Industry in Japan, a Committee for the Promotion of Swedish Production (which it is proposed to convert into a permanent commission), and levies on wool in the British Dominions to support a wool research program. The Reconstruction Finance Corporation in the United States, the Institute of Rediscount and Guarantee in Belgium, and the machinery of the Industries Assistance Act in Queensland, Australia, have given large amounts of financial aid to industry. Subsidies, of course, in one form or another, are a frequent form of government assistance. Even in the Netherlands, where the principle of laissez faire is deeply rooted, there are large items in the budget for assistance to exporters of dairy produce, market gardeners, and bacon producers. The Danish government has subsidized business undertakings on condition that they make a genuine increase in working force. Great Britain subsidizes sugar beets and many other agricultural commodities. Japan subsidizes the industrial guilds in which small producers are organized. Almost every country with a merchant marine supports it by a subsidy. These are only a few out of a great mass of illustrations that might be given. In addition to direct financial aid, there are many forms of disguised subsidy: special exchange rates, special freight rates, remission of taxes, and the whole body of protective tariffs, protective import quotas, and other restrictions on international trade designed to permit local producers to charge local consumers more than they otherwise could.

The extension of national services provides a long list of new governmental economic activities: slum clearance, electrification projects, land reclamation, town and country planning programs, resettlement of workers, new or broader plans of unemployment insurance, old-age assistance, health insurance, and public education. Working-class housing and adequate nutrition are coming to be matters of state concern. Each of these various governmental services could be instanced by examples drawn from many countries.

Many of the measures mentioned involve an indirect redistribution of income. Others, more direct, include the principle of progressive income taxation, which continues to spread, debt readjustment measures for home-owners (in the United States) and for farmers (in most of the countries of Central and Eastern Europe, in the United States, Brazil, New Zealand, and elsewhere). Governmental controls have been used at times to contract and at other times to expand monetary circulation and the general price level. Examples of a contractionist sort were provided by Germany and Italy in the early stages of the depression, and by the Netherlands, Poland and France for a longer time. The methods included general price reductions under pressure from the state, wage-cutting by or on the initiative of the government, forced reduction of interest on loans, attempts to decrease state expenditures, and increased taxation. Expansionist measures, on the other hand, have included "reflationary" open market operations and discount policies by central banks, departure from the gold standard, avowed or concealed devaluation of the currency, and large-scale borrowing for deliberate "pump priming" expenditures on public works or work relief.

All these various governmental measures change the setting within which international economic relations take place. It is unnecessary, after the summary given in Chapter II, to add examples of tariffs, quotas, exchange controls, capital embargoes, immigration and emigration restrictions, and the like, which directly affect the international flow of goods and resources and people. Some national areas live under forms of planned or controlled economy which put all external economic contacts under the direct influence of the state. These systems introduce a new element into world economy that calls for special attention.

External Economic Relations of "Totalitarian" Economies

The U.S.S.R. Thoroughgoing state ownership and control, with nearly complete central direction of all economic activities, is the established order in a territory that covers almost one-sixth of the world's land surface, has a large and rapidly growing population, and includes a variety of natural resources comparable to those of the United States and the British Empire. The Soviet Union was largely a peasant country until a decade ago, but strenuous efforts under successive five-year plans have built a large industrial equipment, trained millions of workers in machine production, and revolutionized the methods of agriculture. Despite internal conflicts, the U.S.S.R. must in the long run be reckoned a factor of major importance in the world's economic and political evolution.

As the only fully-collectivized economy in the world, the Soviet Union naturally carries on external economic relations in a way unlike any other country. Internal production is organized and directed under a central plan, administered from top to bottom by officials of the state, who manage factories, mines, and trading organizations and, less directly, control the policies of collective farms. Imports and exports, lending and borrowing abroad, must also fit into the general economic plan, if they are not to upset other parts of the economy. This would seem to make it unavoidable that the Soviet government should itself direct, organize, and actually carry on all the operations connected with foreign trade, as in fact it does.

The administrative organization for this purpose has evolved through several stages since the initial decree of 1918 that nationalized foreign trade.[4] The present arrangement is considerably more decentralized than the earlier methods. In particular, export-import corporations have been set up to specialize in different commodities. All of them, of course, are state agencies operating within the general framework of a foreign trade plan which is itself a part of the general economic plan. Import or export taxes or subsidies, exchange controls and quotas (in the ordinary sense), have no use in such a system, except as administrative or accounting devices that bear only a superficial likeness to the methods of influencing private trade in other countries. The Soviet economic authorities decide directly what shall be bought and sold abroad, where purchases and sales shall be made, and what terms shall be accepted.

Soviet foreign trade is not large for a country of the size and industrial importance of the U.S.S.R. That is partly the result of a definite attempt to make the economy independent of the capitalist world.

[4] See Karl W. Kapp, *Planwirtschaft und Aussenhandel* (Geneva: Georg et Cie., Librairie de l'Université, 1936), Ch. 7.

> We must build up our economy in such a way that our country shall not be transformed into an appendage of the world capitalist system.[5]

Partly, however, it results from antagonism against the Soviet Union abroad, which has hampered its trading operations and limited its ability to get credit. Long-term capital investments from abroad for the building of local industry, important in the development of other countries, were not available to the Soviets. Successful arrangements were worked out, however, for technical assistance from abroad, and this played a large part in the early stages of large-scale industrialization.

Soviet leaders maintain that autarchy is not their ideal. At the World Monetary and Economic Conference of 1933 Foreign Minister Litvinoff declared:

> My Government has no intention of cutting itself off from the outer world by economic barriers and retiring into its own economic shell. In distinction from other countries, we, with a great increase of our own output, do not aspire to autarchy and do not resist an advantageous import of foreign goods.

Again:

> The Soviet Union has not the slightest intention of breaking off its trade relations with the capitalist world. It is even interested in extending those trade relations, and has the greatest possibilities in the world of enlarging its foreign trade.[6]

Similar pronouncements have been made since.

Fearing, as it does, attack by Japan in the East and Germany in the West, the Soviet Union has seen its economy warped more and more in the last few years away from the earlier emphasis on economic welfare for the

[5] Josef Stalin, in a statement made prior to the launching of the first Five-Year Plan. Quoted in J. D. Yanson, *Foreign Trade in the U.S.S.R.* (London: Victor Gollancz, Ltd., 1934), p. 14.

[6] *Ibid.*, pp. 33-4.

"toiling masses" towards emphasis on war preparation. Probably in no country in the world, except in those actually engaged in war, is such a large proportion of the national income going for war preparedness. Estimates put the figure at somewhere between 27 and 40 per cent of the national income.[7] The frantic quest for security through military power usually tends to put a premium on self-sufficiency and to throttle foreign trade, despite the cost in economic welfare. This tendency is at least as strong in the Soviet Union as elsewhere, and the world will need to be a more peaceful place before the managers of Soviet policy are likely to risk the degree of economic interdependence that would be necessary in order to take full advantage of opportunities for productive exchange with the world economy.

Germany. The events of the War and the post-war years brought state interventions in the economic life of Germany not different in kind from those in other countries of Western Europe. Until 1934 the control of foreign trade was a compound of heterogeneous emergency measures, including import quotas, import and export prohibitions applying to particular commodities, price-fixing measures, export associations encouraged by the government, regulated foreign payments, and the like.

A systematic tightening of state control was inaugurated in the fall of 1934 and early 1935. The Reich Minister of Economics received power to supervise and regulate foreign trade in goods of all sorts. He acted in close coöperation with the foreign exchange authorities, who had to approve all applications for making payments abroad. The purpose of strict foreign exchange regulations, officially stated, was ". . . to prevent the unregu-

[7] William T. Stone, "Economic Consequences of Rearmament," *Foreign Policy Reports* (New York: Foreign Policy Association), Vol. XIV, No. 14, October 1, 1938, p. 165.

lated outflow of foreign exchange and to bring about the purposeful use of foreign exchange that is available or becomes available." [8]

The detailed administration of imports is entrusted to twenty-six control boards, whose authority covers specified groups of commodities. Anyone wishing to import from abroad must apply first to the proper control board and ask for a foreign exchange permit. If the permit is granted, it applies only to one transaction, is made out in the name of the applicant, and is not transferable. With this authorization the importer goes to the Reichsbank or to one of the "Devisen" banks for the necessary foreign exchange. Finally, when the goods actually arrive, the foreign exchange permit must be presented to the customs authorities. In the case of imports of many agricultural products, the goods cannot be disposed of in Germany until they have been offered for purchase to certain state regulating agencies. For other commodities, particularly a considerable number of industrial raw materials, a purchase permit is necessary in addition to the foreign exchange permit.

The export trade is likewise regulated by the state. All goods sent out of Germany must be declared to an agency of the Reichsbank. The foreign money received in payment for any sort of goods or service sold by Germans to foreigners must be placed at the disposal of the Reichsbank or the "Devisen" banks. No other person or agency is allowed to buy foreign exchange with marks. The rate, of course, is officially fixed. It is unnecessary to describe the various measures, some of them quite complex, by which German exporters are either subsidized or enabled to quote prices in foreign currencies lower

[8] "Richtlinien für die Devisenbewirtschaftung," Section I, Paragraph 6, Reichgesetzblatt, 1935, I, 121. Cited in Kapp, *loc. cit.*, p. 122 ff., from which I have gathered much of the information in the text.

than would be possible at the official valuation of the mark. These measures, including special tourist marks at lower rates, payments for exports by "blocked mark" accounts which can be acquired at a discount, "compensation" or barter arrangements by which private merchants are permitted to arrange a trade of, say, American cotton against German optical goods, really mean that the mark has been devalued in fact while the old rate has been nominally retained. The German system makes the actual devaluation different for different sorts of transactions. The real exchange rate even varies from one transaction to another, so that full advantage can be taken of bargaining power.

The far-reaching control of foreign exchange transactions by the German government has led to a network of bilateral clearing and payment agreements and barter arrangements with other governments. The principle of equal treatment in commercial dealings has been frankly abandoned. For example, in the matter of arranging service payments on private debts owed by Germans to foreigners, the governments of countries which bought more from Germany than they sold to Germany were able to get more favorable treatment for their citizens, because they were in a position to set up clearing systems and seize the surplus proceeds of German exports. Political as well as economic bargaining power has inevitably played a rôle in trade arrangements under this system. The formation of a bloc of states in Southeastern Europe politically and economically linked to Germany or dependent on Germany is a part of the same policy.

Germany's method of carrying on international economic relations resembles that of the Soviet Union in some ways and differs from it in others. The two systems are alike in setting aside the market mechanism of international trade. Under both systems import duties lose their importance, and the currents of trade are regulated directly by government decisions. The traditional guarantee of non-discrimination and equal treatment embodied in the most-favored-nation clause comes to have a very restricted application. Trade treaties regulate not only the conditions of trade, but its substance as well. On the other hand, the German system differs decidedly from that of the Soviet Union. The actual transactions in foreign trade are handled by private importers and exporters—though their decisions are closely hedged about by government regulations. No general economic plan is worked out by the government for the coördination of production as a whole, and there is no detailed program for foreign trade as a part of such a plan. The German "four-year plan" is a campaign for discovery of substitutes and a general promotion of self-sufficiency in preparation for war, not a thoroughgoing blueprint for the whole economic system like the five-year plans of the Soviet Union.

If one may hazard a forecast, it is that the differences which separate the German system from the Soviet trading system will grow less important with time. Already, few of the features of the old "capitalist" or free-market economy remain unchanged in Germany. The government has practically taken over the guidance of new investment, and it will have to assume more and more responsibility for direct management of economic affairs. Two quotations from German economic periodicals illustrate the trend:

> If high profits are obtained, they are simply the monetary expression of a high level of State-investment, for which they are again claimed. The acquisition of Government securities by many undertakings is the expression of this state of affairs.
>
> The "free entrepreneur" will not come back. Private undertakings have now become fiefs of the national economy *(volkswirt-*

schaftliche Lehen). The State holds an interest as it were in every German enterprise.[9]

Italy. The "corporative state" in practice means an apparatus of administration run from the top down, not a system of economic representation. Rights of private property and private initiative are retained in principle, but the state controls and supervises and overrules, sets wages and prices, decides whether an enterprise may build a new factory, and regulates foreign trade. All is controlled from the point of view of increasing the military power of the state. In fact, the best short description of the Italian economic system at present is "war economy."

Until the great depression, Italy's foreign trade regulations, except for the usual protective favors to certain domestic industries, were few. The depression led, however, to a system of foreign trade control which has been gradually strengthened, especially under the influence of the Ethiopian War and the economic sanctions applied against Italy.

Exchange restrictions were first authorized by a decree-law of September 29, 1931. A passive balance of payments led to drastic import restrictions by means of a quota system introduced in 1934–35. The Ethiopian campaign brought the usual measures of wartime control, including stricter supervision of foreign exchange transactions, registration of foreign investments, drastic limitations of imports, and measures of economy in the use of scarce raw materials. The country has continued ever since on a war-economy basis. Mussolini has stressed repeatedly that Italy must do everything possible to make itself self-sufficient.

[9] *Frankfurter Zeitung,* "Das Wirtschaftsjahr." 2. Teil, Jan. 1, 1938. *Der deutsche Volkswirt,* August 6, 1937, p. 2191. Both quotations are from the report of the Director of the I.L.O., 1938, p. 33.

The whole nation must acquire the autarchic mentality . . . Any national initiative, no matter how modest, must be encouraged, provided it gives an efficient contribution to the supreme aim of national self-sufficiency.[10]

In comparison with the German system of foreign trade regulation, the Italian seems to be less severe and less thorough, leaving a somewhat greater amount of freedom to the individual firm. But the basic principles are not greatly different.

Japan.[11] The industrialization of Japan since it first came into regular contact with the Western world some seventy-five years ago has been a modern miracle. This development was guided from the first by the government, in collaboration with powerful families that controlled banking and commercial interests. Japan's economic system might be described as modern capitalism with strong feudal survivals. Today the structure of industry and the conduct of foreign trade in particular are being remolded under the dominance of military authority and the demands of war economy.

On December 17, 1931, the Japanese government suspended the gold standard and thereafter established a system of foreign exchange control. The yen was drastically devalued. For this reason, probably, the Japanese government was concerned much less during the depression with restricting imports than with influencing foreign trade in other ways. The low level of the yen was itself an automatic and powerful burden on imports. At the same time, the drastic depreciation of the yen thus early

[10] *New York Times,* October 12, 1937.

[11] See *Japanese Trade and Industry, Present and Future,* by the Mitsubishi Economic Research Bureau, Tokyo (London: 1936); reports and information bulletins on Japan issued by the Department of Overseas Trade in Great Britain and the Bureau of Foreign and Domestic Commerce in the United States; current information in the *Far Eastern Survey,* fortnightly research service of the American Council, Institute of Pacific Relations.

in the depression gave a great stimulus to exports. As has been mentioned in an earlier chapter, this and other measures of the government actually produced an industrial boom while other countries were deep in depression, and the spectacular increase in exports led to restrictions aimed at Japanese goods all over the world.

Among the government measures for assisting traders in the conquest of new markets was the Export Compensation Law of 1930 by which exporters might be partly reimbursed for credit losses incurred on shipments to new or hazardous markets. These credits played an important rôle in the Japanese trade drive in Africa, Latin America, and the Soviet Union. Industrial and export guilds or associations fostered by the government have been active since the initial Export Industries Association Law of 1925. Amendments in 1931 and 1934 strengthened the control of the associations, and of the government operating through them, over the volume and prices of export goods. Tendencies of this sort were very marked after 1933, and from 1933–35 the number of export associations increased from 14 to 85. The operation of this whole scheme of control must be seen against the domestic background of government-sponsored cartellization based on the Major Industries Control Law of 1931. In 1936 the government received statutory powers to enable the associations to limit exports to a given destination. The export associations have helped in the campaign for expansion of Japanese export trade by sending commercial missions to foreign countries, by investigating markets, sponsoring exhibitions, and the like. In April 1934, the Trade Promotion Law gave the government power to restrict imports of specified articles and to impose additional duties, in order to answer discrimination against Japanese trade abroad.

Since the beginning of the war with China, governmental regulation of foreign trade, especially on the import side, has increased very greatly. Characteristic measures of war economy have been applied. These are made more intense in the field of foreign trade by the fact that Japan, even more than Germany and perhaps more than Italy, depends on the import of vital raw materials from abroad. Only materials considered to be military essentials can now be brought in, unless they are to be manufactured and reëxported in exchange for much needed foreign moneys. This regulation is enforced by the so-called "link system" of import permits, under which a manufacturer may buy cotton and other supplies abroad only to replace the same materials contained in finished goods that he exports. The domestic use of various scarce materials such as leather, cotton and many metals is virtually prohibited.

The most far-reaching of all the economic legislation of the last two years was the National Mobilization Law adopted in March 1938.[12] It empowers the government to issue decrees controlling prices, wages, labor disputes, capital investments, foreign trade, production and distribution of vital war materials; to expropriate lands, houses, factories, and other working facilities connected with production of goods needed in war; to confiscate newspapers or other publications violating censorship decrees; and to conscript workers and specialists of all kinds. It has been only partially applied thus far.

Whether the outcome of the war in China is victory, defeat, or stalemate, at least some of these changes in the Japanese economic system will remain. Economic life and international economic relations will be more than ever subject to national political control.

[12] See *Far Eastern Survey,* April 6, 1938, June 29, 1938 and Feb. 1, 1939.

Commodity Controls

While national governments are the most important agencies exerting conscious control over the world's economic activities today, they are not the only ones. Private combinations of capital or of labor often get a firm enough grip on the supply of a particular commodity or a particular resource to influence significantly its output and price, and hence its rôle in the world economy. When this happens it indicates at least some degree of monopoly power. Problems raised by monopoly power in the modern economic system will be touched upon in the next chapter.

Labor combinations usually affect only one part of the world economy directly. Combinations of capital, however, have already become large enough in some cases to control nearly all the world supply of a particular commodity, thus establishing their power to patrol the "boundary" that separates their special commodity-domain from the rest of the world and to supervise all the traffic back and forth. The International Nickel Company of Canada, Ltd., based upon a remarkable mineral concentration in the district where it mainly operates, is the best example. Out of world sales of nickel estimated at 240 million pounds in 1937 the company supplied 207 million, or 86 per cent. It also manufactures nickel and nickel alloy products (especially "Monel metal"), mines more platinum than any other producer and holds fifth place in copper output. In ownership as well as in operations it is international, with its stock held as follows: 18.2 per cent in Canada, 46.4 per cent in the United States, 31.7 per cent in Great Britain, and 3.7 per cent elsewhere.[13]

[13] *Standard Corporation Records,* Individual Reports Section, Vol. 16, No. 3615, July 12, 1938, Section 5.

Much more common than commodity controls operated by one dominant company are those based on coöperation among a number of private producers (cartels), or on inter-governmental agreements. Private controls, sometimes tinged with a large amount of governmental influence, especially where war materials are concerned, have been of international importance in steel and various steel manufactures, aluminum, bismuth, copper, nitrates, sulphur, zinc, electric light bulbs, and other fields. Aside from commodity controls undertaken by one government alone (coffee in Brazil, cotton in the United States, camphor and silk in Japan, quinine in the Netherlands Indies), there have been a number of very significant attempts in recent years at world commodity controls by inter-governmental agreement. Some have survived and some have not; but where a scheme has collapsed, another and broader one in the same commodity has often taken its place. Such important materials as rubber, tin, mercury, silver, tea, sugar, and wheat have been affected, and there is nothing to indicate that the movement is a passing one.

These world commodity controls—private, semi-private, quasi-public, and inter-governmental—have a special significance. In all the welter and confusion of new efforts at conscious control of economic activity, they are among the few that are *super-national.* In the rubber, tin, sugar, and copper controls, as well as in the activities of the Bank for International Settlements, the International Labour Organisation, and the technical committees of the League of Nations, we may see the embryo of future world economic administration and world economic policy—a development that is needed to fit the technological conditions of today. This is not to label the rise of world commodity controls as unqualifiedly a "good thing." Most of their activity has been restrictive, and many of them have done more to cause instability than to relieve the effects of instability. But the world badly needs the habit of working out economic policies on a wider-than-national basis, and institutions go on evolving after they have been established. Instrumentalities like the rubber control represent a trend towards the broadening of economic policy to fit the new conditions of world-wide economic interdependence, despite their origin in producers' demands for restriction of output.

The aim of this chapter has been solely a factual one—to bring to mind the far-reaching changes in economic organization which have been taking place, not just in a few countries, but all over the world in recent times. The growth of governmental economic activity in the countries that continue to depend mainly on a private enterprise system, the rise of "totalitarian" economies, and the multiplication of partly-private, partly-public commodity controls of world significance have been changing the nature of international economic relations. Confronted by new conditions, international economic policy is being forced to explore new paths. Unaccustomed problems appear on every hand. What of the functioning of a system that is partly subject to conscious control and partly subject to the impersonal market forces of competition? What of the relations between countries that have come to have different types of economic systems? These are some of the issues into which the next few chapters must inquire.

CHAPTER NINE

THE SOCIAL THEORY OF LAISSEZ FAIRE AND OF PLANNING

UNDER any economic system that makes use of social coöperation in production—that is, division of labor—there must be some means of coördinating the efforts of specialized producers with each other, and with the wants of consumers. Certain great tasks of organization have to be performed. These include: (1) determining what goods are to be produced, and in what amounts; (2) apportioning available resources of all sorts among the various branches of industry and coördinating them within the industries; (3) sharing the total product of industry among individuals and families; (4) providing for maintenance and improvement of equipment and knowledge; (5) making goods go around until more can be produced.[1]

Two main principles or methods have been combined in different proportions in modern societies for performing these primary tasks of economic coördination. One principle, which we may call "laissez faire" for short, though that does not adequately describe it, relies on the automatic working of a self-regulating market mechanism to achieve coördination. The market mechanism itself depends upon an institutional framework of prop-

[1] Frank H. Knight, "Social Economic Organization," in the *Syllabus and Selected Readings* of the Second-Year Course in the Study of Contemporary Society, University of Chicago (University of Chicago Bookstore, 4th edition, 1935), pp. 125-37.

erty rights, private enterprise motivated by the quest for gain, and free competition among the gain-seekers. Of *conscious* decisions on the total amounts of different commodities to be produced, on the amounts of labor or capital or other resources to be allotted for the use of various industries, and on the other points mentioned above, there would be none if this principle of coördination were applied in its purest form. Thousands of individual decisions add up to social decisions.

"Planning," on the other hand—which we shall use to mean the principle of conscious control of economic activity—relies upon central decisions to answer such questions as how large the total annual output of a particular good shall be, and how much of present production shall be turned into capital equipment instead of into consumption goods. To the extent that this principle is applied, the great primary decisions listed earlier are made at one point or a few points, and they are carried out by administration, not by the impersonal operation of market forces.

Of course, no society that ever existed was so completely "laissez faire" that it lacked all conscious effort to influence the great, over-all economic decisions. Neither has there ever been a society where everything economic was settled by "planning," with no scope at all for small, decentralized initiatives and choices to influence the total result. The chart below places some actual economic systems of the present or recent past along a line which runs from the pole of pure market coördination at the left to the pole of pure planned coördination at the right. The arrangement is solely with regard to the proportion of these two principles, just as one might arrange buildings according to height regardless of color, shape, or content.

THE "SPECTRUM" OF ECONOMIC SYSTEMS

Arranged according to amount of "laissez faire" and of "planning"

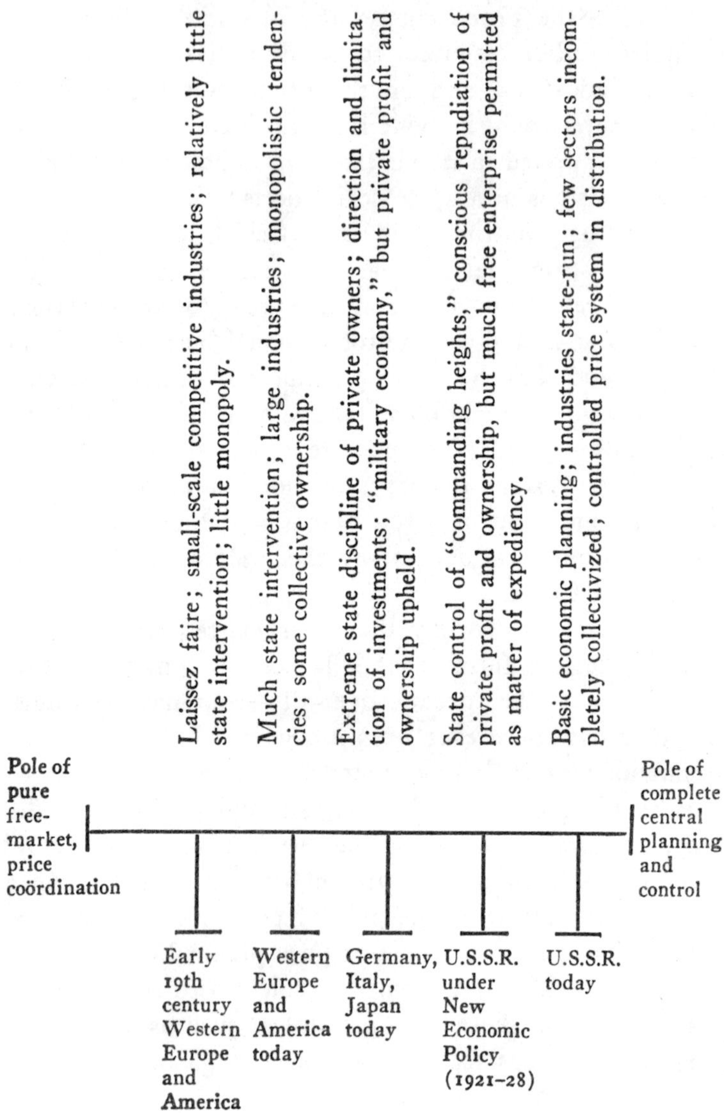

As one moves along this "spectrum" from the pole of free market coördination towards the pole of central planning and control, one seems to move also:

—from private property rights in productive instruments towards collective ownership;

—from governmental functions confined to policing, "refereeing" and maintaining the framework within which the market system operates, towards governmental management of the whole industrial system;

—from relatively distinct political and economic systems connected by a thousand more or less devious ties, towards a merging of economics and politics, at least at the higher levels;

—from great decisions that are totaled up from small decisions in an impersonal market and hence appear as the automatic, unwilled result of "blind forces," towards great decisions that are deliberate, direct, conscious, personal, and willed.

In short, the social and political implications of the means by which economic coördination is achieved are very great. Where the amount of conscious control over economic life is increasing, which means everywhere in the world today, the *kinds* of conscious control and the *purposes* to which they are put are extremely significant for such important problems as the fate of democratic political institutions. These are matters to which we must return later, especially in connection with the discussion of positive versus restrictive planning and planning for welfare versus planning for military power.

The Self-Regulating Mechanism and Its Eclipse

At its theoretical best the principle of economic coordination through the free market offers a self-regulating mechanism which automatically and unconsciously guides society towards the best use of resources. That was the doctrine expounded by such writers as Adam Smith in their campaign to free industrial initiative from mercantilistic restrictions. They maintained that under free competition each enterpriser would find it to his own advantage to try to produce the best goods at the lowest prices. Otherwise he would lose customers to his competitors. And as the raw materials, labor, and capital funds used by each enterpriser in his business could be put to alternative uses by other enterprisers, he would have to bid for these resources against competition and would be forced to pay the full social value for them. Thus, one enterpriser could prosper above others only by combining resources more efficiently—that is, by better methods of production—or by meeting the demands of consumers more exactly.

This is what Adam Smith meant when he argued that given freedom of enterprise, competition, and a reasonable degree of mobility of resources—the "obvious and simple system of natural liberty"—the seeker after private profit would be "led by an invisible hand to promote an end which was no part of his intention," namely, the social welfare. There was nothing mystical about this doctrine, so often misinterpreted by those who have not troubled to understand it. The invisible hand is a metaphor. Perfectly definite forces, namely, competition for the trade of customers and competition for resources to be used in production, operate under conditions of freedom, according to Smith and his followers, to bring the actions of hard-boiled self-seekers into harmony with the general interest. Thus the apostles of laissez faire claimed to have found the key to the solution of a great social problem—how to make the economic interests of the individual coincide with those of society.

Today the conditions of freedom and mobility under

which these happy results are supposed to follow are severely limited in the real world. This results in part, as the advocates of non-interference can rightly point out, from faulty governmental policies which foster monopoly and encourage resistance to needed adjustments in the economic system instead of helping to encourage smoother adjustments. On the other hand, there are elements in modern life—with its greater specialization and greater vulnerability to interruption of traffic, its lack of new frontiers of free land, its new technology which encourages large units and large overhead costs in many lines—which would seem to account for a considerable part of the resistance that keeps the system from being freely flexible, aside from what can be laid at the door of faulty policy.

Even if it were not for restrictions and rigidities, however, both experience and later theoretical analysis should warn us that social welfare cannot be entrusted so entirely to the free market as the more extreme advocates of laissez faire had supposed. (1) There are non-economic values that do not enter into the market price mechanism. (2) Extreme laissez faire under a market system based on private ownership in the means of production must lead, almost inevitably it would seem, to considerable inequalities in the distribution of wealth and income. In the absence of governmental intervention (such as progressive income taxation, subsidized low-cost housing, subsidized education, etc.) this would make pecuniary demand a highly distorted measure of human needs, yet the market responds only to pecuniary demand. (3) Even supposing that the market demand correctly pictures social values, there is bound to be a large class of cases (analyzed in detail in Pigou's *Economics of Welfare*) in which the actions of enterprisers may be correct from the point of view of largest *private* returns for those making the decisions, but incorrect from the point of view of largest *social* benefit. (4) The automatic market mechanism may be highly unstable, as in cyclical disturbances where business men react to mistaken anticipations or react to general pessimism in ways that are rational for the individual firm but disastrous for all firms together and for the community. (5) Competition between large producing units is likely to be "monopolistic competition," which does not lead to the same favorable social results as the type of competition assumed in the theory of laissez faire. Even small units, under certain conditions, show the characteristics of monopolistic competition. (6) It is just as "natural" for a seeker after private gain to try to profit by forming monopolistic combinations, by seeking to influence the action of the state in order to get subsidies, tariffs, restriction schemes, and the like, as it is for him to try to profit by delivering a better product at a lower price. The very motive power of the private enterprise system thus tends, unless the institutional fabric is strong and carefully guarded, to destroy the conditions essential to its functioning—to destroy, that is, free competition.

In the realm of international economic relations, the self-regulating mechanism has had its triumphs and its failures. When new resources became available in North America, the automatic price system, unaided by any conscious long-range plan, brought a flow of labor power and capital to the resources and fitted the resulting new production into the world economy. Higher wages than in Europe attracted labor, higher interest rates attracted capital. As railroads opened up the abundant agricultural resources of the Mississippi Valley, the self-regulating mechanism lowered the price of wheat, made farming less profitable in Europe and made industrial pursuits more profitable, especially as the new purchasing power of

American farm regions increased the demand for industrial goods. Thus labor and capital and enterprise were shifted out of those occupations in which Europe's resources were relatively scarce as compared with America's and into those where its labor and capital could be used more efficiently. There were transition difficulties in Europe as competition with American wheat became possible, but new lines were opening up, and the difficulties proved small and temporary compared with the benefits. The whole process was very much the sort of rearrangement in use of resources that one would have expected from a benign world dictator out to raise the living standards of his subjects, but it was carried through mainly by the response to market forces of thousands of individuals whose only concern was to get better wages, better returns on investments, and better profits.

On the other hand, the record of the self-regulating mechanism in bringing adjustment to the new forces that played upon agriculture after the World War was not so impressive. The opening up of new acres under the influence of abnormal wartime demands, improved methods of production, dietary shifts away from staple grain crops, substitution of tractors and automobiles for grain-consuming work horses, a gradual decline in rates of population growth in many countries, all combined to point towards a need for shifting some human and material resources out of established lines of agriculture into something else. The self-regulating mechanism responded by pushing downwards the price of wheat and other grains, thus setting the price signals at "warning—get out of these lines of agricultural production," but the response was sluggish, and at times a drop in price even brought an increase in plantings as farmers tried to maintain themselves in their traditional occupation. Social factors, and not just governmental interference, would seem to explain a considerable part of the failure of the self-regulating mechanism to bring smooth adjustment in agriculture during the 1920's when expansion in many industrial lines was going forward. As the unsolved "farm problem" entered the depression period it became the center of some of the most radical government interventions in economic life, which in the form they took may or may not have been worse than unimpeded market forces would have been. The relevant point here is that, for whatever reasons, the automatic system was not very successful in bringing necessary adjustments before 1929, and since then has suffered partial eclipse as governments have been forced by political necessity to intervene drastically in agriculture.

In the coffee industry, the fact that trees start yielding only five or six years after they are planted has on several occasions caused the responses of producers to overshoot the mark when price "signals" have called for an increase or decrease of output. Delayed responses of this sort, especially when combined with an inelastic demand for the product, can make an industry inherently unstable under a system of purely individualistic adjustments to market conditions. High prices, signaling a shortage, lead individual enterprisers to expand their capacity for production (*e.g.,* by planting more trees), but without taking account of the decisions of other enterprisers, whose simultaneous actions show their effects only later when all the new capacity starts producing and gluts the market so that even efficient producers go bankrupt. This tendency to rush all together first to one side of the boat and then to the other has been one of the factors that has helped to stimulate insistent demands for interference with the self-regulating mechanism in the coffee industry, the rubber industry, and many others where control schemes have lessened the rôle of the market price system.

A major depression brings out other peculiarities in the response of individual enterprises to price changes which limit the extent to which the "automatic" mechanism can be relied upon to keep the economic system in equilibrium. "When prices begin to fall, it is to the advantage of each individual firm to buy as little as possible. This tends to intensify the crisis. Thus, it is obvious that the automatic reaction of the individual firm does not in this case lead to a reëstablishment of balance. On the contrary, there are certain 'self-inflammatory' tendencies in the economic system which will spread if they are not consciously counteracted." [2]

In the post-war world the self-regulating price system has not been able to function successfully in producing a smooth, regular flow of investment throughout the world. United States investors were attracted by high returns to place huge sums abroad during several years, and then higher returns promised by a stock market boom at home suddenly cut down on foreign placements. After the crash of 1929 the outflow of investment stopped almost entirely, and at just the wrong time from the point of view of the world's economic system it was replaced by a reverse flow. At first the self-regulating mechanism had allowed too large a flow to be well digested; then in the depression years investments that would have been productive from a broad social point of view were not attractive as opportunities for private profit.

But this same set of problems illustrates vividly that many of the failures of the world economy to reach proper adjustment under the self-regulating mechanism

[2] Bertil Ohlin, "The Future of Economic Organization," in the Sir Halley Stewart Lectures, 1937, *The World's Economic Future* (London: George Allen and Unwin, Ltd., 1938), p. 71.

have been due, not merely to new difficulties created for the mechanism by modern conditions, and not merely to unusual burdens imposed by post-war readjustments, but also to bad types of "planning." Governmental action, instead of facilitating fundamental adjustments that needed to be carried through and smoothing the way for them, so as to lessen transition disturbances, has too often sought to sidestep the necessity for adjustment. At other times the mechanism has been strained to the breaking point by contradictory policies of governments. The attempt of the Allies to collect reparations from Germany, and of the United States to collect war debts from the Allies, while both were raising barriers against goods that had to be the final means of payment, helped to produce such events as the German currency collapse of 1923, the cracking of the world's currency structure under depression strains, and the discarding of both political democracy and the free-market system in Germany.

Today the self-regulating mechanism seems to be in decline, certainly on the defensive. The amount of central organization and conscious control in economic life is increasing. The movement in this direction, while extraordinarily rapid during the depression emergency (and no doubt temporary in some of its emergency aspects), is a long-term phenomenon which antedates the depression and even the World War. "The chief characteristic of change in the organization of society in the last half-century," in the words of Professor Bertil Ohlin, "has been the growth of central organization and control," represented by the rising influence of trusts and cartels, the spread of governmental enterprise and governmental supervision, and the tendency of large-scale enterprise and financial control to increase.[3] The growth of control has been based in part on fundamental economic changes

[3] *Ibid.*, p. 66.

which have increased the need for conscious direction in economic life. Among these changes Ohlin lists: technical developments tending to increase the economies of large-scale production and to encourage larger business and financial units, the changes in the conditions of competition caused by the greater rôle of fixed costs, the lessened flexibility of the labor market due to labor organization and the declining international mobility of labor, and the greater seriousness of depressions in recent years. At the same time, the ability to organize is greater now than formerly, due to better systems of communication, efficient tabulating and calculating machines, and improved methods of large-scale management generally. Likewise, the attitude of business men and the public has shifted from confident belief in uninterrupted economic progress to a demand for more security—a shift which may be explained in part by decline in the automatic growth factors of the last century, such as new lands for settlement and rapid growth of European populations. Finally, the resources of the state have increased enormously.

All these factors are mutually related, as interacting causes and effects, to the growth of new attitudes towards conscious control and the self-regulating mechanism. "That there is a certain inherent necessity in this development can hardly be doubted. Many people regard the interventionism of our days as an entirely mistaken policy, due only to the stupidity of politicians, but for such an interpretation of history there is no foundation." [4] On the other hand, there is no doubt that the eclipse of the self-regulating mechanism would not have been, and need not have been, as severe as it is today if the aftermath of the World War had not imposed unusual and impossible tasks upon it, and if governments had not indulged so extensively in bad types of "planning."

[4] *Ibid.*, p. 74.

Why Has Planning Been Restrictive?

Those who look to planning for the improvement of economic welfare have in mind systematic, rational, co-ordinated efforts directed towards the more effective use of resources in meeting human needs. Only a small part of the vast mass of conscious economic control surveyed in Chapter VIII fits that description.

It is a moot question whether much of the control actually seen in recent years should really be called "planning" at all, for planning ordinarily suggests something carefully thought out. Most of the intervention in economic life by governments and by organized groups has been notable for its hit-or-miss character. Action on one problem has had little relation to action on other problems. Everywhere there have been stop-gap measures, contradictions, and confusion. Measures of this sort belong in our discussion because we have defined "planning" very broadly as the principle of conscious control in economic life, in contrast with the principle of unconscious adjustment through the market. But, clearly, planning can be consistent or inconsistent, good or bad.

Only a small part of the measures of conscious intervention in economic life during the last few years has been directed towards more effective use of resources. Planning has been defensive and restrictive. Organized economic interests have sought privileged positions for themselves and shelter from depression storms—usually by measures to maintain the scarcity-value of their products—at the expense of each other and the general public. This has been true domestically. In the United States today a grave problem of "internal protection" is being widely discussed—barriers contrived by the states to shield their producers against competition from other parts of the United States, milk-shed regulations to exclude competition from outside, and the like.[5] Internationally, the restrictive type of planning that wastes resources and promotes maladjustments has been even more characteristic. One of the most widespread forms of governmental effort in Europe is the encouragement of staple food crops in the industrialized countries. This uses land and labor for producing things that could be brought from overseas much more cheaply, while diet studies show a great lack of "protective foods" such as green vegetables that need to be grown locally. The triumph of Mussolini's "battle of the grain," the British subsidy to sugar beets, the German emancipation from the lard of corn-fed Iowa hogs, and the French success in raising wheat at controlled prices four or five times the price for which it could be bought in Canada are all examples of deliberate control in directions exactly the opposite of those called for by economic welfare. The counterpart of agricultural restrictionism in Europe is the attempt of many overseas countries to limit farm output and to find an outlet for unemployed resources by developing manufactures. To encourage manufactures the import of finished goods from Europe is then restricted, and consumers must pay a higher price for home-produced articles while European factories have fewer orders and less employment.

Why is it that so much of conscious economic control is restrictive and serves to make the general community

[5] Consult Frederick Eugene Melder, *State and Local Barriers to Interstate Commerce in the United States: A Study in Economic Sectionalism* (Orono, Maine: University of Maine Studies, Second Series, No. 43, 1937); Raymond Leslie Buell, "Death by Tariff: Protectionism in State and Federal Legislation," originally in *Fortune* (August, 1938), reprinted as *Public Policy Pamphlet* No. 27, University of Chicago Press, 1939; and recent publications of the Council of State Governments, including its monthly magazine *State Government* and proceedings of a national conference on interstate trade barriers which it held in Chicago on April 5-7, 1939.

poorer rather than richer? Several reasons may be given. First, governmental policy these days is dominated by the fear of war. Military power must be given precedence over economic welfare, and, as we shall see in Part IV, those planning measures that are necessary for military power, especially when the test may come next week or next year, are often quite the opposite of planning measures that would be called for in the interest of economic welfare.

Second, emergency needs have dominated planning measures during the depression. Impromptu intervention to forestall collapse, rescue work rather than construction, has been the rule.

Third, the efforts of governments in the economic sphere have been in very large part new and therefore amateurish. To be sure, there has been a long-run trend towards more efficient methods of administration, better civil services, larger technical staffs. But the troubles of the post-war and depression periods descended upon governments that were ill equipped for such vast problems and for such technical problems. One result was that governments had to depend for advice on persons with direct interests at stake, since disinterested experts on the details of economic life were hard to find.[6] The influx of university professors into Washington in the "brain trust" days of 1933 was essentially a hurried attempt to get disinterested experts. Another result of governmental

[6] Sir Arthur Salter has written that "it is the most serious, and the most unjust, obstacle to the schemes not only of Socialists but of all those who desire any system in which the public interest is adequately protected by public control, that the present commercial policies of the world constitute a kind of bastard socialism, conceived not in the public interest but pressed upon harassed governments by strong sectional organisations. Nor is this accidental or fortuitous. It results inevitably from the unsuitability of the present procedure and traditions of representative government for the economic tasks of the present period." *The Framework of an Ordered Society* (New York: Macmillan, 1933), p. 17.

unfamiliarity with problems of industry that suddenly demanded attention was, naturally, many honest blunders.

Fourth, economic planning has been restrictive and anti-social because it has been interest-group planning. Business firms and business combinations have always made their plans primarily for their own profit, and where a certain amount of monopoly power gives them room to maneuver they generally find it worth while to restrict output, within limits, to maintain the scarcity-value of their products. Governments, too, have generally been forced into economic planning by one pressure group after another, and schemes for restriction of output or "protection" against competition have been the typical remedies demanded by these groups. For each interest-group separately, artificial scarcity seems a good thing. Finally, to be fair to all, production is restricted all around. Thus, the manufacturer gets import tariffs and cartels, and the farmer gets crop controls.

Fifth, planning has been done piecemeal. When attention is concentrated on one industry at a time, one crop at a time, it is easy to conclude that the trouble is "over-production" and the remedy some sort of restriction to keep the product scarce enough so its price will cover the producers' costs. It takes a wider view to see that it is the product of one industry that buys the product of the other, and that the fundamental remedy for "over-production" of textiles and cotton is to be found in raising output and buying power in all industries generally.

Finally—and this is really only a special case of piecemeal planning—most economic planning has been *national,* even on problems that are clearly international. The reason is easy to see. Authority to act vigorously and decisively on social problems in the modern world is lodged with national governments. There is no world government, save for the weak beginnings of one in the League of Nations, the International Labour Organisation, and a collection of official and unofficial international unions for specific purposes. Even the League, the I.L.O., and the other organizations are powerless to act effectively on most questions except through national governments. Hence, when urgent economic problems put people into the "something-must-be-done" frame of mind, it is to national governments that they turn.

There are two reasons why separate national planning on problems that have international aspects generally tends to be restrictive. Like business firms or interest-groups acting for their own immediate gain, national governments acting separately are likely to find a temporary advantage in maintaining scarcity-values for products in which their land has monopoly power, and in beggar-my-neighbor policies generally. Policies that might profit one country at the expense of the world community if only that one country used them, become collective ruin when all try the same game. Yet, lacking means for coördinated action, it is hard to abandon these policies. Country A raises tariffs and installs quotas in order to put some of its unemployed to work at producing goods now being imported. But A's imports are B's exports, and this kind of "planning" does not solve the unemployment problem; it merely shifts some of it to B. Then B "solves" its problem by deciding to produce at home goods formerly bought from A. There is as much unemployment in both countries as before, probably more, with the difference that the *best* industries of each country (those able to export and hold their own in world markets) have been sacrificed for the sake of whatever employment gain has been registered in the relatively weak industries now shielded from foreign competition.

This, repeated a thousand times, saps the productive power of all countries.

The second reason why national economic planning tends to be restrictive goes even deeper. In dealing with problems like the low price of wheat, or depression unemployment in the textile industry—problems that are international in scope—national governments are unable to do anything about those causal elements that lie outside their own jurisdictions. Joint action by dozens of separate governments is too difficult to organize, too unwieldy and slow even if final agreement might prove possible. So governments are pushed into doing what they can within their own territories, *and if their national action is not to be nullified by uncontrollable economic influences from outside, they may have to restrict economic contact with the rest of the world.* Thus, French farm prices cannot be raised independently of the rest of the world unless a wall against outside farm products is put around the French market. If one country wants to use monetary expansion as a method of combating a world depression it may find it impossible to do so (unless the rest of the world is willing to go along) without cutting many monetary and trade ties. In short, the area over which economic interdependence is permitted cannot be larger than the jurisdiction of the controlling authority, if there is to be successful economic planning. As the demand for planning advances ahead of international government capable of planning, world economy finds itself being lopped off to fit the Procrustean bed of nationalism.

The Worst of Both Principles

The more extreme advocates of laissez faire sometimes cite as typical examples of planning all the restrictive measures we have been discussing and on this showing condemn the whole principle of conscious control. At the same time, they complain against identifying their ideal system—a flexible, competitive system of free enterprise—with the actual results of profit-seeking economy in an environment of monopoly, rigidity, and state interference. On the other side of the debate some advocates of social planning—that is, planning in the social interest—point to chaotic conditions that have arisen under the system of market coördination as typical examples of the way laissez faire works. Restrictive measures by the state and by private groups, they say, are the natural fruit of the "anarchy of self-interest." Blaming the profit system for the failure of most "planning" to promote the social welfare, they protest against identifying their ideal with present restrictive measures.

The truth is that what each side sees to criticize in the other's system is also, outside the realm of the ideal, a part of its own system. Indeed, a marriage of the worst in the principle of laissez faire (monopolistic combination and the corruption of public authority) with the worst in economic planning (aid to special interest groups at the expense of the community) has produced a progeny of which the admirers of neither system can be proud.

Because polemics from both sides confuse the issue by trying to put the blame for present troubles at the door of the other party's system, it is important to see clearly the identity in the worst features of both systems. Consider first the workings of laissez faire. If profit-seeking monopolists are let alone, they are *not* led by an invisible hand to promote the public welfare. This has long been recognized; it is the basis of the traditional opposition of classical economics to monopoly in all its forms. But recent developments in economic research have shown that important departures from the best social use of resources, and serious instabilities in the economic system, may result from degrees of monopoly power that do not approach complete control over the supply of a commodity in the old sense of the term "monopoly." In fact, competition of a kind may be very intense between holders of partial monopoly power. But there is a strong tendency for "monopolistic competition" or "imperfect competition" to take socially wasteful forms like competitive sales pressure and competitive advertising, and to result in restriction of output even without any collusion between the parties which could be pointed to as "restraint of trade."

Any enterpriser who has a choice in determining at what price he shall sell his product holds some degree of monopoly power in the sense used by the modern analysis of monopolistic competition. This monopoly power may result from controlling a substantial part of the supply. Thus, no single copper company has a monopoly in the sense of complete control over output, but any one of the few large competing copper companies is important enough so that the decisions of its executives have an important influence on the market price. No single producer in a purely competitive situation is able to affect the market price. The individual cotton-grower, for example, has only the choice to sell or not to sell at the day's quotation, and whether he sells all his stock or only a part of it will make no difference in the price he can get.

Monopoly power may also result from product differentiation, including artificial differentiation by means of trade-marks, labels, and advertising. There is no monopoly of soap, but by spending enough on advertising a firm may build up a public preference for a particular brand of soap—over which it does have a monopoly. Once such a situation has been brought about, and if it can be maintained against rivals who must now spend money on advertising campaigns to defend their own positions, the firm has a choice of selling more at a lower price or less at a higher price—the typical characteristic of monopoly power.

Good business practice, motivated by the wish to make the firm's earnings as large as possible, may not always lead, under conditions of partial monopoly, to an output lower than the theoretically best social use of resources, but it seems safe to say that it will usually do so. Also, the producer's ability to choose whether to sell more at a lower price or less at a higher price is likely to increase the instability of the economic system. When demand falls off during a depression, those who have such power often sacrifice output rather than prices, and this extends the vicious circle of unemployed resources.

Monopolistic conditions would be much less widespread than they are if governments did not grant special privileges and did not shield favored groups against competition by protective tariffs, import quotas, and the like. But a considerable amount of partial monopoly of the type analyzed would seem to be inseparable from large-scale production and from modern business methods. The conclusion follows that, since even partial monopolists are not led by the invisible hand of competition to serve the public interest as they might, laissez faire alone cannot be relied upon for bringing the best social use of resources.

To the extent that monopolistic competition brings restriction of output by individual firms, socially wasteful employment of resources, and policies that intensify economic instability, we have results identical with the worst forms of economic planning. Indeed, the "competitive wastes" of rival advertising, unused plant capacity, and the like (which are really traceable to monopolistic elements and the *absence* of perfect competition) may lead business men to the conviction that the industry needs a cartel, an NRA "code," or some other form of "planning." This often brings further restriction of output by private or governmental means, "in the interest of the industry."

Interest-group planning—that is, conscious economic control administered by private groups in their own interest or by government for the primary benefit of only a part of the people affected—leads to wastes and instabilities of the same kind as those from monopolistic laissez faire. Control schemes run by producers or by governments in the interest of producers (rubber, tea, tin, copper, aluminum, cotton, nitrates, coffee, silk, etc.) have the power to choose between more sales at lower prices or fewer sales at higher prices, just as do private monopolists, and they are tempted in the same way to restrict output below the level called for by the general interest. "Planning" by protective tariffs and import quotas seeks protection for a favored group by methods that cause loss and instability in other parts of the system. The wasteful selling costs characteristic of monopolistic competition appear in government efforts to help their producer-groups crowd out other producer-groups in markets abroad. Some day we may see gigantic rival campaigns of commodity control boards: "drink tea" versus "drink coffee," "use copper" versus "use aluminum." Planning that looks to the interests of just one part of the world, or one section of the community, when much wider interests are also affected, is almost sure to waste the community's resources.

Herein lies the fallacy of schemes for "self-government in industry." All planning by producers whose income is directly affected by scarcity-values of the goods being planned is bound to have an anti-social bias. Furthermore, if done on a large scale it would be likely to cause so much friction between organized groups as to require a dictatorship to keep order.

The worst of laissez faire is monopolistic laissez faire, and the worst of planning is interest-group planning. The two are not far apart. In fact, we may say that monopolistic laissez faire *is* interest-group planning.

The Best of Both Principles

The ideal world imagined by the exponents of a flexible, competitive, free-enterprise system, regulated smoothly and automatically through the play of prices in the market, is remote from the real world of today with its rigidities, barriers, large-scale monopolistic enterprises, and its determined resistance to productive readjustments. The ideal world imagined by the exponents of a social planning that should do away with depressions and unemployment and use industry at full capacity in ways best calculated to meet human needs, is no less remote from the real world of interest-group planning. The two ideals are in fact closer together than either is to actuality. Poles apart as to method, the final arrangement of resources if each system succeeded in working perfectly would be very much the same in either case, supposing that each started with the same resources and sought to gratify the same wants. The income distribution under the two systems would doubtless be different enough to affect the wants to be gratified, so we should not exaggerate the extent to which their ideal working would give identical results in detail. But basic problems in international economic relations, such as movements of goods and resources, their direction, kind, and volume, would have to meet with essentially similar answers. As an advocate of social planning has put it: "The economics of a planned world would resemble in the character and volume of international trade the imaginary world of the laissez faire economists." [7]

May it not be reasonable to suppose, then, that a considerable amount of planning and a considerable amount of laissez faire can exist side by side in the same economy without either making the other unworkable? This is a grave issue, which has not had enough systematic attention from economic thinkers. It can be argued that a "mixed" system in which there are large elements of free enterprise and also large elements of social control must work badly, that one or the other must be crowded out if the system of economic coördination is not to "fall between two stools." Specifically, it can be urged that government economic action in one industry or one country has both economic and political repercussions that create a need and a demand for new interventions elsewhere, and that the process has no end. Also, it may be urged that government action to equalize the distribution of income, and government competition with business, will tend to stop the flow of capital into private enterprises. On the other hand, it can be argued that so long as private enterprise for profit is permitted, the political influence of the business class, and the political influence of organized labor groups with a special interest in particular commodities—indeed, the influence of all groups with political power and special interests—may be used to prevent or to pervert genuine welfare planning. Practical examples can, of course, be found to reinforce all of these points.

Practical examples can also be found to make one very suspicious of logic-tight arguments which seem to prove that mixed systems of private enterprise and conscious

[7] G. D. H. Cole, *Principles of Economic Planning* (London: Macmillan, 1935), p. 282.

control must work badly. Sweden has become a symbol of the "Middle Way," and it gets along more happily than most countries. It seems to thrive on a mixture of private capitalism, monetary management, socialist housing schemes, strong trade unions, state competition with business to regulate monopoly, a strong coöperative movement also concerned with furnishing competition for private monopolies, and planned programs of public works to counteract depressions. In fact, if we look about us for experiments in "mixed economy" we may be as surprised as Molière's *Bourgeois Gentilhomme,* who discovered that he had been talking prose all his life without knowing it. In the United States there are two large industries that have long been socially planned and administered in the public interest, not run on free-market principles, and which have assets and employees exceeding those of most private industries. Yet no one will contend that the existence of a publicly-managed "education industry" and a publicly-managed "highway industry" has made the United States less suitable for private enterprise.

On the whole, the best practical view of the matter would seem to be that the possibility of having laissez faire and planning work well side by side in the same economy depends upon the kind of laissez faire and the kind of planning. *Social* planning and *competitive* laissez faire can be fitted in together in different parts of the same system. Interest-group planning and monopolistic laissez faire are disruptive elements, and it is only a question of how much of them any system can stand before it breaks down.

CHAPTER TEN

PROBLEMS OF THE "MIXED" ECONOMY

A NUMBER of "grand solutions" have been offered by uncompromisingly logical advocates of this or that system of eonomic organization: a world of free enterprise and cosmopolitan free trade; a world plan on collectivist lines; a world of national plans, with some kind of exchange among the national entities. As a matter of fact, no one of these in its full-blown perfection is likely to sweep the field in the near future. Yet elements from each are almost sure to be part of the world economy in coming decades.

The grand solution which looks to the reënthronement of the self-regulating market system in a flexible world economy built almost entirely around individualistic private enterprise is impossible even if it were desirable. Modern economy has evolved beyond the stage of atomistic competition. Vested interests have grown up by now in monopolistic controls, special state protection, and public economic action of all kinds. Labor organizations and trade associations, giant corporations and large business and financial units of many kinds, social security measures, wage laws and crop controls—these things cannot be wiped out by any such negative-appearing policy as "non-interference" and "back to individualistic competition." Paradoxically, it would seem unlikely that anything short of a political dictatorship could liquidate these social tendencies completely enough to remove the rigidities and inflexibilities that make a purely automatic market system unworkable today.

As for freeing trade between nations, the direct attack on trade barriers has not lacked persistence and resourcefulness over the last two decades. It has been aided by the excellent technical services of the League of Nations, and by general recognition of economists and statesmen that, in principle, the world would be better off for more trade. Yet the story of "Post-War Efforts for Freer Trade" [1] has been a melancholy one:

> The difficulties encountered in abolishing import and export prohibitions in general led to an endeavor to concentrate on certain specific products. The unsatisfactory results of strictly limited negotiations led back to the idea of a general concerted action, to be initiated by a general tariff truce. Repeated failures on the world plane suggested the idea of the apparently less ambitious scheme of an union purely European. More recently and more generally, the discouragement engendered by the impossibility of securing any measure of significant agreement by means of multilateral conventions has caused most Governments to fall back on the time-honoured, but far more modest form of bilateral treaties.

Yet it is very important in the modern world (or so it seems to the author) that the principle of laissez faire and free private enterprise should be encouraged—maintained or restored—in all those parts of the economic system where it can be made to work in a socially efficient way. The free enterprise principle, where it can work competitively and efficiently, avoids the dangers to democratic political institutions that would be bound up with far-reaching control of economic details from the top, and it contributes valuable elements of productivity and economic progress which should not be lost to society. Likewise, it is very important that international trade should be much increased over present levels and that ob-

[1] William E. Rappard, *Post-War Efforts for Freer Trade* (Geneva Research Center, Geneva Studies, Vol. IX, No. 2, March, 1938).

stacles to trade should be decreased—this for reasons that have been stated at length in Part II. Is not the best economic strategy, however, one which takes as its slogan not "non-interference," but *positive and coördinated action* designed to facilitate economic adjustments and to maintain a framework of over-all stability within which decentralized private enterprise can work? The enemy of free enterprise and of other freedoms is not "planning" as such, but restrictive, interest-group planning, whether under public or private auspices. Positive planning in the general public interest is likely to be the best defense against the pressures that make for socially wasteful and restrictive measures which, if unchecked, will cause repeated breakdowns and lead eventually to some form of totalitarian, regimented planning.

Another "grand solution," the one which looks to a world plan on collectivist lines, is impossible in the absence of a central authority capable of planning and getting the plan accepted and executed. Certainly for this generation any practical progress towards economic welfare and peace will have to rest on methods that fall short of such completeness. Nothing but a cataclysmic struggle which would root out nationalism and capitalism could bring us quickly to a really comprehensive world plan, and the result, if created by such a struggle, would probably not be the progressive, humanitarian society desired by social planners.[2] On the other hand, though a com-

[2] Observe that I do not raise the theoretical objection against a collectivist world society that the "problem of economic calculation" would be insoluble in the absence of a free market system. This argument, advanced by Ludwig von Mises and others in *Collectivist Economic Planning* (F. A. von Hayek, ed., London: Routledge, 1935) and adopted by Lionel Robbins (*Economic Planning and International Order,* London: Macmillan, 1937), by Walter Lippmann (*The Good Society,* Boston: Little, Brown and Company, 1937), and by others, seems highly artificial and unconvincing.

Professor Pigou in *Socialism versus Capitalism* (London: Macmillan, 1938) does not accept the "economic calculation" argument as valid. Might he not have been justified in adding that the technical possibilities

plete world planning system is out of the question today, there must certainly be a great increase in conscious co-operation and a considerable amount of positive economic planning on a world basis if modern economy is to work at all well.

A third "grand solution" has sometimes been proposed or implied: a world of national plans, each national state dealing as an economic entity with the others. This would be a world of national socialist states, most likely, as free enterprise internally would hardly co-exist with absolute control of dealings abroad (though that is a theoretical possibility). That such a world of independent national economic units could exist for long is very doubtful, mainly because of the political conflicts that would be inevitable.

Suppose, first, that the most important national planning boards decided to go in for self-contained autarchy. Then the causes of war discussed in Chapter VI would indeed have free play. Economic opportunity would coincide with political sovereignty for certain. The world could expect more bitter struggles than ever for access to raw materials, for trading areas that would permit industrialization demanded either by growing popula-

---

of rational economic calculation in a collectivist state would very likely be greater than the possibilities of accurate social valuation through an automatic market system, because of knowledge based on centralized accounting information from every enterprise? Whether these technical possibilities would be wisely used or not is another question, and chiefly a political one.

In an excellent analysis which, so it seems to me, effectively disposes of the original contention and goes beyond to make a positive contribution to social planning theory, Oskar Lange thus summarizes the result of the controversy that has raged around the economic calculation issue: "In 1911 Professor Taussig classified the argument that 'goods could not be valued' among the objections to socialism that are 'of little weight.' After all the discussions since that time no reasons can be found to change this opinion." (*On the Economic Theory of Socialism,* Minneapolis: University of Minnesota Press, 1938, p. 90. Originally published as two articles in the *Review of Economic Studies,* Vol. IV, October, 1936, and February, 1937.)

tions or awakened desires for higher living standards, not to speak of the psychological desires for "a place in the sun." There would be tremendous pressure for the building up of larger empires; states would have to amalgamate or be gobbled up; war preparedness, not welfare, would have to be the main object of economic planning.

Suppose, however, that the national planning units engage in trade.[3] Since the tin-export plan of one government could not be carried out except as part of the tin-import plan of another, and since tin exports and tin imports would be a vital part of the total economic plan in each nation, no country could make its plan independently of the others. The most rational solution would be a central coöperative organization, which, if it were allowed to work efficiently, would be nothing else but the world plan mentioned earlier, based on national units. Were great national states the basic planning units, however, the danger from head-on clashes and from use of monopolistic power for bargaining would be considerable.

Even more dangerous, probably, would be a world system of inter-governmental trading without any attempt at central coöperation, but with each government bargaining from week to week with all the others on a bilateral

[3] This is *The New Internationalism* predicted by Clark Foreman in a small book of that title (New York: Norton, 1934).

"International coöperation will take place not between individual citizens but between nations as units. Cobden, in advocating free trade and capitalist internationalism, called for the least possible relations between nation and nation, and the greatest possible relations between man and man. The new internationalism as it is working out shows the opposite tendency, that is, the coöperation between man and man of different countries through their state government rather than directly." (p. 130.)

The new system need not completely supplant the old, however: "Capitalist internationalism dominated the world without being completely practiced. The new internationalism will obviously exist for some time side by side with the dying remains of the others. Before the new system is accepted universally, still another new system may be taking its place. For the next few generations, however, an internationalism based on national planned economy and inter-governmental trade seems definitely scheduled." (pp. 128-9.)

basis. Each would be tempted to exploit any monopolistic powers that nature had given it; none could feel quite safe when including external resources in its own domestic plan; political power and the threat of force would be constantly in the background of economic bargains.

> The close association of the power of the government with the competitive economic struggle involves danger in innumerable ways. The closer the association the greater the danger. It is a primitive and dangerous form of commerce when the trader goes with his goods in one hand and a pistol in the other. . . . The more the activities of the world come into touch with each other not by contact at national frontiers but by cutting across them, the broader the foundation of peace.[4]

Nevertheless, the strong tendency towards nationalization of economic activities means that national economies must be important elements in any workable world policy for the immediate future. The problem is how to fit them into a world system and to keep them so far as possible to economic functions that are best handled on a territorial basis.

None of the total, logical, neatly packaged solutions that advocates of this or that system are likely to suggest is really available to this generation. A world of free enterprise and cosmopolitan free trade is as remote from our grasp as a collectivist world plan, while a world of purely national plans would soon disintegrate into conflict and chaos. Each, however, has elements out of which the "mixed" system of the immediate future will have to be

[4] Sir Arthur Salter, Williamstown Institute of Politics, typewritten records, 1925. In the same connection: "It is better that men should think of themselves more in terms of their occupations, professions and businesses, and meet the nationals of other countries on that basis, and be less conscious in all their activities of their differences as Englishmen, Germans or Frenchmen. The identification of all the interests and activities of a country with its political sovereignty, and the political authority which controls its armed forces, is the greatest of all the ultimate dangers." Salter, "The Future of Economic Nationalism," *Foreign Affairs* (New York), October, 1932, p. 18.

composed. The problem of statesmanship is to find as nearly as may be the proper rôle of each.

Under What Conditions Can Free Enterprise and Planning Work Side by Side?

The world economy of the future will be a "mixed" system in two senses. In the first place, some branches of industry, trade, and finance will be run mainly by private enterprise under a market system, while in other branches there will be collectivism, or at least strong elements of public control.[5] In the second place, the world economy will be mixed as between different countries. Widely divergent systems of carrying on economic activity exist in different parts of the world today, and it is unlikely that economic evolution will close these gaps very soon. Hence, the world economy of today and tomorrow must include means of making free enterprise and public planning work harmoniously side by side in the same country and means of carrying on exchange between countries whose economic systems are organized on different principles.

There is no more important area for economic re-

[5] "Apart from the Soviet Union—which falls into a category of its own—the countries of the world are at present attempting to find some half-way house between laissez-faire and collectivism; some system which shall as far as possible avoid the disadvantages and combine the benefits of both individual enterprise and management by the State. That this in effect is the situation is not always recognized. Fervent partisans of the Left or of the Right are convinced that the present stage is purely provisional and that there must soon be either an advance to full-fledged collectivism or a return to 'economic sanity.' So far as visible facts and present dispositions indicate, there would seem as little justification for one view as for the other. No country—the U.S.R.R. always excepted—is proposing to eliminate private enterprise altogether; and no country considers it practicable to leave the running of the economic system to private initiative alone. For the present in any case it is within the framework of the 'mixed system' that economic planning is called upon to operate." (P. W. Martin, *International Labour Review,* Vol. 35, February, 1937, p. 180.)

search today than the theory of the mixed economy. Under what conditions can conscious guidance or control—"planning"—in some sectors of economic life work together with free enterprise and the play of market forces—"laissez faire"—in other sectors? What kinds of government intervention upset the functioning of the market mechanism in the sector supposedly left to free enterprise, and what kinds do not? What kinds of free enterprise are permissible and useful as parts of a social planning policy?

The author ventures to suggest below a few principles which seem important for the proper working of a mixed system. So much spade work has still to be done in this field of thought that these must be regarded as only tentative explorations.

In the first place, the mixed economy must have enough over-all planning in the realm of monetary management and in the relation of savings to investment so that the system as a whole does not get into a cumulative, contracting process. Readjustment must be sought in ways that will make unnecessary an extreme deflationary pressure on any important part of the world economy. Unless these conditions are met, neither the market sector nor the planned sector will work well. Free enterprise will be paralyzed, and state intervention will be of the stop-gap, defensive, and restrictive sort. This need points towards monetary coöperation on a world scale, coördinated public works programs in emergencies, and the like.

In the second place, the planning that is done must be positive rather than restrictive. It must promote change, rather than resist change. It must actively stimulate readjustments to more productive uses of resources when inventions or discoveries or economic development in other countries create a new situation. The aim must be to achieve more smoothly, if possible, and with less cost of transition, end results very similar to those that long-run market forces would also arrive at, if they were able to work ideally according to theory. For example, if planning is directed to the defensive and restrictive end of maintaining the colonial market for an obsolescent British textile industry, a process of readjustment which ought to lead to better social use of resources is indefinitely postponed. Positive planning would meet the situation by allowing the production of textiles in Japan to increase, though not under the artificial stimulus of an extreme devaluation of the currency, and would replace some of Britain's textile production by production of machinery and other articles requiring a higher level of industrial skill and experience. This would mean, in Britain, a program of developing new industries and expanding the more efficient old ones, retraining workers, and redirecting capital. Planning measures of this sort would work with, rather than against, the socially desirable tendencies of market forces. They would help to release private enterprise rather than to repress it. If state interventions in economic life are consciously directed according to the principles of good social economy, they will be allies and not enemies of the "best" in free enterprise.

Third, the technical means used by the state when it intervenes in economic life must be chosen in such a way as to mesh well with the market system. Import tariffs, even when they are high, are much less objectionable from this standpoint than quotas or other direct quantitative restrictions on imports.[6] A tariff, if reasonably stable, can be taken into a merchant's calculations along with other factors affecting his estimate of supply and

[6] *Cf.* G. Haberler and St. Verosta, *Liberale und Planwirtschaftliche Handelspolitik* (Berlin: Junker und Dünnhaupt, 1934), p. 84 ff.

demand. An import tariff, in fact, has exactly the same effect as higher transportation costs. Quotas, on the other hand, throw the price mechanism out of gear. Market forces no longer decide *who* is to import, and the government is faced with the double problem of distributing import permits by countries and by firms within its own country. Those who get these scarce permits make a special profit, and as a result importing becomes less of an economic activity calling for the constructive talent of the merchant and more of a scramble for monopolistic favors. Here is an authentic instance: A dealer in Austria (before Austria ceased to be independent) had a permit under the quota law to import *one* automobile each year from the United States. Early in January he would bring in the car. It cost him about $1,200, including duty. Because of the artificial scarcity maintained by the quota law, he was able to sell it the next day for about $2,400. The rest of the year he hunted and fished.

In the economic relations between countries the allocation of import quotas and exchange control funds is also a matter of handing out favors. It is very difficult to apply quantitative regulations of this sort in a non-discriminatory way. If quotas are distributed according to some "normal" period in the past, they become less and less applicable as economic conditions change, and there is no way of adapting them to the fluctuations that occur among countries and among firms from year to year. They become more and more uneconomic. Import taxes, by comparison, can be uniformly applied to goods from all sources. They permit readjustments in the flow of trade to take place automatically when basic conditions change drastically enough. In other words, the market system still operates, though part of the data on which it operates is the government's decision to impose a burden on movements of goods. If government regulation of imports is necessary, it should be done either by import duties as moderate as possible or by direct importing through government-controlled corporations. Either of these methods is better than quantitative controls over private transactions, unless in temporary emergencies, and both keep for the government the extra profit created by raising domestic prices artificially above outside prices.

Fourth, in the market sector competition must prevail. Monopolistic elements must be kept at a low enough level so that the "wastes of competition" (which are mostly wastes of imperfect or monopolistic competition) do not offset the gains from private initiative. Competition centering on price and quality is essential if free private enterprise is to be a social benefit. Otherwise, restriction of output, wasteful use of resources, exploitation of the consumer, and general instability are the results of laissez faire. Where competition of the right sort is not present, public action to restore it or to substitute public control for the private control given by monopoly power is needed.

Fifth, and finally, the methods used to control the monopoly power that inevitably arises in modern industry must be carefully chosen. Monopoly power in itself is not necessarily evil. It often results from real economies in large-scale operations, sometimes combined with a chance location of resources which makes unified operation easy (as in the case of the International Nickel Company's monopoly based on the Sudbury deposits in Canada). The evil to be guarded against is not monopoly as such but the use of monopoly power for the benefit of part of the community at the expense of the whole. In other words, the danger arises where there is *private* monopoly. Monopoly power used for the benefit of a single firm or a group of firms or for a large group of producers banded together in a commodity control scheme may lead to exploitation of consumers or workers or to price policies which promote instability in the economic system as a whole.

Economists have done much research on the question, "What policy as to price and output will be pursued by a private monopoly in quest of maximum net profit?" Little has been done, by comparison, on a question which has great practical importance at this stage of economic evolution and which is scientifically just as interesting, namely, "What price and output ought to be pursued by a social monopoly managed in the general interest?" [7] It is conceivable that a monopoly, such as the International Nickel Company or any of the great international control schemes in rubber, tin, tea, and the like, might be managed in the social interest with results better in some cases than could be obtained by free competition. Tentatively, the difference between the price policy of a social monopoly and a private monopoly might be expressed this way: In normal times the social monopoly would aim to expand its output up to the point at which additional production would cost more than consumers would be willing to pay for the extra amount. That is, enough should be put on the market to make marginal cost equal

[7] The controversy over the problem of economic calculation in a socialist society has produced some analysis which may also throw light on the problem of a social monopoly operating in the environment of a mixed economy. See, for example, the work of Oskar Lange cited earlier in this chapter.

The analysis in such works as Joan Robinson's *The Economics of Imperfect Competition* often skates along the edge of the problem, but never quite admits social monopoly as an alternative of equal theoretical interest with private monopoly and perfect competition.

Perhaps the most difficult technical problem for the conduct of a social monopoly in a mixed economy is the question of what it should do in booms and depressions. Critical studies of raw material control schemes and cartels, like the chapter by J. W. F. Rowe in *International Control and the Non-Ferrous Metals* (W. Y. Elliott, ed., New York: Macmillan, 1937, Ch. 3), have made a beginning here.

to price. A private monopoly, on the other hand, would restrict output below that point if the conditions of demand were such that the greater scarcity-value at a smaller output would more than make up for the reduced volume of sales. During times of boom and depression, the social monopoly would take into account in setting its price and output, not only the effect of its decisions upon its own net income but also the effect upon general economic stability.

The real problem of monopoly in the world economy, then, is to find means for either (1) restoring effective competition, or (2) converting private monopoly into social monopoly. One good way to make competition more effective than it is now as a regulating device is to widen the area of competition. The advance of the technology of distance helps to do this where it is not counteracted by trade barriers. Thus, the coal trade in England between the northern counties and London was dominated from 1771 to 1845 by a combination of mine-owners generally known as The Limitation of the Vend. Its dissolution was the result of the widening of the area of competition brought about by the steam railway.[8] A freer world market would be one of the best antidotes to the growth of monopolistic competition in advanced industrial countries. Another method of making competition more effective is for the government itself or consumers' coöperative societies to launch producing enterprises that will either serve as "yardsticks" for public regulation or will force down monopolistic prices by themselves pursuing an active competitive policy.

Where conditions of production or other reasons do not permit effective competition, private monopoly must

[8] Paul M. Sweezy, *Monopoly and Competition in the English Coal Trade, 1550–1850* (Cambridge: Harvard University Press, 1938), pp. 47-8, 119-20, 145, 147-8.

be converted into social monopoly. This may be done through outright public ownership or through various devices which make the managers of the monopolistic enterprise responsive to social needs rather than to the quest for maximum net earnings in the undertaking itself. Representation of the public on the boards of directors of such undertakings (the so-called "mixed" corporation) and the increase of a professional spirit with emphasis on public responsibilities among managers themselves are devices of this sort.

Of all the ways of handling monopolies, domestic and international, the method of leaving the management in the hands of private enterprise to be run for profit and then setting up a public authority to regulate the private enterprise would seem to be the worst.[9] It is widely used in the United States where both the method of public competition and the method of public ownership have to combat a strong prejudice against "government in business." The combination of private management for profit

[9] "Public regulation of private monopoly would seem to be, at best, an anomalous arrangement, tolerable only as a temporary expedient. Half-hearted, sporadic, principle-less regulation is a misfortune for all concerned; and systematic regulation, on the basis of any definite and adequate principle, would leave private ownership almost without a significant function or responsibility to discharge. Analysis of the problem, and examination of experience to date, would seem to indicate the wisdom of abandoning the existing scheme of things with respect to the railroads and utilities, rather than of extending the system to include other industries as well. Political control of utility charges is imperative, to be sure, for competition simply cannot function effectively as an agency of control. We may endure regulation for a time, on the dubious assumption that governments are more nearly competent to regulate than to operate. *In general, however, the state should face the necessity of actually taking over, owning, and managing directly, both the railroads and utilities, and all other industries in which it is impossible to maintain effectively competitive conditions.* For industries other than the utilities, there still remains a real alternative to socialization, namely, the establishment and preservation of competition as the regulative agency." (Henry C. Simons, *A Positive Program for Laissez Faire: Some Proposals for a Liberal Economic Policy.* Chicago: University of Chicago Press, Public Policy Pamphlet No. 15, 1934, pp. 11-12. Italics in the original.)

with public boards to determine allowable prices and profits makes for inflexibility, rigidity, and duplication of effort. It invites corruption of government by creating a situation in which the profits of the private owners depend as much upon their ability to influence the regulating authority as upon other considerations. Executive talent is diverted from the task of organizing efficient production to the task of influencing "public relations." The costs are paid by the public. The regulating authority, on its side, can do little but obstruct. Lacking positive control, it cannot cause an industry to expand when good business cycle policy would call for expansion. It may defend the consumer against obvious exploitation, but it cannot make use of price policy as a means of promoting stability in the general economic system.[10]

If there is planning for over-all stability to prevent extremes of inflation and deflation, if planning measures are positive rather than restrictive, if public intervention takes forms that mesh with the market system, if competition prevails in the market sector, and if monopolistic elements are met either by methods that restore effective competition or by public control, then the principle of laissez faire and the principle of planning may work harmoniously in the economic world of today.

[10] "No longer is public policy toward monopoly power concerned merely with fair prices or prices which prevent exploitation of the public and waste of resources. It is also concerned with the problem of *harmonious* prices and *harmonious* price changes, the problem of prices which do not intensify and prolong fluctuations in the economy . . . It is . . . clear that the present effort in the way of public regulation . . . is from this standpoint quite useless and perhaps worse." (J. K. Galbraith, "Monopoly and Price Rigidities," *Quarterly Journal of Economics,* Vol. 50, p. 474.)

Under What Conditions Can Countries with Different Systems Coöperate? [11]

One important area of the world, the Soviet Union, is operating under the most complete application of the planning principle yet seen. It may be called for practical purposes a fully-planned economy. Other countries, like Germany, Italy and Japan, have adopted a system which we shall call here "controlled economy," meaning that the structure of private ownership and private enterprise is left at least partially intact, but that close state regulation has replaced many of the former functions of the market. In the United States, Great Britain and the Dominions, France, Belgium, Switzerland, Scandinavia, most of the Latin American countries—in fact, over most of the industrialized world—the private-enterprise market system is still dominant, though it is strongly modified by various admixtures of planning. We shall refer to the type of organization in these countries as "market economy," remembering that the term is used only by contrast with the fully-planned and controlled economies, for every market economy today is really a mixed system. What is the effect of these divergent forms of economic organization upon international economic relations?

The relations between two regions or countries both under the market system have been analyzed in great detail by most of the literature on international economics. Efficient use of resources depends on the working of the price mechanism and on freedom of private firms to buy where cost of production is cheapest and to sell where

[11] See the discussion of the problems treated in this section in Karl W. Kapp, *Planwirtschaft und Aussenhandel* (Geneva: Georg et Cie., Librairie de l'Université, 1936). I have drawn upon this useful study frequently.

demand is strongest. Trade takes place between individual firms, and is naturally multilateral rather than bilateral. The balances paid by United States importers to Brazilians for coffee are turned over to English manufacturers for woolens and finally sent back to the United States for, let us say, business machines and cotton. Governments influence the movement of goods and of capital funds mainly by taxes or subsidies which affect the prospects for profit of private enterprises. Trade treaties between governments are made simply to establish the general conditions under which private firms shall operate. Under the international system of market economy it is left to the private importers and exporters, as a general rule, to decide in what countries and in what amounts they will make purchases or sales.

The economic relations of two fully-planned economies with each other must depart widely from this pattern. The same fundamental social reasons for exchange exist between planned economies as between market economies, namely, differences in the abundance and scarcity of various types of resources in relation to the home demand for them, making it possible for each economy to gain by exporting products that embody its relatively abundant resources, receiving in return products made up of resources that are relatively scarce to it but abundant to the other economy. However, the external economic relations of a fully-planned economy must necessarily be part of its general economic plan, and even though they may be administratively decentralized they must come under the ultimate control of a central authority. The government, therefore, will not influence trade merely by such indirect means as taxes and subsidies on imports or exports, but will conduct the trading operations directly. Trade agreements between the governments of two fully-planned economies would not merely fix the conditions under which trade should be carried on but would go much farther and determine the direction and quantities and terms of each exchange in detail. In other words, inter-governmental agreements would determine the *substance* of economic relations, not merely, as under the market system, the framework within which they would be carried on by private parties. In effect, trade negotiations between fully-planned economies would represent a certain amount of *joint planning,* for each would be adjusting its plan to the other's plan. Unless some sort of a multilateral clearing system or a joint international planning agency could be set up among a number of fully-planned economies, exchange between them would tend to be balanced on a bilateral basis, thus reducing the flexibility and the social productivity of trade, though in a "mixed" world economy one planned economy might buy more from another than it sells to it, settling the balance in funds which could be used in the market economies of the world.

What new problems arise when a fully-planned economy and a market economy enter into economic relations? The fact that they have different forms of economic organization does not remove the fundamental possibilities for productive exchange between them, supposing that they both want economic welfare. (Remember that the whole discussion here concerns the *means of attaining economic welfare,* not, for example, the means of building an economic base for military power. The very great importance of this distinction will become apparent in Part IV.) The social productivity of trade between regions does not depend upon the use of any particular system for carrying on trade. However, the peculiar conditions under which trade would take place between the private firms of a market economy and the government agencies of a fully-planned economy would create certain difficulties for each side, which might be balanced by certain advantages. In the first place, from the standpoint of the market economy, the possibility of sudden large shifts in policy by the planned economy might be considered a disadvantage. Political reasons might lead to a complete suspension of trade relations on short notice, or there might be an unexpected change in import or export policy. Such sudden changes would be less likely in dealing with thousands of individual firms in another country. Furthermore, an individual firm in the market economy would find itself dealing with agents of a huge monopolistic combination on the other side, whose very size might give it power in bargaining. On the other hand, the orders received from the planned economy might be very large and correspondingly economical for the private firms of the market economy on account of lessened sales cost and assurance of large output. There would also be the advantage that no separate credit investigation would be necessary in dealing with different agencies of the planned economy. Future orders might be known a considerable time in advance, and, so far as the planned economy succeeded in preventing waves of boom and depression, the orders would be steady in volume (except for political factors, as suggested already).

From the standpoint of the planned economy, what are the advantages and disadvantages resulting from trade with a market system? In the first place, its ability to offer very large orders to competing firms in the outside world—that is, its monopolistic purchasing position—might enable it to get favorable price bargains. On the export side, likewise, many commodities over which the planned economy happened to hold some degree of monopoly power could be disposed of on terms only possible under unified control. Dealing with a market economy might present certain disadvantages, on the other hand, in that it would not be possible, when drawing up the import and export plans, to be sure that price conditions in the outside world would remain unchanged during the period of its execution. Booms and depressions in the market economy, especially, might upset the calculations of the economic authorities in the fully-planned country. Thus, the great depression of the 1930's suddenly reduced the prices that could be obtained for Soviet raw material exports, such as oil, on the world market, without reducing in like proportion the prices that had to be paid for imports of machinery to be used in the program of industrialization.

Many of the traditional devices of commercial policy apply only in part to trade treaties between governments that represent a market economy on the one side and a fully-planned economy on the other. The planned economy, of course, would have every reason to desire a pledge of non-discrimination (the most-favored-nation clause) that would apply to the tariffs levied on its goods when entering the market economy. But for goods flowing the other way, while a pledge of non-discrimination as to any taxes that might be levied would be desirable from the point of view of the market economy, it would not be sufficient. The most-favored-nation clause would have meaning only in connection with such matters as administrative treatment and in assuring equal rights for the citizens of the market economy to reside and carry on trade negotiations in the territory of the planned economy. The planning authorities, by a mere change in their buying orders, might alter the currents of trade just as unfavorably to the market economy as though a high discriminatory tariff had suddenly been erected against it. For this reason, commercial agreements between governments of planned and market economies must tend to take the form of the recent agreements between the

United States and the Soviet Union, in which the United States agreed to admit goods from the Soviet Union on the same terms as goods from other countries in return for a pledge to purchase at least a certain minimum amount in the United States during each year of the agreement. This is safe for both sides so long as there is sufficient competition in the market economy among the suppliers of those goods which the planned economy would wish to buy, and so long as the planned economy sells its goods abroad at a reasonably steady valuation, without spurts of price-cutting to disorganize its competitors and permit monopolistic exploitation later.

The external economic relations of countries like Italy, Germany, and Japan, where a system of "controlled economy" prevails, raise many of the same problems that we have just been discussing. When every transaction is subject to the approval of the government, through exchange-control and licensing and quota systems, tariffs levied on imports cease to be the main subject of commercial treaty negotiations. The government of a market economy will not be content with assurances of equal treatment as to import taxes. It has to have guarantees in quantitative terms, so that it can count on a certain amount of foreign exchange being released each year by the authorities of the controlled economy for purchases in its market. What is "fair" and "non-discriminatory" in this respect is not easy to define. Past proportions of purchases in different markets give some indication for the first few years, but as conditions change, this is less and less useful. The allocation of funds by the controlled economy becomes a direct matter for bargaining. Exports from the controlled economy likewise present special problems because of open or concealed subsidies.

In the relations of controlled economies with each other, governmental approval of each transaction on each side converts trade treaties into instruments that, just as in the case of fully-planned economies, settle not only the conditions of trade but its substance as well. Treaties of this sort cannot be signed and then left unchanged for years at a time. Commercial negotiations between the governments must be continuous. The system of controlled external economy, as we have already noted, tends towards bilateral balancing of exchange between each pair of countries, thus reducing the social productivity of trade. A multilateral clearing system among controlled economies is technically possible; it is not so much technical difficulty as the great rôle of bargaining where governments exercise a minute control over trade that tends to result in bilateralism.

The whole system of "controlled economy" suffers from inherent waste. It is inefficient in much the same way that public regulation of privately owned monopolies is inefficient. When every transaction must be considered first by a private enterprise from the point of view of its profit and then by a government control board from the point of view of public policy, there is enormous duplication of effort. It seems safe to predict that the long-run trend in the controlled economies will be either towards outright state management of industry and foreign trade, dropping the pretense of private enterprise and taking on the characteristics of the "fully-planned" economy of the Soviet Union, or towards restoration of free enterprise under general governmental regulation (that is, not regulation of each transaction). Some combination of the two is conceivable. Public corporations might import and export directly in some lines felt to be particularly important, and effective private enterprise might be restored in other lines under conditions defined in general terms by the state. In countries with the political outlook of Germany, Italy, and Japan, however, the strong chance is that the economic system will gravitate towards the fully-planned form rather rapidly.

The conclusion of our analysis is that the same fundamental reasons of social economy operate to make exchange of resources and of goods productive whether between countries under divergent economic systems or between countries under similar systems. Mutually beneficial economic coöperation is theoretically possible *if the dominant wish in both countries is to promote the economic welfare of the people.* This is a very important qualification, as will be emphasized in Part IV. Coöperation and exchange between different systems are made more difficult, however, by new complexities in the forms which economic relations must take. New techniques will have to be developed to meet the new world problem of divergent systems. International organization and permanent methods of international administration must play a much greater rôle than under the old conditions where the world market could serve as the connecting link between all countries of industrial civilization.

CHAPTER ELEVEN

POSITIVE VERSUS RESTRICTIVE PLANNING

NO ONE is happy over the present situation in world economy. As we have seen, it combines large elements of the worst in laissez faire with the worst in planning. If types of economic control most common today—restrictions on output, barriers to trade, defenses against competition—are to be continued indefinitely, it will be at the cost of sacrificing economic progress, and probably even at the cost of standards of welfare already reached.

On the other hand, many controls that are admittedly wasteful and restrictive when viewed in a long-run perspective have arisen out of attempts to meet serious, sometimes even desperate, human problems. While one of the main tasks of economic policy at present is to get rid of a mass of restrictive measures, a simple return towards laissez faire would not be likely to give the desired social results, nor is it a prescription that has a real chance of being applied. In the words of J. W. F. Rowe:

> As a surgeon, laissez-faire cuts unnecessarily deep, while its treatment in general is so rough that the whole constitution of the patient will be undermined, and in any case it is so brutal that the patient will run away.[1]

In the actual world as we know it the solution has to be sought in substituting positive for restrictive planning. The question today is not whether to plan or not to plan,

[1] *International Control in the Non-Ferrous Metals,* W. Y. Elliott, ed. (New York: Macmillan, 1937), p. 74.

but *what* to plan for, *how* to plan, and *where* to plan (that is, the proper scope of planning and free enterprise). One of the tasks of positive planning should be to create conditions of stable economic progress in which a considerable amount of laissez faire can work effectively for the social welfare.

It is not conducive to clear thinking to argue as though any planning at all must be completely regimented planning, with all that would imply in loss of precious freedoms.[2] Indeed, the persistence of democratic political institutions and democratic freedoms generally will depend very much on success in making "mixed" economies work effectively, which means there must be conscious attempts to coördinate policy, to maintain a framework within which enterprise can function smoothly, and to stabilize the economic system. "Conscious attempts to foster social adjustment" [3] describes in brief the positive planning policy which—in contrast to futile advocacy of non-interference on the one hand and to regimented, totalitarian planning on the other—is the best economic defense of democracy. Democratic societies must lay particular stress on social devices by which conscious fostering of social adjustment may take place otherwise than through au-

[2] "When . . . economic planning is held to mean all-embracing, all-coördinated centralized planning, reinforced by public control extending to the uttermost details of economic activity, . . . we are in the realm of theorizing . . . It seems to me utterly false to assume that unless one commits himself in advance to such an extreme of 'planned economy' no significant progress in economic planning is possible." Again: "Those who envisage such an ideal, in their enthusiasm for economic planning, are visionaries; and those who base on this notion their fear of economic planning, or their hostility to it, are seeing ghosts or attacking a 'straw man.'" (Joseph S. Davis, "On Economic Planning," contained in a volume of essays *On Agricultural Policy, 1926–38,* Stanford University, California: Food Research Institute, 1939, pp. 48, 45.)

[3] The phrase is borrowed from Abbott Payson Usher, "Laissez Faire and the Rise of Liberalism," *Explorations in Economics: Notes and Essays Contributed in Honor of F. W. Taussig* (New York and London: McGraw-Hill, 1936), p. 411.

thoritarian decisions at the center executed by administration from the top down. Coöperative undertakings illustrate one such device, regional planning conferences another. Careful study of problems, widespread discussion of goals and the means of attaining them, may have an important coördinating influence without any coercion on individuals at all.

Positive planning must differ from restrictive planning in its attitude towards economic change. Instead of a defensive attempt to prevent new developments in other parts of the world from causing readjustments at home, it must seek to anticipate and smooth out the path of readjustment. One of the most inspiring examples of the way to meet difficult problems positively is the story of Denmark's agricultural transformation in the latter part of the nineteenth century. Floods of cheap grain from America were ruining its trade, and about the same time defeat in war, with loss of the rich territory of Schleswig-Holstein, had dealt blows both to its economy and its national feelings. Yet the very American competition that had ruined Denmark's old agriculture gave it a new opportunity, as cheaper staples made possible higher living standards for the people of manufacturing countries like England. The opportunity was in dairy farming, raising premium quality bacon and eggs, making first-grade butter and cheese. This is the road that Denmark took, under the conscious guidance of the new coöperative movement and the Danish Government, and with the important aid of a unique adult education movement (the Folk High Schools).[4] Denmark's achievement, starting from a background of depressed tenant farming, was the building of a partly rural, partly urban economy with one of the highest living standards in the world, and a nation

[4] See Frederic C. Howe, *Denmark, the Coöperative Way* (New York: Coward-McCann, 1936).

second to none in the genuine democratic culture of its people. Under the same difficult circumstances another kind of program might easily have led the Danes by way of defensive, nationalistic economics and swashbuckling militarism to quite a different destiny.

Positive planning must be made to differ from restrictive planning in other ways. For haphazard, stop-gap, emergency interventions it must try to substitute coördinated, purposeful, foresighted action. As the best defense against the political necessity of yielding to antisocial pressures from interested groups it must set up a broad, forward-looking program. If genuinely grounded in the common interest and outlined clearly enough, such a program would be a touchstone by which public opinion might test specific proposals, and it would be a rallying-point for the defense of the community against predatory groups. Instead of controls that defend the interests of special groups by maintaining the scarcity-value of their products, positive planning must seek to substitute higher levels of consumption and greater leisure. Where there is a real case of over-capacity in a particular industry, positive planning must seek to encourage the transfer of excess workers and other resources out of that industry into more productive employment, rather than to maintain them in partial idleness by subsidies and limitations of output and part-time work.

In economic relations between nations, positive planning must look to greater coöperation rather than to a defensive cutting of contacts as the proper means of attaining stability and security. It must seek to encourage new productive developments, and, by coördination of the economic programs of different countries, to minimize transition costs. It must make wider use of the opportunities for international division of labor through exchange of characteristic products. It must seek to provide a solid basis for peaceful political relations in the form of a world-wide program for raising living standards. The outlook for world peace, for economic welfare, and for the rights of the individual in the modern world depends upon whether or not the people and the governments of the major countries are willing to carry through such a program of economic coöperation.

PART FOUR

THE CHALLENGE OF WAR

CHAPTER TWELVE

ECONOMIC PREPAREDNESS FOR TOTALITARIAN WAR

THE preceding parts of this book have been written on the assumption that what people want from the world's economic system is a plentiful supply of the means of good living at a minimum cost in human toil—that is, that the purpose of economic policy is to increase economic welfare. Part I showed how the advance of technology has had the effect of enlarging the area within which economic coöperation can and must take place. Part II drew attention to the benefits of interregional exchange which flow from the fact that it makes possible more efficient use of resources and thereby helps to raise living standards. Part III has been occupied with some of the new problems in world economic relations arising from recent changes in the structure of economic systems. Throughout these chapters the "best use of resources" has been understood to be that which gives the highest living standards.

Undoubtedly, the "best use of resources" in this sense is the aim which most of the peoples of the earth would wish to have economic policy pursue. Yet the state of the world today is not one in which economic welfare can be given first consideration in the actual decisions of statesmen. The political prerequisites are lacking. Humanity is faced with a challenge to the whole ideal of a constantly rising level of economic welfare—the challenge of war and insecurity.

Instead of the ideal of economic welfare, a competing ideal is thrusting itself into economic decisions everywhere —the ideal of *power*—of military potential, of war preparedness. This is an era of totalitarian war. The armed forces, as someone has put it, are only the cutting edge of a modern military machine. The whole of industry and all the economic activities of a people have to be geared into a modern war effort, and preparedness for war means shaping the whole economic system to meet war needs. Under a world political system which forces each country to be prepared to defend itself, the economics of power tends to displace the economics of welfare—that is, resources are viewed more and more as a basis of military power and less and less as a basis of peacetime living standards.

The economics of power, not of welfare, offers the true explanation for most of the "inevitable economic conflicts" one hears about—for example, in connection with alleged needs for self-sufficiency and demands for political control over areas that supply raw materials. "Economizing" is a matter of relating means to ends. Resources can be used to increase military power, or they can be used to increase economic welfare, but economic policy will be different when the ends in view are different. Much confusion arises from a failure to make this important distinction. Power economy seeks to provide industrial backing for military forces in order to insure victory in war. It therefore looks first of all to such factors as self-containment (at least potential self-containment) within the area likely to be subject to military control in time of war. Welfare economy, on the other hand, tests its success by the standards of living of the people. That economy which gives the most to eat and wear, the best housing to live in, the most leisure, is the best from the point of view of welfare. Not self-containment, but exchange with the widest possible area is desirable for welfare economy, because exchange makes for production on a larger scale, for more specialization, lower costs, greater output, and greater real income. Power economy must judge a source of supply in terms of its availability in case of war. Welfare economy calls for using the sources of supply that are least costly.

It can be argued that in the long run much attention to the dictates of power economy weakens a country, and that a nation which builds a sound, healthy economic system on principles of welfare will ultimately prove the stronger, too. That may be true *in the long run.* If it were only the possibility of a war twenty-five years from now against which nations were preparing, the conflict between power economy and welfare economy would not be important. But when war is imminent, power economy clashes head-on against welfare economy at point after point.

Why do statesmen these days yield to the dictates of power economy when a decision must be taken that involves weighing more power against more welfare? There are two reasons. In the first place, state power is an ideal with some rulers. They prefer it to economic welfare for their people, and they subject the people to a monopoly of propaganda which permits no criticism of the official thesis. Usually the propaganda includes the argument that only military power can enable the nation to be prosperous. The standing refutation to that argument is the prosperity of countries like Denmark and Sweden, though one must admit that (as shown in Chapter VI) the nationalistic economic barriers throughout the world have done much to make such propaganda plausible. In the great majority of states, however, neither the people nor their rulers crave military power and conquest. But even in non-aggressive countries preparations for war must take precedence over welfare, because, as crisis follows crisis, responsible statesmen are more impressed with the imminent menace of war. "Defense," said Adam Smith, the apostle of economic liberalism, "is of much more importance than opulence." So long as each nation must depend on itself for its own defense, there is no escape from the logic of power economy—and little hope in a world as small as ours for substantial progress in economic welfare.

Economic Consequences of Power Economy

International trade is one of the first branches of economic life to feel the impact of war preparedness. Normal peacetime demands are distorted, so that a precarious boom develops in some types of commerce, while other lines, where consumption has to be curtailed or where home substitutes are set up under subsidy for strategic reasons, tend to languish.

It is good economy from the point of view of welfare for each country to buy abroad (that is, to pay for by additional exports) products that it can get more cheaply through trade than by home production. But from the point of view of power economy it may not be at all sound to become dependent on the outside world. Even if a country can reasonably expect to be in command of the sea in time of war, the risk of counting on foreign industries for vital supplies is very great. In England, for example, it is a grave question of policy at the present time whether English agriculture should be diverted now, in time of peace, from the production of live-stock and vegetables, where it is best employed from a welfare point of view, to the production of cereal crops and sugar. These staples can be had much more cheaply from abroad, but what would happen if imports from America and elsewhere should be interrupted in time of war?[1] For countries lacking in sea power the military argument for self-containment is even stronger.

Here we have the greatest obstacle at the present time to the success of efforts like the United States trade agreements program for liberalizing international trade. When the United States pushes the trade agreements program it is in more than a metaphorical sense proposing to other nations that they join in a move towards economic disarmament. But disarmament in the field of trade, like disarmament of other kinds, cannot proceed far so long as the only security of nations lies in their own preparedness to defend themselves. Deciding to import American cotton or pork or machinery or copper wire or chemicals, instead of excluding them to subsidize a more costly production at home and in the colonies, is for statesmen in many countries today almost like deciding to cancel the plans for a new anti-aircraft gun or a new tank. It may make their defenses more vulnerable in case of a war this year or next year, for industrial preparedness and potential self-sufficiency have now taken on prime importance in military preparedness.

If trade is diverted from welfare channels by the dictates of power economy, permanent investment is no less distorted. Every great power today must have its own aluminum industry, its own aircraft factories, its own sources of gasoline (even if they have to be established by synthetic production at great cost), its own plants for nitrogen fixation—and so on and on. The costs in terms of economic welfare are immense. There is enormous international duplication of plant, raising problems of

[1] Keith A. H. Murray, "Food Supplies in Peace and War," Lloyds Bank, Limited, *Monthly Review,* October 1938, makes a convincing case for meeting the problem by accumulating large reserves rather than by subsidizing home-grown supplies in time of peace.

excess-capacity and "over-production" to disorganize industry now and in the future. The net protection in Germany in favor of home-produced motor fuel is estimated at nearly 350 per cent over the cost at which it could be bought from outside, and since May 1937, rubber imports, hitherto duty free, have been subjected to taxes which encourage home production of substitutes by practically doubling the price to consumers.[2] But what is today's standard of living against the ability to wage war tomorrow?

At the beginning of the World War, says a French economist, France experienced a tragic and instructive lesson on dyestuffs. It turned out that the chemistry of dyestuffs is the twin sister of the chemistry of explosives, and France came near to defeat in September 1914, for lack of explosives. It is understandable that the French government has since taken measures to encourage dyestuff factories, protecting them against foreign competition. The same is true for chlorine and many other vital products.[3] In other words, the American or the German or the British chemical industries cannot expect to expand their market in France, or in other countries that fear war, no matter how efficiently they produce.

Power economy dictates the transfer of whole industries from exposed locations to ones more easily defended, regardless of the ordinary considerations of cost and convenience which enter into welfare economy calculations. Some examples of the "war economy landscape" are: arms industries moved outside the London area; Poland's "safety triangle" near Sandomir; heavy industries of the U.S.S.R. developed in the Urals and western Sibe-

[2] A. S. J. Baster, "Some Economic Aspects of Rearmament," *International Labour Review,* Vol. 37 (June, 1938), p. 188.

[3] Henri Hauser, *Economie et Diplomatie* (Paris: Librairie du Recueil Sirey, 1937), p. 41.

ria instead of the Ukraine; border regions left undeveloped.[4]

Even population policy follows power rather than welfare lines. At first thought it seems inconsistent that a state should put a tax on bachelors, encourage early marriages, reward large families, prevent its citizens from emigrating and then complain of "population pressure" and demand more territory. These things are inconsistent if the object of state policy is the economic welfare of the people, but not if the primary object is the power of the state.

So far we have been discussing the consequences of power economy in terms of its effect on measures taken by governments. But individuals and firms must also make their plans conform to the war orientation. When they see their governments acting as though war might start any week, it is no wonder that business men send "hot money" scurrying from one market to another in a nervous quest for safety, that long-term plans for developing trade opportunities hang fire, that investments in industries which prosper from peace demands rather than from war demands are not undertaken. The resulting misdirection of economic activity (from the standpoint of peacetime welfare) makes itself felt in some degree in every branch of manufacturing, agriculture, and mining, in raw materials and in finished goods, in finance and in trade, in countries far and near. Taken together with the industrial preparedness policies of governments, this distortion of the whole structure of *peacetime* production is the greatest economic cost of modern totalitarian war. This point is so important that it must be developed further.

[4] See Friedrich Lenz, "Wirtschaftliche Wirkungen des Rüstungswettlaufs," *New Commonwealth Quarterly,* June 1938, pp. 46-47; Eliot G. Mears, "Strategy in Industrial Location," *Harvard Business Review,* Autumn, 1938, pp. 9-14.

There are persons—many of them in the United States—who still feel that if a country can "avoid war" in the sense of not actually sending troops to do battle it can avoid the main social and economic and political costs of war. Nothing is farther from the truth. The main costs of war today—and we shall speak of economic costs only, though the same would probably apply to social and political costs as well—come from living in a warlike world. In an era of highly complex industrial organization, economic interdependence, and totalitarian war, the costs of war can be divided into three kinds: (1) direct costs of the fighting itself and its direct effects; (2) indirect costs that come from the after-effects of a particular war on the economic system; (3) direct and indirect costs of the menace of war in general, not of any one war in particular—in other words, the costs of power economy. Of all these costs, the last weighs more heavily on economic welfare in the modern world than either of the other two.

The direct costs of the World War were immense, but its indirect costs have undoubtedly been still greater. For example, if one sets out to explain the troubles of practically any metal industry during the 1920's and the vulnerable position of many in the depression of the 1930's it is necessary to start with wartime distortions of demand and wartime effects on old and new sources of supply. Whole counties in certain western states of the United States are still suffering from economic problems that began with over-stimulation of local mining enterprise during the War. American farmers know from experience how two-dollar wheat during the War encouraged over-capacity which plagued the industry all during the 1920's. Cubans could tell a similar story of war demand and later maladjustment in sugar. The monetary disturbances of the World War and its aftermath of debts and trade barriers certainly had much to do with the severity of the depression of the thirties. These indirect losses from the disturbing effects of war on economic life are huge today because modern wealth production, depending as it does on smooth flows, on "keeping the traffic moving," is particularly vulnerable to disorganizing shocks.

With the appalling direct and indirect economic costs of the World War fully in mind, we must still reckon that the costs to most countries of living in a warlike world (costs of power economy) will overtop the losses from the World War in a few years' time, unless conditions change. The burden on economic welfare which results from the present menace of war naturally cannot be calculated exactly, but here are some of the items: (1) direct costs of military and naval preparations; (2) costs of preparation for civilian defense against air raids and gas attacks; (3) costs of attempting to be more self-sufficient in raw materials by subsidizing expensive home production, thus burdening consumers and also distant producers (such as hog-corn producers in Iowa); (4) costs of preparedness in manufacturing industries, including duplication of facilities, over-investment; (5) wasteful interference by government in private business enterprise, far beyond what would be needed for purposes of welfare economy; (6) misdirection of inventive genius and organizing genius into the arts of war instead of the arts of peace. This last item may be the greatest economic cost of all in the long run. Granted that the stimulus of war has helped to develop technology in the past, incidental benefits of this kind are less important under modern conditions, while the disorganizing effects of the war menace have become far greater. The progress of invention nowadays depends on fundamental science, which requires peace and quiet and funds for research, and, above all, a mental atmosphere of intellectual freedom in the search for truth. The preparation for modern totalitarian war tends to destroy these essentials of scientific progress. Can anyone doubt that science would move ahead more rapidly today if more talented persons were at work on the problem of bombarding atoms and fewer on the problem of bombarding cities?

There is probably no single factor which does so much to hold down living standards today as the insecurity of modern international relations. Release of the world from the insecurity of the war danger would be likely to unleash a volume and variety of scientific progress unparalleled in the history of mankind; it would clear the way for the immediate application to the arts of peace of thousands of technical ideas we already have, but which are not now profitable because of war-scare distortion of industrial demands and because of war-scare raw material prices; it would do more to raise real wages, lower taxes, and relax industrial tensions than can possibly be done by the most successful direct attack on these problems so long as the war menace lasts. Even in our relatively most prosperous times we are in a constant depression, compared with what we might enjoy could we remove from the path of progress the boulders piled there by international insecurity.[5]

Political Consequences of Power Economy

The quest for power, rather than the quest for welfare, lies back of most of the so-called economic causes of international conflict. "Economic" causes of war are important more because economic resources are major constituents of fighting power than because of any irremediable conflict between the economic welfare of one country and the economic welfare of another. The economic welfare of all countries can increase at the same time. Economic power, however, is a relative matter, so that the gain of one is the loss of another. Economic welfare calls for coöperation; economic power is essentially

[5] From the author's *War Losses to a Neutral* (New York: League of Nations Association of the United States, 1937), pp. 65-6.

competitive. Conflicts of interest in the field of welfare, when they do arise, can be settled by compromise. It is hard to think of any gain in economic welfare which could be attained by a modern war and which would be worth the price. Conflicts of power, on the other hand, can hardly be compromised. Yielding on the slightest point is quick to be interpreted as a sign of weakness and to entail a disastrous loss of prestige, which may soon require new yielding or an appeal to force. The whole matter has never been better stated than by Mr. R. G. Hawtrey in his little book on *Economic Aspects of Sovereignty:*

> We are accustomed to think of economic ends in terms of welfare, but in matters of public policy that is never the whole story. To each country power appears as the indispensable means to every end. It comes to be exalted into an end itself.
>
> So long as welfare is the end, different communities may cooperate happily together. Jealousy there may be, and disputes as to how the material means of welfare should be shared. But there is no inherent divergence of aim in the pursuit of welfare. Power, on the other hand, is relative. The gain to one country is necessarily loss to others; its loss is gain to them. Conflict is of the essence of the pursuit of power . . .
>
> So long as international relations are based on force, power will be a leading object of national ambition. There results a vicious circle. When a political leader says that war is necessary in his country's vital interests, what he usually means is that war is necessary to acquire or to avoid losing some factor of national strength. The interest is only vital in the sense that it is vital to success in war. The only end vital enough to justify war is something arising out of the prospect of war itself . . .
>
> If . . . wars are made for material aims, the reason is that those aims are thought of in terms not of welfare but of economic power . . . When I say that the principal cause of war is war itself, I mean that the aim for which war is judged worth while is most often something which itself affects military power . . . Diplomacy is potential war. It is permeated by the struggle for power, and when potential breaks out into actual war, that is

usually because irreconcilable claims have been made to some element of power, and neither side can claim such preponderance as to compel the other to give way by a mere threat.[6]

The political consequences of power economy are seen in the domestic field as well as in the relations between nations. Gigantic armament programs and the need for the broadest form of industrial preparedness in an era of totalitarian war are forcing governments everywhere to impose great sacrifices on their people.

In order to accomplish its purpose, the state is forced to appropriate a larger share of national income, accelerate its own investment activity, intervene in the operations of the national economy, and suppress civil liberties. For the democracies, the ultimate cost of unlimited armament competition may be the loss of their free economies and the undermining of democracy itself.[7]

[6] R. G. Hawtrey, *Economic Aspects of Sovereignty* (London: Longmans, Green, 1930), pp. 26-7, 105, 107.

[7] William T. Stone, "Economic Consequences of Rearmament," *Foreign Policy Reports* (New York: Foreign Policy Association), October 1, 1938, p. 172.

CHAPTER THIRTEEN

FROM POWER ECONOMY TO WELFARE ECONOMY?

THE world must rid itself of the menace of war or of modern industrial technology. The two do not fit together. The same technology that makes economic progress possible also makes war totalitarian, and in an era of totalitarian war the mere threat of war sets a dry-rot going that, if it proceeds far enough, changes the whole character of the economic system from welfare economy to power economy. Power economy undermines the foundation of world economic coöperation, which rests on the mutual benefit (from a *welfare* point of view) of exchanging different kinds of resources. Under the influence of a frantic quest for the economic means of military power the world economy begins to crumble into competing nationalisms or imperialisms. Economic productivity is held in check by restricted market areas and restricted supply areas and by continual insecurity. Cultural values dissolve in the moral preparation for war. It is no overstatement, but a sober weighing of the forces at work, to say that within the near future the world must take a decisive turn either towards a type of world organization able to make war only an occasional local problem or towards a period of chaos and disintegration during which scientific technology, having been proved too potent for man's use, will eventually be smothered in a new Dark Ages.

The problem of abandoning power economy and turning towards welfare economy has two aspects. In the first place, there is the political problem of removing the overwhelming necessity for each nation to possess the means of independent self-defense. It must be made possible for nations to cease thinking frantically of war preparedness. In the second place, mobilization of economic resources for war has gone so far already that if stable peace were suddenly to "break out" tomorrow there would be ticklish problems of transition in redirecting large sections of industry all over the world towards peace needs instead of war needs. This is the problem of economic demobilization.

Making Welfare Economy Politically Possible

How can it be made possible for nations to lose their present feelings of insecurity and to turn from the economics of military preparedness to the economics of peaceful welfare?

In the very long run, of course, there is much truth in the view that the solution to the problem of peace must come from the development of an atmosphere of coöperation in a forward movement of social and economic progress, the fruits of which are shared in a manner felt to be reasonably just for all nations and all classes. What the world must achieve in order to have peace is not some static, ideal justice, under which everyone is forever content, but a dynamic justice of peaceful evolution. There must be reasonable promise for the dissatisfied that their legitimate grievances will be done away with in time. Feelings of frustration must give way to the exhilaration of healthy development. This is the broad meaning of "peaceful change," and it is with the economic aspects of peaceful change in this sense that the analysis and the proposals of the present volume are chiefly concerned.

But starting from where the world finds itself today, long-term policies of economic adjustment are not enough. The plain fact is that the long-run benefits of economic coöperation cannot be had until certain political prerequisites are met. A first essential of economic coöperation is that a reasonable amount of order and security be established in the world. Anarchic force must be tamed; otherwise the dictates of power economy will continue to dominate the scene and policies looking towards economic welfare will not have a chance. They will be smothered in frantic economic preparedness for attack or defense before they have time to work. It will prove more and more difficult to have them applied at all. To prescribe that nations coöperate for economic welfare and thereby achieve the security that comes from a general sense of "justice" or well-being overlooks the most important facts of the present world situation. Nations cannot coöperate very far or very effectively for economic welfare until most of them are assured of more security against attack than they have now.

Some social reformers make the mistake of supposing that to remove the influence of munition-makers or capitalist investors, or to change the internal balance of social forces in some other way, would enable nations that now live under the fear of war to turn from power economics to welfare economics. The evidence is all against such a view. Every nation today, whether it be a capitalist democracy with strong socialist labor opposition, like Britain and France, or a completely socialist Soviet Union, or a fascist Italy, or a progressive, socalist-inclined democracy like Sweden, or a New Deal United States, or a nationalist China, is armed and arming within its capacities and in accordance with the intensity of the threat that it feels. Not internal pressures, but the consciousness of insecurity is the cause of the boom in armaments, and every country, no matter what its social system, is finding that "defense is of much more importance than opulence."

Given the conditions of today, a new start towards welfare economy will be possible only if concerted guarantees against attack, backed up if need be by the overwhelming force of the world community, can be made to supplement, and ultimately to take the place of, the present necessity for national preparedness. In other words, the only alternative to power politics and power economy is community organization.

Can the peacefully inclined peoples of the world organize some protective system to free themselves from the overwhelming need for separate national defense, so that they can have security to plan in terms of welfare rather than in terms of power? The economic bases of power for doing so are still in their hands. There is no doubt about the superiority of the resources under the control of the democratic and non-aggressive countries, and this gives them an ultimate superiority of force. Japan could not carry on its present aggression in China without aid from the United States, Great Britain, Holland, and France. Italy could not have conquered tiny Ethiopia, let alone stand up against the League Powers that it threatened to attack, had the League Powers dared to put oil on the list of sanctions and to close the Suez Canal, and had the coöperation of the United States been assured for the oil sanction. Italy and Germany could not have intervened in Spain, and Germany could not have seized Czechoslovakia had there been a solidly organized system of resistance to aggression, backed by a united world community.

What a former president of the United States, Theodore Roosevelt, said almost three decades ago applies with even more force today:

... It would be a master stroke if those great powers honestly bent on peace would form a league of peace, not only to keep the peace among themselves, but to prevent, by force, if necessary, its being broken by others. The supreme difficulty in connection with developing the peace work of The Hague arises from the lack of any executive power, of any police to enforce the decrees of the courts. In any community of any size the authority of the courts rests upon actual or potential force; on the existence of a police, or on the knowledge that the able-bodied men of the country are both ready and willing to see that the decrees of judicial and legislative bodies are put into effect. In new and wild communities where there is violence, an honest man must protect himself; and until other means of securing his safety are devised, it is both foolish and wicked to persuade him to surrender his arms while the men who are dangerous to the community retain theirs. He should not renounce the right to protect himself by his own efforts until the community is so organized that it can effectively relieve the individual of the duty of putting down violence. So it is with nations. Each nation must keep well prepared to defend itself until the establishment of some form of international police power, competent and willing to prevent violence as between nations. As things are now, such power to command peace throughout the world could best be assured by some combination between those great nations which sincerely desire peace and have no thought themselves of committing aggressions. The combination might at first be only to secure peace within certain definite limits and certain definite conditions; but the ruler or statesman who should bring about such a combination would have earned his place in history for all time and his title to the gratitude of all mankind.[1]

Economic Demobilization

According to a survey made in the fall of 1938, world expenditures for armament had more than trebled within the preceding four years, rising from a total of five billion dollars in 1934 to more than fifteen billion in 1937 and an estimated 17½ billion for 1938 (not counting the

[1] "International Peace," by Theodore Roosevelt, an address before the Nobel Prize Committee. Delivered at Christiania, Norway, May 5, 1910.

sudden increases after the Czechoslovakian crisis in the fall of 1938). Even allowing for changes in price levels, current military expenditures were found to be more than four times as large as they were in 1913. "The rate of acceleration is without precedent in modern times except for the period of actual hostilities during the World War." [2] Since publication of that survey successive crises have continued to step up the pace of military preparation.

The huge expenditures on armament and its rapid rate of increase have become major factors in the world financial and industrial situation. Rearmament has coincided, for the most part, with a recovery movement of the business cycle, and has introduced a dangerous element of instability into world economy. It disorganizes government budgets and imperils the stability of currencies. It is likely to be financed by means that become more and more inflationary as time goes on. It produces a distortion of demand that affects the structure of industry not only in the countries spending the most on arms but also in the outlying raw material countries and the great "neutral" purveyors of all sorts of wartime and peacetime commodities, like the United States. Furthermore, the urgency of defense preparations, the difficulties of finance, the necessity of imposing sacrifices on the people, and the need in many countries for foreign exchange with which to buy armament materials are everywhere working a transformation in economic systems. Where government control over economic life is strongest it becomes still stronger, more centralized, and directed still more towards power and less towards welfare. In the countries where free enterprise still has an important rôle economic

[2] William T. Stone, "Economic Consequences of Rearmament," *Foreign Policy Reports,* October 1, 1938, pp. 158-9 (New York: Foreign Policy Association).

systems come more and more to resemble the totalitarian economies of wartime.

It is obviously impossible to continue forever piling arms upon arms. Yet a sudden stoppage of the huge outlays now being made, if nothing positive were done to ease over the transition for industry and finance to demands of a more peaceful kind, might well touch off a new depression. Perhaps even a mere slowing up in arms expenditures, or a slowing up in the rate of increase, would be enough to start a downward spiral. The danger is especially great because booms and depressions normally revolve about fluctuations in the capital goods industries, and these are just the industries where armaments produce the most direct expansion.

This situation immensely complicates the problem of statesmanship in seeking to turn from power economy to welfare economy. Beating swords into ploughshares is not a simple business when the sword has come to be the whole power of an industrial production system turned in the direction of war economy. No one can say without prolonged and careful study of concrete facts just what measures might be best for easing the transition from armaments to peacetime industry, should it become politically possible to make such a transition. Certainly there will have to be economic clauses in any political truce that is reached. Otherwise some countries, at least, will face the dilemma of pushing the arms race to its logical outcome in general war or entering a period of economic depression. What those economic clauses might contain may be briefly suggested: (1) coördination of national public works projects, and launching of some international public works projects, with particular attention to finding useful peacetime outlets for the heavy industries and other industries now occupied with armament orders; (2) coördination of central bank policies in order to counteract any general deflationary spiral that might be set going by the decline in armament orders; (3) direct stimulation of international trade in capital goods by the launching of international development projects in the Orient, South America, Africa, Southeastern Europe, or elsewhere; (4) arrangements for investments "in kind" by countries too weak financially to participate by cash investment in international development projects, but whose heavy industries have been developed beyond normal peacetime needs (*e.g.*, Japan, Germany); (5) general development of international trade, by removal of restrictions, increased facilities for medium-term credits, a world survey of resources and industries to provide information for new lines of trade, and the like.

The whole problem of the transformation from power economy to welfare economy which is the great need of the world today can be symbolized thus: How is it possible to create social conditions under which scrap steel from America and rubber from the East Indies, now going into China in the form of Japanese bombs and military trucks, can go instead for the building of bridges and schools and factories? How can economic effort be turned from rendering human life unendurable to giving it opportunities for development?

The problem which has to be faced first, however, is the problem of some mutual defense system to stop the trend towards the rule of force in the world. Almost everything constructive that might be done in the field of international economic relations in order to raise the level of economic welfare waits on a political prerequisite: some means of banding together to stop the progress of aggression, and thereafter to promote the common peaceful solution of common problems.

PART FIVE

PROBLEMS OF POLICY IN A "MIXED" SYSTEM

CHAPTER FOURTEEN

THE PRACTICAL BASIS OF WORLD ECONOMY TODAY

WHAT might be done to work towards the ideal of peaceful and intelligent use of the world's resources for the benefit of the masses of ordinary people? The aim of the next several chapters is to bring together the threads of the analysis thus far by applying the general principles developed earlier in the book to concrete questions of policy. These chapters do not pretend to lay down a blueprint for statesmen to follow; their aim is, rather, to put certain problems in perspective. Concrete suggestions do emerge, and no doubt some of them will be thought "Utopian." The author holds, however, that an academic student of these problems can make a useful contribution by exercising, within limits, the freedom that lack of responsibility gives him to look around and ahead, to explore various avenues, and to turn up ideas here and there.

Starting from Where We Are

In discussing policies that are proposed for application in the reasonably near future, certain stubborn facts have to be accepted as "given" data.

The first of these is the planetary nature of modern technics. This is a fact that can hardly be altered except at the price of a cataclysm capable of reversing the whole trend of our civilization. Furthermore, it is a fact that is on the way "in"—growing stronger. Far from slackening off, the conquest of distance by technology seems still to be moving forward at a pace as great as at any time in the past. More specialized production, and important economies of large-scale production, will continue to demand a market covering a very wide area in order to get maximum efficiency. Developments in metallurgy, the rapid growth of such modern industries as electrical communications and aviation, and the general tendency of "neotechnics" to put emphasis on the exact adaptation of material to function continue to increase the advantages for economic welfare of a world-wide raw material supply area.

This is true despite the frantic and in some cases successful attempts of military economies to develop synthetic substitutes for strategic materials. In view of all these continuing trends, is not the wisest policy to seek to turn to social advantage the new possibilities raised by an advancing technology of distance, by an advancing technology of production, and by a more discriminating use of raw materials, rather than to retreat into the unreality of a fantasy world where nations can pretend to be as far apart and as independent as they used to be?

Another stubborn fact in the present-day world is the important rôle of the nation and the nation-state. Sentiments and traditions, vested interests, and the lack of any strong world government make the nation-state the chief agent of economic control and the fundamental governmental unit through which most measures of constructive action in the near future must be executed. This fact is undoubtedly a survival from old conditions of civilization now rapidly giving way to new conditions. The all-supreme nation-state, like the coal-driven locomotive, is on the way out, but in the meantime we have to depend on the coal-driven locomotive to pull most of our freight cars and on loyalties to the nation-state as the chief basis for government.

From the point of view of securing the most peaceful and intelligent use of world resources the supremacy of the nation-state is a fact to be regretted. It differs from the fact of world-wide technics in this regard. We should have a more prosperous and happy world if nationalism meant what we now mean by regionalism, and if nation-states were like member states of a world federal union. But we cannot build a practicable program for today upon the rapid realization of such a vision. A "given" fact at present is the habit of thinking in national terms and the necessity of executing public decisions mostly through national governments. However, this is one given fact that it should be the purpose of constructive statesmanship to alter—gradually, of necessity, but steadily.

The fact that the nation-state must be accepted as the main unit of economic policy, even on problems that are really world-wide, need not prevent constructive action. The self-interest of every nation is fundamentally on the side of economic coöperation and exchange, if national efforts can be directed towards improving the lot of the people rather than towards a competitive struggle for power. The more enlightened the self-interest the more clearly does this appear. Even in a world of self-centered nations, all have more to gain *in terms of economic welfare (not power)* by a concerted forward drive to better use of resources than by snatching unreal or temporary advantages from each other in a game of beggar-my-neighbor.

A fourth fact that colors the world economic situation of today is the necessity for defense. If we had a peaceful world to start with, or one with nerves less on edge and less accustomed to seeing its worst fears come true, this point could be disregarded. We might even hope that economic coöperation would be enough by itself to bring stable peace. The trouble is that economic coöperation cannot be tried to the full except in the shelter of a world political system that offers some effective guarantee of security other than the ability of each nation to defend itself. So long as statesmen and peoples are convinced that there is danger of war and that the chief support of each country in case of war will be its own armed power, there can be no hope of great or long-continued success in promoting world economic coöperation.

The necessity for defense, so long as it rests upon each nation individually, brings us up before a factual situation different from any of the others we have been surveying. A planetary technology creates new difficulties of economic organization, but they are not insurmountable. National traditions and political organization based on nationalism interfere with the best use of the world's resources in many ways, but a workable world economic system could be reached without requiring the destruction of national feelings. Economic coördination in a mixed economy, partly through conscious planning and partly through a market system, is theoretically conceivable on certain conditions. But there is no way to fit the requirement for great national preparedness and strong national military power into a picture of world economic welfare built upon the peaceful interchange of world resources.

The economics of power and the economics of welfare do not mix—not in an era of totalitarian war. The chapters that follow are therefore written on the assumption that measures of political coöperation will be put into effect by means of which nations that want peace may be relieved of at least part of the overwhelming necessity they now feel for war preparedness. On no other assumption is it possible to plan for economic welfare in the modern world.

The Dictatorships

What about economic coöperation between the rest of the world and those countries known as the "dictatorships"? Can it be grounded in mutual benefit? Should it be sought now?

The difficulties that cause these questions to be raised wherever current world economic policies are under discussion have two roots. One comes from the systems of economic organization that have been introduced in the dictatorship countries, and especially the control of external economic relations by the state. This has been discussed in Part III, where the conclusion was reached that fully-planned and controlled economies raise novel problems in a world economic system, but that these problems need not be insoluble.

The real difficulty in dealing economically with the dictatorships stems from their political philosophies rather than from their methods of economic organization. The world can afford to tolerate very divergent economic and political systems in different countries and to adapt itself to getting along with them. But there is one thing that it cannot tolerate if the peoples of the world want to pursue economic welfare. That is external military aggression or the threat of it by any member of the family of nations. Aggression or the threat of it forces even the peacefully minded people to adopt the practices of power economy, with a result that is eventually ruinous to the world economic system. Above all else, the growing *power* of the aggressively inclined has to be checked in the interest of preserving any possibility at all of constructive coöperation for welfare in the future. This, and not the technical difficulties of reconciling the methods of different economic systems, makes fruitful economic coöperation with the dictatorships impossible under present circumstances. Economic concessions to them now, unless part of a general settlement that included solid political guarantees, would simply be to strengthen the forces which threaten to make the whole world economic system unworkable, and which even now are subjecting all nations to economic costs comparable to those of war.

Two elements must be part of any effective method of meeting the threat of violence from the dictatorships. In the first place, there must be a willingness to go very far indeed to coöperate economically on a peaceful basis, as part of a general settlement which assures freedom from further attacks and which assures certain elementary rights of man. In the second place, there must be a firm and previously announced determination to meet violence with a collective defense which would leave an aggressor who resorts to violence little chance for success. Such a method of meeting the problem of violence is possible only in an organized community where all the important members of the community, especially the ones least likely to have a selfish "axe to grind" in any immediate quarrels, are coöperating. Unfortunately, the world has never become an organized community to the extent necessary to apply such policies with success where major powers are concerned, and what partial success had been attained under the League of Nations now seems to have been sacrificed in general abandonment of the League system for pre-1914 diplomacy.

Probably the most practical way to start re-forming the lines of the world community is for those governments that are genuinely concerned for the peace and the economic welfare of their peoples to join in a sort of "economic club," to begin practicing among themselves as many of the principles of peaceful economic progress as may be possible in view of the threat to their security and the necessity of preparedness, and to throw their joint economic power to the support of those threatened by aggression. Membership in the club should be open to all, regardless of economic system, but with one requirement: renunciation of aggressive political designs, backed by actions that show the pledge to be sincere.[1]

The Form of Future World Economy

The international economic system of the future is likely to have three sectors: the market sector, the intergovernmental sector, and the sector of international public or quasi-public authorities. The market sector will consist of economic transactions carried on by private enterprises. It will overlap, of course, with the other two sectors. The intergovernmental sector will include transactions of the planned or controlled economies of the world among themselves—for example, trading agencies of the Soviet Union in dealing with those of Japan, Turkey or Germany—and also transactions between public corporations set up in countries of mixed economy. The sector of international public or quasi-public authorities will be made up of such existing agencies as the International Rubber Regulation Committee, the tea and tin and copper control groups, the shipping conferences, and regulating agencies that may develop in cotton, wheat, and other lines.

In all three sectors the need for continuous and intel-

[1] For discussion of a somewhat related proposal see the memorandum prepared by Professor Michael A. Heilperin for the tenth International Studies Conference, *The Monetary Aspect of the Raw Materials Problem and the Revival of International Trade* (Paris: International Institute of Intellectual Coöperation, 1938), p. 36.

ligent *international* coöperation is clear. The market sector cannot function effectively without "rules of the game" designed to check anti-social tendencies and to make the private quest for profit operate as nearly as possible in the social interest. Providing these rules is a function of government, and in the present era of world economic interdependence it requires coöperation among governments. International loan contracts and the law to be applied to them in the settlement of disputes, the taxation of international businesses, international questions of patents and copyrights, unification of the laws on bills of exchange, standard methods for the collection of statistics on trade, prices, production, and occupations have all been the subject of international conferences or treaties in recent years under the auspices of the Economic Organization of the League of Nations. Other technical services of the League, such as the Transit and Communications Organization, have dealt with related subjects. The International Labour Organisation has developed conventions on conditions of work. Private international bodies, such as the International Chamber of Commerce with its arbitration courts for the settlement of commercial disputes, are also helping to create a world code for the regulation and protection of private enterprise. The code must expand, and ultimately some of it should be administered directly by world agencies.

In the intergovernmental sector the need for permanent methods of coördination is great and will continue to grow. "Commercial policy" in the past concerned tariff rates, treaties guaranteeing equal treatment for private enterprises, and the like. In the future, as governments and governmental agencies participate more in economic life, commercial policy will be a matter of continuous negotiation among governments, involving monthly, weekly, even daily decisions. Inevitably there will have to be new and more effective means of regular international coöperation.

The sector of international public or quasi-public authorities may be expected to grow in importance, and its development may counteract to some extent the exaggerated importance of the national unit in world economics. However, the outlook of international control authorities at the present time is dangerously restrictive, and there is need for some international public supervision able to speak for the world's consumers. Perhaps the appearance of international development projects for particular regions, international public works coördinating committees, and the like, may introduce a more positive note into this sector.

CHAPTER FIFTEEN

INTERNATIONAL MONEY PROBLEMS

WHAT should be the respective rôles of laissez faire and of planning in the world's system of international money relations? In other words, what should be left to the working of the automatic market forces and what should be handled by conscious public control? Towards what ends should the controls that are used be directed, and how should they be organized?

The task of the money mechanism is, of course, to aid in the exchange of real goods and services, and it gets its great importance from that fact. A breakdown in the money mechanism is the greatest of all barriers to trade and resource movements—or, at least, it runs a close second to the disorganization caused by war and the prospect of war. Because problems of the money system have such a close connection with the great problem of economic stability and instability, they are fundamental in all efforts to bring about better use of the world's resources for economic welfare, and they are closely tied to problems of political peace. Many kinds of adjustments can be made smoothly and peacefully in a stable, progressive economy that cannot be made at all in an unstable, contracting one. The core of the world's monetary problem, then, is to see that smooth functioning of the currency and credit system shall help to keep goods moving, to encourage steady increases in production, and to avoid the disastrous contractions and deflations that make productive, peaceful adjustments impossible.

Aims and Methods

Starting from where we are, there are certain factors that have to be taken into account. The first is the tradition of an automatic, self-regulating gold standard which, merely by the observance of a few simple rules, provided an international money. The persistence of that tradition, in the face of changes that have removed many of the conditions that made an automatic gold standard workable, is one of the obstacles to reaching a new permanent system of world money on the basis of positive planning. The idea of a money linked to gold still has a certain psychological value, and perhaps gold will long be a convenient technical device for international reckoning, but the real responsibility for the total amount of money in the world and for the ratio of one national money unit to another is now in the hands of conscious administration, and will remain there. The philosophy of "back-to-something"—in this case, back to the self-regulating gold standard—can merely hinder progress on the real problem, which is improving the conscious administration of the world's money system.

A second factor in today's situation is the recent experience of extreme monetary instability, uncertainty, devaluation, fluctuation. Panic movements are therefore easy to start and hard to stop. Fear affects international movements of funds more readily than prospects of profitable and useful investment, so that "hot money" and capital that flow "upstream" from regions of high interest rates to regions of lower rates vex the world's monetary authorities. Reluctance to enter into long-term contracts that involve transfers from one currency unit to another prevents healthy foreign lending, and hinders trade in goods by making it risky to enter into commitments even a short time ahead.

A third element in the problem is the fact that monetary intervention, universally practiced, is everywhere carried on by *national* authorities. Even though the devices of monetary management now in common use—manipulations of the discount rate, open market operations, devaluation, sterilization of gold flows, changes in bank reserve ratios, exchange controls, equalization funds, public works programs—obviously have world-wide repercussions of great importance, they are wholly under the legal control of national governments. In practice there are more and more consultation and coöperation, especially since the tripartite monetary understanding worked out between Great Britain, France, and the United States in September 1936. Coöperation of this sort must not only be encouraged, it must be institutionalized.

What are the objectives towards which international monetary coöperation ought to aim? The most important is the maintenance of conditions that make possible stable production and employment. Concerted efforts on an international scale are necessary if monetary policy is to contribute effectively to this end. Not only is one country acting alone unable to control all the conditions that affect its prosperity, but in default of common action to meet a world economic crisis the interest of any one country acting alone is to play beggar-my-neighbor, unless it takes an unusually long-range view of its interests. The lack of organized means for common action of a positive sort in the great depression of the nineteen-thirties goes far to explain why emergency needs led to many mutually harmful measures of monetary nationalism. If all countries together can embark upon expansionist programs to counteract the downward spiral of deflation in time of depression, and can act together to control booms, then the conflict that is often supposed to exist between stability in monetary relations with other countries and internal stability loses its seriousness.[1] World coöperation in monetary policy is the only real alternative to mutually destructive measures of monetary nationalism. In this field, as in so many others, the issue is no longer whether there shall be planning or not, but whether it shall be coöperative, coördinated, and *positive,* or nationalistic, haphazard, and mainly restrictive.

International monetary policy should aim at stability in the ratios of national money units to each other. But if it is necessary to choose between a partial retreat from this position and drastic deflation for some particular country, then retreat in the form of devaluation of the country's currency by *international agreement* may well be preferable. The important thing is to provide for continuous coöperation of a sort that will enable such measures to be carried through, when necessary, without starting a chain of defensive or competitive devaluations, and without leading to new trade barriers. A world policy directed towards preventing deflationary tendencies from carrying the whole world economy downwards in a depression spiral can do much, however, to remove the need for action of this kind. That is, if world price trends can be kept fairly stable, adjustments to the ordinary shifts in demand, changes in production technique, and other disturbances that occur in a progressive economy can be made by the country most affected moving slightly ahead or slightly behind changes in the world price structure. Only in unusual cases would the dilemma of drastic deflation or devaluation arise. So long as great disturbances do occur, however, and considering that there is not the same freedom of movement for goods and per-

[1] See Michael A. Heilperin, "Monetary Internationalism and Its Crisis," in *The World Crisis,* by the Professors of the Graduate Institute of International Studies, Geneva (London: Longmans, Green, 1938), pp. 347-51.

sons and capital between countries as between different regions of one country, it is not feasible to maintain a rigid relation between currencies at all times, and it is not desirable to make the attempt at the risk of drastic deflations. Economic welfare calls for distinguishing as well as possible between permanent disturbances to which adjustment must be made and temporary disturbances that need to be resisted or smoothed over. Such a distinction can only be made in view of the world economic situation as a whole, and the plan of action decided upon should be a joint plan for concerted international efforts.

Coöperation of the central banks and the governments of the leading trading countries in their use of equalization funds, discount and open market policies, public works programs, and other devices of control is obviously the main practical method today for seeking the objective of greater monetary stability in world economy. While such coöperation between national authorities is all to the good, it is not enough on a longer view of our problems. There must be conscious development in the monetary sphere of more effective world institutions differing in structure and outlook and methods from joint national action in the way that federal action in the United States differs from joint action by the separate states. The Bank for International Settlements is useful today as a clearing house for information, as a secretariat for technical studies of money problems from a world point of view, and as a meeting place for the central bank authorities of different countries. Its power to form policies and to execute them in part by actions of its own should gradually be increased, until it becomes a real central reserve bank of the world.

Large movements of funds not directly connected with movements of goods—as when capital raised in one country is invested in another, or when debts are paid—may put serious strains on the international money mechanism and on the internal money systems of individual countries. Post-war history has shown what evil results can follow from setting heavy tasks of this sort for the mechanism while cramping its normal working by barriers to trade. The obvious moral is the need for better coördination between trade policies and policies on debt collection and investment. The United States, for example, followed incompatible policies when it encouraged large-scale investment of American capital abroad, presumably with the hope of return payments, tried to collect on the Allied war debts, and at the same time raised higher barriers against imports. The Hawley-Smoot tariff, boosting import duties in 1930 just at the time that the crisis had strained money systems everywhere and when the sudden stoppage of new foreign investments had made the situation of debtor countries particularly acute, helped mightily to hasten financial collapse and to deepen the depression.

Large capital movements, under a system of fixed currency ratios, ordinarily are "transferred" with the help of price movements that induce trade shifts: upward price movements in the lending country, downward price movements in the borrowing country, inducing an outflow of goods from the lending country and an inflow into the borrowing country. When net repayments begin the mechanism works in just the reverse manner, helping to induce a flow of goods to the creditor country that constitutes its "real" payment. Under certain conditions, when the capital transfers are large and sudden, the working of the transfer mechanism is thus likely to involve an appreciable amount of deflation in the lending or repaying country, inflation in the borrowing or receiving country. When many costs and prices are rigid or "sticky,"—as they are under modern conditions of large-scale enterprise, cartel agreements, collective wage bargaining, and state controls—this might help to set off a depression, or an unhealthy boom that ends in depression. The internal price shifts and hence the disturbances caused by the working of the transfer mechanism in cases of capital migration need not be very great if there is a large volume of international trade. But "the smaller the volume of trade the more violent will be the inflation in the borrowing and deflation in the lending country consequent upon the movement of a certain sum of money capital, or, if exchanges are allowed to vary, the more violent will be the fluctuations in the exchange rate." [2]

In periods of instability and difficult readjustment, when the problem is to set trade and capital moving again in a healthy way, the central banks or other monetary authorities of the different countries need to watch capital transfers closely. There is even much to be said for a permanent supervision over large-scale capital movements as a part of monetary planning in the interest of stability. When necessary, part of the burden of international capital tranfers could be taken off the money mechanism, leaving it freer to function for ordinary trade, by arranging that great international projects for development and reconstruction launched in, let us say South America, Africa, or China, should be supplied with some of the needed capital "in kind." That is, some countries might participate in a joint international loan by furnishing steel or machinery rather than cash.

Exchange Controls, Clearing, Barter

A transition problem of great importance is the question of methods by which the restrictive aspects of ex-

[2] Gottfried von Haberler, *Prosperity and Depression* (Geneva: Economic Intelligence Service of the League of Nations, 1937), p. 312.

change controls now existing in many countries can be done away with. Exchange controls are restrictive because they make international trade cumbersome and inelastic. A large part of the time of the merchant has to be spent studying the latest regulations, waiting on government offices, and filling out endless forms. Correspondingly less energy can go into the regular economic function of the merchant, namely, moving commodities from places where they are more abundant or less in demand to places where they are scarcer or more in demand. Furthermore, exchange controls and the clearing agreements and barter devices often associated with them are restrictive because they tend to make trade bilateral. The invention of money was a great step forward in economic technique because it made possible trade between A, who has shoes and wants a coat, and B, who makes coats but does not want shoes. By use of money, "multiangular" trade could be substituted for simple barter. Modern nations, setting up elaborate machinery for bilateral swaps—as when the proceeds of Yugoslav sales to Germany can be used only to buy German goods, or when an American cotton exporter wanting to sell to Germany under the "compensation" arrangements must first find an American importer willing to take the right quantity of optical goods—have in effect renounced part of the technical gains from the money system. That this may have been the only course open in emergency conditions created by the depression breakdown of the money system does not lessen the fact that bilateralism is a great step backward, lowers the world's productivity, and limits economic welfare. Dr. Schacht himself, chief architect of the complicated German external economy, has said that against his own wishes he found himself obliged to substitute a terrible bureaucracy for the normal play of exchange and credit, adding, in an interview, that "it is barbaric to be forced to barter machines for cereals or radio apparatus for tobacco, like a negro who exchanges his ivory for glassware or his rubber for cotton goods."[3]

It has been suggested by some that the exchange controls and clearing agreements of today offer a new and useful "planned" basis for the organization of international trade. They need to be developed on the positive side, the argument runs, as by working out means of multilateral clearing, and when that is done they can well supersede the old "anarchic" international money system. Governments would "plan" trade by supervising all transactions. Advocates of this view even urge that countries like Great Britain and the United States, which do not have exchange control, should institute it in order to get these supposed advantages.[4] The present writer, after weighing these arguments carefully, is completely unconvinced. It seems to him that the best way to get rid of the restrictive aspects of exchange control and clearing agreements is to do away with these devices wherever they exist, as rapidly as the fundamental conditions which made them necessary can be removed. There should be substituted for exchange control either outright public operation of export and import enterprises by government agencies, or permission for free buying and selling by private enterprises in foreign trade (subject only to indirect controls through tariff and monetary methods that fit in with the market system, as explained in Chapter X), or a combination of the two methods. The first method would fit best in an economy that is to be run more or less on the Soviet model. As we have noted,

[3] Quoted by Professor Bertil Ohlin in his report to the Joint Committee of the Carnegie Endowment for International Peace and the International Chamber of Commerce, *International Economic Reconstruction* (Paris, 1936), p. 94.

[4] Cf. Paul Einzig, *The Exchange Clearing System* (London: Macmillan, 1935).

the economic systems of Germany, Italy, and Japan show a strong drift in that direction. The second is more suitable in the countries where the market system still predominates. Either free enterprise, regulated by competition, or direct government operation, presumably regulated by the government's sense of the public interest, is preferable to the exchange control system in which profit-seeking enterprises carry on transactions but government officials check and double-check every move. The reasons are the same as those which suggest that public regulation of privately run utilities is the worst of the many forms which may be given to the relation between government and monopolistic enterprise (Chapter X). Such methods encourage duplication of effort, restrict initiative or misdirect it, waste energy in a tangle of red tape, and if they do not produce outright corruption, at least give higher rewards to the kind of talent which can influence the government than to the kind which can improve the efficiency of production and trade.

Schemes have been worked out for making exchange-clearing systems more flexible by means of "compensation checks" or some similar device.[5] No doubt a plan of this kind is to be preferred to the rigid, trade-throttling types of exchange control and bilateral clearing, and it might be of some use among the controlled economies until they can be reintegrated into a world money system. But to the extent that a scheme of this sort is perfected—made flexible and inclusive, providing, for example, as its expounders have suggested, for a rise and fall in the value of the "checks" on a certain country to bring demand and supply into equilibrium, and providing for loans and capital investments—it becomes more and more like the regu-

[5] See especially the various works of Professor Edgard Milhaud, *La Compensation Organisée* (Paris: Sirey, 1935), *Le Chèque-Compensation International devant l'Opinion* (Paris: Sirey, 1936), etc.

lar international money system, with the same advantages and the same troubles. Checks on France and checks on England would behave like francs and pounds. Nothing would be gained by going from the present money system to exchange control in order to work back through "compensation checks" to something like the present system again, unless exchange control is desirable in itself, which it is not. The better plan is to concentrate on improving the use of existing monetary controls. It has been well said that "the most efficient clearing system and the most simple, too, is the monetary system."[6]

Countries now under restrictive exchange control régimes can be brought back into a satisfactory system of money relations with the rest of the world only as the difficulties that led to the imposition of exchange controls are removed. This means that there must be lowering of trade barriers and coördinated efforts to preserve world monetary stability. But the countries concerned must also be willing to steer their own policies in the direction of international coöperation, particularly as regards readjustment of currencies whose official value is too high, willingness to let trade be multilateral, and willingness to work for other economic ends than war preparedness. Finally, the policies of the countries in a strong financial position, especially the policies of the United States with its huge accumulation of gold, will largely determine whether transitions can be made without too much risk of monetary instability in the financially weaker countries. The United States must definitely seek a passive balance of payments, allowing Americans to receive more goods and services from abroad than they send abroad and paying for the balance by exports of the huge surplus stocks of money (gold) now accumulated in the United

[6] Ludwig von Mises, "The Disintegration of the International Division of Labor," in *The World Crisis* (cited earlier), p. 267.

States. This will be easier if education in the principles of economic welfare can disabuse the public mind of common fallacies, such as the notion that an "unfavorable" balance of trade is bad, or that increased imports lessen total employment in a country.[7]

In conclusion, the monetary sphere is one in which the rôle of conscious control is likely to be very great, indeed. In order that it may be positive rather than restrictive in its effects on the use of world resources it must be coöperative and international. The Tripartite Monetary Agreement and its extensions, the Bank for International Settlements, the International Public Works Committee which met for the first time in June 1938, under the auspices of the I.L.O., the Delegation on Economic Depressions set up recently by the League of Nations, and the work of the Economic, Fiscal, and Financial Committees of the League and their sub-committees, all stand for tendencies that need to be encouraged. Concerted efforts to lessen economic instability by world-wide direction of monetary policy have a key importance in world economic coöperation today. It should never be lost from sight, however, that monetary policy alone cannot keep a system running smoothly, nor can it make up for bad policies in such fields as trade and investment.

[7] The half-truth in this latter fallacy will be recognized by readers of Chapter V as the problem of "costs of transition."

CHAPTER SIXTEEN

INTERNATIONAL TRADE, LABOR STANDARDS, PRODUCTION CONTROLS

The Future of Trade

THE character of international trade may change. Specialty goods of all sorts, particularly capital goods, are likely to increase their relative importance as living standards rise and as the simpler machine processes for producing articles of mass consumption spread more evenly over the world. Methods of carrying on international trade may change. We are likely to see an increase in the amount of trade by governmental agencies, by coöperatives, and by commodity control authorities. But the fundamental principles which make interregional and international trade productive do not change. International trade in the future, as in the past, will offer a very important means for raising standards of living, and humanity will be the loser if by reason of world anarchy, it proves impossible to take full advantage of this means.

Trade in goods is fundamentally a method of exchanging the more abundant resources of each region for resources that are scarce to it but relatively abundant elsewhere. Trade in raw materials often comes close to being direct trade in natural resources. For example, nickel from the remarkable deposits in Canada flows to Germany and the rest of the world, while potash from the rich German deposits flows to Canada and other countries. Even such simple goods as raw materials, however, have "wrapped up in them" many different kinds of resources, including natural advantages of climate or geological formations, resources in capital equipment, knowledge and techniques, managerial ability, technical labor, skilled labor, and unskilled labor. The wheat which flows out of the Mississippi Valley and the great farms of the northwest United States carries to foreign countries the peculiar advantages of flat prairie land, good soil and temperate climate, and also the advantages of mechanical ingenuity and large-scale machine farming in which North America has shown special abilities. The more refined types of goods—semi-finished and finished goods—are also, in essence, nothing but more or less complex combinations of primary resources. The relative proportions of different kinds of resources in a particular region determine its fitness for specific industries. Each region is best equipped to produce the goods which require large proportions of the resources relatively abundant there, and least fit to produce the goods requiring large proportions of resources which it has only in relatively small quantities. Trade allows industry to adapt itself to the geographical distribution of material and human resources, and promotes the welfare of all regions by placing the demands of each in touch with the best available sources of supply.

But even if there were no differences between the resources, human and material, of different regions it would still be good social economy to have trade. This is because trade permits specialization of products, of equipment, of techniques, of managerial and labor skills. It has already been pointed out in Chapter I that the economies of large-scale production depend upon having a very wide market area, especially if the more durable and highly specialized types of capital goods are to be produced by mass methods. In addition to economies of large-scale production within a single enterprise, a wide market also makes possible what are called "economies of concentration." These result from the grouping of large amounts of similar kinds of work in one locality. They help to explain the preëminence of Paris in the world of fashion, of the Detroit-Flint-Toledo district in automobiles, of Jena and Rochester in optical goods and photographic supplies. "When an industry has thus chosen a locality for itself, it is likely to stay there long," so great are the advantages of neighborhood for similar skilled trades. "The mysteries of the trade become no mysteries; but are as it were in the air. . . . Good work is rightly appreciated, inventions and improvements in machinery, in processes and the general organization of the business have their merits promptly discussed . . ."[1] Subsidiary trades grow up, testing and research laboratories and training schools are established near by, buyers come regularly from a distance, and different firms can draw upon the same pool of trained labor with less unoccupied reserve. In many industries economies of this type depend upon the large market made possible by world trade.

Finally, an abundant international trade makes for smoother readjustments when men and capital and knowledge move from place to place. Abundant trade simplifies the task of developing new territory as men migrate into the few unexploited areas that are left; it facilitates capital movements and the introduction of better techniques in the less advanced regions and lessens the problem of absorbing new production into the world economy. Thus there are three distinct ways in which trade in goods promotes better social use of resources: it makes it more possible than otherwise to shift primary resources themselves from place to place without prohibitive tran-

[1] Alfred Marshall, *Principles of Economics* (London: Macmillan, 8th edition, 1922), p. 271.

sition costs; it acts as a substitute for resource movements where they cannot take place or where they take place slowly, bringing the demands of one locality into direct touch with other localities where the necessary resources are most abundant; and it makes possible increased economies from specialization, large-scale production and concentrated production. Trade in the future, as in the past, will offer these fundamental advantages.

Laissez Faire and Planning

A program of constructive action to promote economic welfare must make use of considerable amounts of conscious control in such fields as monetary management, guidance of investment funds, spread of knowledge and techniques, and the organization of human migration. Trade in goods, by contrast, can be left more largely to private enterprise and the principle of laissez faire. International trade for private profit, directed only by market forces, may be expected to work reasonably well in the social interest if three conditions are present. The first is over-all stability of the world economic system—a matter closely linked with monetary policy, with private and public investment, with barriers that impede trade readjustments. The second is the absence of war and war crises. The third is competition. Given a chance by an environment at all favorable in these three respects, private international trade is a powerful instrument for improving economic welfare through promoting better social use of the world's resources. Indeed, it is the most powerful we have available for operation between different countries. Furthermore, international trade in goods and services, as compared, for example, with international investment and international migration of persons, is an aspect of economic relations in which the pursuit of private interest by individuals and firms is relatively unlikely to have repercussions that are contrary to the social interest. An import-export house that makes a profit is usually performing a useful social function with at least a fair degree of efficiency. Huge fortunes these days are not ordinarily founded on international mercantile enterprises, which goes to show that this branch of economic life is by and large quite competitive and in a situation where the motive of private profit operates to serve the public rather than to exploit it.

The main problem for positive planning in the sphere of international trade in goods is how to remove the obstructions that keep private enterprise from working as effectively as it might—in other words, to get rid of antisocial, restrictive "planning." Existing obstructions to trade are partly the result of uncertainties created by depressions, monetary instabilities and the fear of war. In part they have been deliberately erected by national governments in response to emergency conditions, or to promote self-sufficiency in the event of war, or in response to pressure groups whose appeals are reinforced by erroneous protectionist beliefs on the part of the public. The lowering of these barriers—tariffs, quota restrictions, and the like—by any method which is effective and which can be applied in a way to minimize costs of transition is the great task of positive planning in international trade at the moment.

Secretary Hull's reciprocal trade agreements program is the most important effort in this direction now being made. The method is to deal one at a time with country after country, considering in detail the commodities that most concern the United States and the other country in the two-way trade between them. When reductions in the barriers that affect the flow of some of these commodities can be agreed upon by both sides, a pact to that effect is signed, but the concessions mutually made are not exclusive. They are immediately generalized under the most-favored-nation clause.

There are many advantages in the Hull method of attacking trade barriers. It is capable of being applied a bit at a time, with gradually cumulative effects. It makes possible careful attention to both the immediate and the long-run consequences for every industry affected. When honestly and intelligently applied, as it certainly has been in the United States, it permits at least an approach to a just balancing of probable permanent gains against probable transition costs. The study of detailed trade and tariff problems under the administrative organization in charge of the trade agreements program has been the most thorough, public-spirited, and scientific ever applied to such problems in the United States.

A great advantage of the Hull method over unilateral tariff reductions, both from the point of view of minimizing transition costs and from the practical standpoint of getting some reductions actually accepted, is that every reduction made on import barriers is accompanied by concrete, simultaneous reductions in the barriers encountered by exports. Of course, when the United States reduces its barriers against imports it automatically creates conditions under which its own exports will sooner or later expand. More dollar purchasing power goes to pay foreigners for the goods they supply, and sooner or later, given monetary stability, this purchasing power must flow back to the United States to pay for exports.[2] But this effect takes time, and the immediate effect of unilateral tariff reductions (that is, without the concessions on exports which are part of the Hull system) is deflationary. This may be an important disadvantage under certain

[2] Exports must here be understood to include services, and other "invisible" items in the balance of payments.

business conditions. Furthermore, the process by which exports ultimately expand as a result of increased imports is not direct and simple enough to be grasped readily by public opinion, especially when the propaganda of interested groups is at work. Hence the great advantage of reciprocal concessions which increase both imports and exports simultaneously.

Finally, the reciprocal trade agreements method, using the unconditional most-favored-nation clause to guarantee non-discrimination, is bilateral in form but multilateral in effect—if the items on which reductions are made are not too narrowly defined. The tendency to make concessions very specific, so that in fact the goods on which duties are lowered can be furnished by only one or a few countries, is a danger to the whole principle of equal treatment. If narrow definitions of commodities are not allowed to defeat the purpose of the program, however, every new agreement between the United States and another country, and every new agreement by any country already included in the network of agreements, yields some concession, great or small, which is generalized to all countries in the network to the advantage of world trading opportunities. Thus, a pool of reasonableness can gradually spread and deepen if the governments of the world wish to make that happen.

Governments can help to make the market sector of international trade operate more effectively in the social interest by certain other measures. They can improve the public facilities that make trade more efficient—international roads, airways, canals, radio and postal communications, banking, means of access to investment funds. A project that deserves consideration whenever a propitious moment for progress in international organization arrives is an international "consular service" to gather and distribute trade information through direct representatives in all the great cities of the world. This service should provide information to the managers of private enterprises and governmental agencies in all countries impartially. Organizationally, it might well be an extension of the Economic Intelligence Service of the League of Nations. But charges of favoritism towards particular countries might arise to hamper the work of an official body, so perhaps an international commercial information service could best be built up at first by a voluntary organization like the International Chamber of Commerce.

In addition to (1) trade carried on by private commercial enterprises in response to market forces, international economic relations in the future will probably include (2) government-controlled trade, (3) government-operated trade, (4) trade carried on by consumers' coöperative societies, and (5) trade influenced by private combinations, cartels, producers' coöperatives, and other associations of producers, including governmental or intergovernmental commodity control schemes.

Little positive gain can be expected from extending the method of government control of private transactions (number 2 above). It has already been argued that exchange control and the clearing and barter devices connected with them are essentially defensive measures, perhaps justifiable in an emergency, but better done away with as soon as possible in favor either of greater freedom of trading for private firms or direct government-operated trade.

Governmental trading (number 3 above) is doubtless here to stay. In view of the trend towards more and more public authority in economic matters, it is likely to increase in importance. This does not mean that private enterprise will disappear in the "mixed" economies, or that a government monopoly of foreign trade, however essential in a fully-planned economy of the Soviet type, will become the characteristic form of trade organization in the near future. But in Germany, Japan, Italy, and perhaps in other countries it would not be surprising to see the present façade of private enterprise removed, whereupon minute governmental control of external trade would become forthright management. The trading might still be carried on by decentralized government-operated corporations, perhaps under existing firm names. The firms might simply become public corporations in fact by a gradual process of subordinating more and more types of managerial decisions to state control. This process has already gone very far in the countries named.

In the "market" or "mixed" economies there is likely to be some increase in the amount of foreign trading carried on by government corporations, but not to the extent of superseding the market system. There is no reason for nationalizing foreign trade in general in these countries. In fact, quite the opposite is desirable, both on grounds of economic efficiency and for political reasons. A highly decentralized conduct of trade by private specialists who know their lines and who react quickly and competitively to changes in demand and to new supply possibilities is much more efficient than a large, bureaucratic foreign trade organization for countries where internal economic organization is not centralized. The government, where necessary, can influence foreign trade in the large by influencing the "supply and demand" situation to which traders react, and it might need to intervene to encourage competition. But it does not need to manage transactions in detail in this field.

International trade carried on by consumers' coöperative societies (method 4 above) is a fairly new development. It is oldest and has reached greatest volume in the imports of the wholesale societies of England and

Scotland. In the Northern Countries the Scandinavian Coöperative Wholesale Society, founded in 1918, represents the consumers' coöperatives of Sweden, Norway, Denmark, and Finland. It is the largest import agency in Northern Europe for such overseas products as coffee, fresh and dried fruits, rice, spices and tea. It also imports large quantities of raw materials for the use of the factories run by the coöperative movements of these countries, including soya beans and copra for the manufacture of oils and margarine, rubber for galoshes, hides, hemp, wheat, and sisal. The coöperative wholesale societies of Northern Europe not only enter the world market as buyers, but they have established the first internationally owned coöperative factory: the Luma electric light bulb factory in Stockholm. Launched originally to bring down the monopolistic price charged in these countries by an international electric bulb cartel, an endeavor in which it was quite successful, Luma now supplies bulbs to coöperatives abroad. Thus it exercises a restraining influence on monopolistic practices far beyond its main sphere of operation.[3]

If international economic relations are allowed to develop in conditions of peace and stability, the general economic importance of the consumers' coöperative movement and its rôle in world trade are likely to increase considerably. Certainly this would be a desirable development from the standpoint of world economic welfare. In the first place, coöperative purchase through coöperative wholesale societies controlled by retail societies that are in turn owned and controlled by consumer members is an efficient way of organizing trade. It brings together a large block of stable demand, and avoids some of the

[3] Herman Stolpe, mimeographed memorandum on "Consumers and Monopoly Concerns," Swedish Memorandum No. 1, International Studies Conference, Tenth Session, Paris, June 28–July 3, 1937.

waste of competitive sales pressure. In the second place, strong consumers' coöperative societies, especially when they are able to go into production on their own account, are one of the best means of restoring competitive conditions under which the profit-seeking of private enterprise can once more work in the public interest. All-inclusive coöperative organization of a trade or industry is not necessary in order to get this result. In Sweden, it has been adequate as a rule for the coöperatives to control anywhere from ten to twenty-five per cent of the total output of an industry in order to check monopolistic practices.[4]

Third, and very important, the influence of organized consumers in world economics is much more healthy, from the point of view of making planning positive rather than restrictive, than the influence of organized producers which is now such a strong factor. In the field of nationalistic trade barriers—protective tariffs and the like—organized consumer influence in a number of countries is already beginning to make itself felt. Thus, in 1930 there was no manufacture of vegetable oils (used in making margarine) in Sweden, though two factories had earlier been erected for the purpose. Under the influence of an international cartel, they had closed down and declared that they could not resume operations unless the Swedish parliament put a tariff on vegetable oils. In 1932 the Swedish coöperative wholesale society bought the mill at Karlshamn and not only operated it without tariff protection but soon put it on an export basis. Similarly, in 1937 the coöperatives took over the largest porcelain factory in the country, which had been clamoring for protection against Finnish competition, rationalized it,

[4] Mauritz Bonow, *Kooperationen och folkförsörjningen* (Stockholm: Kooperativa Förbundets Bokförlag, 1936), p. 166.

and withdrew the demand for a tariff.[5] The Consumers' Union of the United States, a rapidly growing organization whose main activities are in the line of testing and rating products offered on the retail market, has lately shown a tendency to interest itself also in the treatment meted out to consumers in tariff legislation.

The influence of production control schemes on international trade (method 5) will be considered later in this chapter.

Labor Standards

There is a mixture of truth and falsity behind the fears that are so easily aroused in high-standard countries over the effects of trade with countries on lower wage and living standards. As usual, confusion arises out of differences between long-run permanent gains and short-run transition costs, and out of conflicts between the general welfare and the welfare of particular groups.

The gain from international trade for any country consists in the fact that it is thereby enabled to get the things it imports more cheaply than they could be produced at home. Trade is socially productive just *because* it takes advantage of differences in production costs for particular goods in different places. This, by the way, shows what a mockery is the so-called "scientific" tariff formula of "equalizing costs of production at home and abroad." A tariff just high enough to equal the difference between production costs at home and abroad is just high enough to stop trade completely and prevent all social gain from trade. It is an embargo.[6]

[5] Stolpe, *op. cit.; Vi* (organ of the Swedish coöperative societies), May 29, June 19-26, 1937, and information supplied by Dr. Mauritz Bonow of the Swedish coöperative organization.

[6] "What the world needs are moderate tariffs *(sic)* at levels which represent no more than the difference in cost of production between home and abroad," said ex-President Herbert Hoover in a radio address giving his program for peace, January 15, 1938. (*New York Times*, January 16, 1938.)

If a country like China, where the efficiency of labor is very low, is to be able to trade at all it must be able to sell something abroad. The production costs of *some* things in China must be lower than the production costs of those things elsewhere. So long as the efficiency of Chinese labor is very low, the wages of labor have to be very low in comparison with other countries; otherwise, no Chinese goods at all could be sold in competition with the efficient producers of Europe or the United States. As it is, even with extremely low wages in China, there are only certain industries in which production cost *per unit of output* is low enough for China to export to the United States, and these are industries using large proportions of crude labor power. In such lines the low Chinese wage level can have its full effect, and the characteristic advantages of the United States in mechanical skill, capital, and organization do not have full play. Hand-made rugs offer an example. When it comes to making motor cars, however, the United States undersells the world while paying three times the hourly wages of automobile factories in other countries. The situation is similar in such lines as mechanical refrigerators, typewriters, machine tools, and many others peculiarly well adapted to American methods and American resources.

In other words, differences in wage levels express differences in the average efficiency with which labor is applied to production. The best-adapted industries of a country—those that use high proportions of its most characteristic resources, such as the automobile and radio and wheat industries of the United States—apply labor to production with even more than the average efficiency of the country. Therefore, even when paying the highest wages, these industries are able to undersell competitors abroad and to export their goods, for their costs of production *per unit of output* are less. Other industries, where the comparative efficiency of labor applied to production is not so high as the average for the country, find difficulty in producing at as low a cost per unit as is possible abroad while paying their country's wage level. These are the industries that complain of competition from "low-standard" countries.

What is the remedy? If industries where labor works at relatively low efficiency are subsidized by a protective tariff the effect is to put labor out of the high-efficiency industries (the export industries, which cannot sell abroad unless there is two-way trade), in order to keep it in the low-efficiency industries. That is not the way to raise wage levels. And furthermore, the whole process has to be paid for by consumers, who are forced to subsidize the less efficient industries by paying more than the cost of the same articles imported from abroad.

The promotion of economic welfare demands a different procedure. In the first place, if the inability of the complaining industries to produce at low cost while paying high wages is due to poor management, or if it is possible to invent new methods of production that lower costs enough so that no subsidy is needed, the remedy is obvious. If the inability comes from the fact that these particular industries need large proportions of factors of production that are much more scarce domestically than they are abroad, then the industry is not well adapted to the country. It ought to decrease in size, perhaps it ought to disappear altogether. The labor employed in it ought to be retrained and transferred as rapidly as possible to industries that *can* pay high wages while meeting all comers in competition. The expansion of these latter industries will be encouraged, of course, by the very fact of importing goods formerly made by the less efficient industries—for the fundamental fact about trade is that it is a *two-way* affair, and increased imports must be paid for by increased exports.[7] Thus, as pointed out in an earlier chapter, real wages in the United States as well as in China are made higher by trade that permits the United States to get its hand-loom rugs made in China in exchange for radios, machinery, wheat, or gasoline.

So much for the falsity of the notion that trade with low-wage countries imperils the standards of high-wage countries. The pressure on wages comes only in industries that are not up to the average level of efficiency of the country in their use of labor, and long-range positive planning calls for meeting the situation by encouraging the transfer of resources to the better-adapted industries.

Now we come to the truth in the notion. *When the efficiency of labor is rapidly rising in low-wage countries,* and this happens when new capital and techniques and better organization are being introduced, the relative cost situation in certain industries may change quite suddenly. Japanese and Chinese textiles start underselling European and American textiles, first in foreign markets, perhaps later in the home markets of the established producing countries. Here we have in an acute form one of the costs of transition that accompanies all economic progress. There must be readjustment in established industries. If the readjustment can be made smoothly and positively, the end result is a better division of labor and a more productive use of world resources, with higher living standards for all concerned. But in a world economy already unstable, and with restrictive measures impeding the expansion of new and old industries that ought to help to take up the slack when changes occur, the difficulties created in some countries by improvements in others

[7] Unless a country gets credit from abroad, or uses up purchasing power that it has accumulated in the past (such as a gold hoard, or accumulated investments abroad). But all these are temporary methods, and even the accumulated purchasing power depends on past exports. Exports, of course, include services as well as goods.

may be serious. Hence, there is all the more reason to anticipate such difficulties by continual international study of industrial changes, so that transition problems can be met constructively.

It should be noted that the transition problems created for established industries by growing efficiency of labor in low-wage countries are no different from the problems created by any kind of improvement that lowers production costs elsewhere. The discovery of a new mine from which ore can be dug more cheaply than from existing mines, or the invention of a new process for making tires which renders existing factories obsolete raises the same problems. There is no special "menace" looming over the world from the industrialization of the low-wage countries. This is just one of many challenges to plan constructively so that economic progress may be had without a totally unnecessary amount of conflict and suffering.

Aside from encouraging parallel readjustments in the older industrial countries, this challenge of new industrialism can be met constructively by methods that the International Labour Organisation is already practicing, namely, by efforts to see that labor standards and wage levels rise along with labor efficiency in countries entering upon rapid development. Modern techniques of worker protection should be introduced along with modern techniques of production. There can be no question of equalizing wage levels all over the world, however, until the margin of efficiency at which labor works is more nearly the same in all countries.

Cartels, Large Firms, Commodity Controls

Many kinds of goods, especially raw materials, move in international trade today under the influence of great combinations or cartels or governmental and inter-governmental commodity control schemes. The facts have been described briefly in Chapter VIII. Little will be said here about the problems raised by these controls or about the policies that might be pursued towards them, because that would be to duplicate parts of a work prepared by the present writer for the 1937 International Studies Conference.[8] The following summary may be quoted from Chapter 7 of that report:

The question of the social desirability of raw material control devices is not one which can be answered in general terms for all commodities under all conditions, for the answer depends upon the *relative* desirability of unhindered price reactions and whatever control might be applied in the particular case. There is a great difference in the efficiency with which the price system can bring about necessary adjustments in raw material industries of different sorts. Industries characterized, for example, by very inelastic demand accompanied by fluctuating crops, or excessively immobile factors of production, or a great tendency to overcompensation in response to price signals, are less well adapted than others to adjustment under the price mechanism and therefore offer the most promising field for control experiments. Incidentally, they also offer the greatest temptation to exploitation of consumers by producer-managed controls.

The possibilities of control schemes, on the other hand, are extremely various. Factors which will determine whether control will be better or worse than unhindered price adjustments under given circumstances include: the degree of price flexibility in the economy as a whole in the absence of controls; whether the control is managed wholly in the interests of producers and from their point of view, and is therefore likely to use any available monopoly power to the limit, or whether there can be strong representation of a wider public interest in determination of control decisions; the

[8] Eugene Staley, *Raw Materials in Peace and War* (New York: Council on Foreign Relations, 1937), Chapter 7 on "Raw Material Control Schemes," and a long appendix in which a summary history of efforts at control is given for each of the following commodities: aluminum, bismuth, camphor, coal and coke, coffee, copper, mercury, molybdenum, newsprint, nickel, nitrates, petroleum, pineapples, platinum, potash, quebracho, quinine (cinchona bark), radium, rubber, sandalwood oil, silk, silver, sisal, steel, sugar, sulphur, tea, tin, tungsten, wheat, wood, zinc.

degree to which control techniques have been perfected, and their applicability to the problems of the particular raw material industry in question; the good or bad foresight and general competence of the personnel placed in charge; whether or not the control is likely to be dominated by a particular national interest. The public ideal respecting control policy calls for efforts to achieve the same results as those which would be obtained by ideal operation of the free competitive price system, but with mitigation of its wastes and rigors, and attention to human elements not taken into account by a pecuniary calculation. The private ideal for profit-seeking producers engaged in managing or influencing the management of a control scheme calls for the maximum exploitation of monopoly power consistent with preserving that power. These two ideals are not compatible, and under producer-managed controls of the type common today the first is not likely to be determining.

The essence of the problem of commodity control schemes in international trade, from the standpoint of fitting them into a program of positive rather than restrictive planning, is *who* does the controlling. A control run by or for producers of the commodity in question, persons whose pecuniary interest is on the side of a high scarcity-value for that particular commodity, is practically sure to be biased on the side of socially undesirable restriction. This is not to say that collective restriction of output, especially in certain emergency situations, is never desirable (though it ought to be only temporary, while more fundamental, positive readjustments are being worked out). What it does say is that persons who get their income from the sale of a particular product are never the proper judges to determine when it is in the social interest to increase or decrease its total output, or to raise or lower its price. They should be represented in any organization having such authority, or at least their interest should be weighed in deciding what is in the social interest, but they are the last persons to whom exclusive control should be given. In practice, however, it is largely the producer interest that runs the world's commodity controls.

Power to determine total output or price is the essence of a monopolist's power, and that same power is inevitably tied up with any commodity control arrangement that works. Monopoly need not always be anti-social. The evil results of monopoly flow from the fact that it is generally *private* monopoly, or is used in the interest of only one part of the public. A *social* monopoly might function better in the public interest under some circumstances than the free market—if the power that monopoly gives is truly used in the public interest. The whole strategy of a statesmanlike program for meeting the issues raised by the increasing number of control schemes of world-wide effect should be based, therefore, upon seeing to it that where such controls continue they are run by representatives of the public interest rather than representatives of only a part of the public. This means (1) that a commodity must not be controlled by or for producers only, and (2) that a commodity of international importance must not be controlled by representatives of one or a few countries only.

The point of view taken here is quite contrary to that expressed in the Draft Annotated Agenda drawn up by the Preparatory Commission of Experts for the 1933 Monetary and Economic Conference. There were sharp differences of opinion within the Commission, but the report as drafted said, under the head of "Organization of Production and Trade":

> We consider that, generally speaking, international economic agreements [i.e., cartels and commodity control schemes] have more chance of success if their formation is left to the initiative and free discussion of the producers concerned, for whom they represent an already advanced stage of industrial organization.
>
> Some of us, however, think that the governments might usefully

take the opportunity of the coming Conference to discuss the attitude they should adopt in regard to these agreements, particularly in cases where the intervention of governments is necessary to insure the organization of the production of, and trade in, certain staple products, especially in cases where the producers are not at present in a position themselves to regulate the production and distribution of their products.

Note that the "success" of commodity control schemes is in this view presumed to be measured by their satisfactoriness to producers, while the rôle of governments is to help producers get what they want. Of course, in part this reflects the conditions of 1932–33, in which the producers of raw materials were faced by sharply falling demand which had depressed prices far below normal. But more fundamentally it reflects the unconscious bias of those who have an interest in high pecuniary values for particular products, and hence in scarcity—a bias which runs through the economic attitudes of our civilization and accounts for much of the tendency towards restrictive rather than positive planning. The warped, anti-social viewpoint which unconsciously rejoices in scarcity for the sake of the producers' pecuniary values is characteristically reflected in the pages of business journals. In D. H. Robertson's phrase, "The *Economist* of 30th November, 1929, told me in three successive paragraphs that there was too much tin in the world, too much tea, and too much oil; and of course I already knew that there was too much coal, too much rubber, and too many ships!" [9]

It is true that a later passage in the Preparatory Commission's report does say that the object of governmental policy towards production controls should be "not only to adjust the interests of the producing countries, but to safeguard those of the consuming countries." But even

[9] "How Do We Want Gold to Behave?" in *The International Gold Problem,* by a study group of the Royal Institute of International Affairs (London: Oxford University Press, 1932), p. 23.

here it is tacitly assumed that the interests of the producing countries as a whole are identical with the interests of the producers of the particular products in question, overlooking the fact that there may be consumers of wheat or coal within countries that produce these commodities.

The endeavor of constructive policy should be to insert public representatives into the boards of world trusts and cartels and control schemes. The first step is to establish some system of supervision or registration which will require publicity for their operations. Public regulation might be a useful expedient in some cases, though on grounds already stated it is generally better to make all organizations that exercise a large degree of monopoly power into public corporations or into "mixed" corporations, where the public interest participates in management directly. Obviously, the problem of world commodity controls and world monopolies in general cannot be met adequately until permanent world organization is developed to coördinate these tasks of economic administration.

Conclusions

The aim of wise policy should be to encourage a large volume of international trade, flowing in the most productive channels. That is, each type of good should move out of the regions where the resources from which it is made are more abundant than elsewhere (in relation to local demand) into regions where those resources are relatively scarce (or more in demand). This means that each region would export products containing large proportions of its most abundant resources and would import products containing large proportions of its scarcer resources. Trade of this sort between regions, including those regions that happen to be separated by political boundaries, is desirable, not as an end in itself, and not for the profit of traders, but because it is among the most powerful means of promoting the general economic welfare of the peoples of the world, and because without it differences in economic opportunity would accumulate into political tensions and wars.

Such productive trade can be carried on by many different methods. Trading done by government agencies will increase in importance, particularly for those countries where internal economic life is most fully controlled. It is to be hoped that private trade regulated in detail by governments will be replaced either by government-operated trade or by greater freedom of private trade. If the small quantity of international trade carried on by organized consumer groups can be increased, and if organized consumer influence on trade conditions and trade policy in general can grow, that will be all to the good. The bulk of international trade is still carried on by private enterprises, however, and the most important means at the moment for getting better performance of the important social function of trade between countries is to remove the obstacles, political and economic, which hinder the flow of private trade. Most of the detailed conduct of trade can safely be left to the market sector of economic life. The great task of public policy is to create a framework of economic and political stability.

Contrary to widespread belief, there is nothing about trade between regions on widely different standards of living which tends to pull down the general wage level or the labor standards of a high-standard country. So long as the trade proceeds steadily and regularly, so that both countries adapt themselves to it, the result is to raise real incomes on both sides. The real problem is the problem of rapidly increasing labor efficiency in low-standard countries. This makes transitions necessary in the industrial structure of other countries, in exactly the same manner as do new discoveries or new processes that increase productive efficiency. The pr blem must be met positively by measures that make modern labor standards follow rapidly where modern methods are introduced, and by constructive international efforts to encourage the development of new industries to meet the new demands that should be released by improving efficiency.

Commodity control schemes already play an important part in world economics, and constructive statesmanship must be used to prevent them from being managed solely in the interest of producers.

CHAPTER SEVENTEEN

SPREAD OF CAPITAL AND TECHNIQUES

The Future of International Investments

THE productivity of capital movements from one country to another rests on the fact that those regions where savings can be accumulated most easily are not always the ones where additional capital equipment is most needed in order to improve the output from labor and natural resources. Loans from countries relatively rich in capital to countries where capital is a scarce resource, repaid later out of the increased productivity they make possible, result in more efficient use of the world's resources in accordance with the general principle of social economy. If the lending and repaying can be carried through in ways that keep to a minimum the economic and social transition costs discussed in Chapter V, then the shift of capital resources from regions of lower yield to regions of higher yield can benefit the economic welfare of the whole world immensely.

It is sometimes argued that capital investment, however good for the receiving country, means a loss in economic welfare for the people of the lending country. The argument is that the proportion of available capital to labor is reduced by capital exports, thus making the productivity of labor and real wages somewhat lower than they might otherwise be. The answer is, in the first place, that lending is a process of giving up the immediate use of some economic good for the sake of higher returns in the future. If the investment is wisely made and turns out well, the original capital will be repaid with interest (presumably at a higher rate of yield than might have been had at home) so that the end result is to increase the wealth of the lending country. The investment abroad, whether made by private persons or by public agencies, will thus make possible a still more abundant capital supply in the future for use either at home or abroad. Secondly, development of productive resources abroad helps to raise the real income of workers at home by decreasing the price which they must pay for imported goods, including imported raw materials that enter into domestic production. Thus, the very large loans by the English economy to the American economy during the nineteenth century were not only repaid with interest (despite some losses and defaults), but the development of American railroads which English capital made possible raised the standards of living of English workmen by greatly reducing the cost of food and other essential commodities. Thirdly, one of the great problems of the highly industrialized countries today is how to stabilize the flow of new investment so as to keep the capital goods industries working steadily, thus avoiding one of the main factors in general economic depression. An intelligent and coördinated program of loans abroad for developing the less well equipped regions of the earth would be one of the best ways of meeting this problem—certainly better than "investment" in armaments.

Capital-receiving countries sometimes find serious disadvantages of a non-economic kind bound up with the coming of investment from abroad. Chief among these disadvantages are, first, the risk that foreign capital may be made the instrument of foreign political penetration, and second, the social transition costs that may result from the strain of rapid industrialization and from new ways of life. Both these disadvantages are unimportant in the case of investment in countries like Canada and Australia, where the political situation is stable, and where the people are already familiar with modern methods of organization. These particular dangers are most likely to be important in regions like China or Iran, regions of political weakness and non-industrial civilization. Nevertheless, the introduction of modern methods and modern equipment holds out the only promise for raising the standard of living in these countries.

The size of the transition costs connected with the international migration of capital depends very much upon the circumstances under which the movement takes place, upon its direction and timing, and upon the flexibility of the economic system in the countries immediately concerned and in the world as a whole. As better equipment increases the productivity and the purchasing power of new regions, there must be readjustments in established currents of trade. The readjustments, if successfully carried through, will leave both the older industrial countries and the newer ones on higher levels of economic welfare than before. It is in facilitating this process of readjustment that there is great scope for positive planning by means of concerted international efforts in the modern world. Conscious attention to these problems has been made all the more necessary by the growth of barriers against trade in goods and by other sources of inflexibility in the world economic system, such as "sticky" prices and wages and general lack of mobility within the domestic economies of many countries.

It has often been pointed out of late that industrial developments in the past century, including the profitable use of European capital for building up overseas countries, were connected with a very rapid growth in population, and that now population growth in the Western world has slowed down. The next few decades may bring an actual decrease in the numbers of people in many countries of Europe or of European origin. Thus, there will no longer be an automatically expanding market for agricultural products, especially for the great staple foodstuffs, and there will no longer be an almost automatic assurance of returns on great sums of capital put into railroads, canals, telegraph lines, and other equipment for "opening up" vast new reaches of agricultural land. The recent great improvements in agricultural technology add to the strength of this argument.

These observations are quite valid and pertinent if they are intended merely to demonstrate that the usefulness of international capital investment will be in a different direction in the future from the past, and that lines of future development will be more complex. No longer will international investment be mainly a process of building railroads in new countries which will pay for the loans by raising foodstuffs to feed the hungry mouths of rapidly growing industrial populations in the old countries. But any implication that international investment in the future must necessarily be less productive socially than in the past is unwarranted. Agricultural development to feed a growing population is not the only process of economic expansion. Why cannot a rapid rise in the standard of living all over the world increase the demand for industrial products in the future just as the rapid increase in the numbers of population increased the demand for foodstuffs and other primary essentials in the old days? In fact, the international campaign for better nutrition now being conducted under the auspices of the League of Nations shows that even in the realm of foodstuffs, especially the "protective" foodstuffs, there is still room for a great increase in production. However, economic expansion based more on rising living standards and less on population growth is likely, for a number of reasons, to require greater delicacy of adjustment and more coöperative planning and deliberate control if its total social results are to be good.[1] Investments will have to take new forms and new directions, but the fundamental social economy of a more even development of world resources will continue to make capital movements productive.

> The dynamic economic world of the future will present innumerable opportunities for new industrial development in different countries, and so long as savings available to finance such progress are unevenly distributed between countries, international investment must play an important part in world economics. Provided that the investment takes forms suitable to the circumstances of each particular case and that the limiting conditions connected with the balances of payment of creditor and debtor countries are observed, there is no reason to deprecate and every reason to encourage it.[2]

Constructive action regarding international investment in the future must be grounded on the lessons of the past. These lessons are of two sorts. First, experience has shown that capital movements can add greatly to the productivity of the world, helping to increase the standard of living both of the countries that lend and of those countries that borrow. Great movements of European funds into the United States, Canada, Australia and South America hastened the development of these regions, and the necessary readjustments in Europe were on the whole successfully made. Then came the great disrup-

[1] See the discussion on the relation between population growth and the character of demand and the "bumpiness" of economic progress in "Problems of Economic Insecurity," by A. Loveday, in *The World's Economic Future* (Sir Halley Stewart Lectures, London: George Allen and Unwin, 1938).

[2] *The Problem of International Investment,* by a Study Group of the Royal Institute of International Affairs (London: Oxford University Press, 1937), p. 103. This study has been drawn upon freely in the pages that follow.

tions of the World War, and a second sort of lesson emerged from the experience of the post-war period. International investments took place in a new environment. At first it was not sufficiently recognized that conditions were no longer the same. There were higher barriers to trade, economic life was less flexible, political insecurity continued to be great. New lending from the United States took place without the tempering of the long experience and tradition accumulated in older centers like London and Amsterdam. There were elements of recklessness, irresponsibility and high-pressure about some of this lending that played into the hands of other factors making for instability. Also, the rise of American lending brought a creditor nation onto the scene that had not yet learned how incompatible is the desire to keep out foreign goods by a high protective tariff with realization of the income from investments abroad. Collapse of the post-war international investment structure after 1929 was a notable feature of general economic collapse. Now, nearly ten years later, we still find relatively little resumption of international long-term capital movements.[8]

Long-term capital movements of any great importance for raising the world's economic welfare cannot take place in an atmosphere of political insecurity such as we

[8] "Nowhere in the world," says the Bank for International Settlements in its Seventh Annual Report, 1936–37, "are there any real signs of the revival of new long-term capital issues for foreign countries. Not only lending to public authorities but also direct investment in new enterprises has remained at minimum figures. In the United States new foreign issues amounted to $20 million in 1936 as compared with $1,330 million in 1927, and in England foreign issues (for countries outside the British Empire) were only £3 million in 1936 as against £56 million in 1927—even for British overseas countries, the total new issues amounted to only £28 million in 1936 as compared with £95 million in 1927." (P. 88.) The latest report adds that ". . . new foreign issues at long term remain generally at a low level although there has been a certain revival in Switzerland and the Netherlands." (Eighth Annual Report, 1937–38, p. 67.) *Direct investments,* however, have been increasing despite all the difficulties which have beset international relations in recent years. (Pp. 72-3.)

have today. But if the fundamental conditions for international investment can be improved so that it is possible to have a resumption of large-scale lending, what are some of the lines of a socially desirable policy based on past experience?

First, there must be greater attention both by private investors and by governments to the interrelations between trade currents, trade barriers, monetary conditions and the making and repayment of loans. The idea that "capital movements create their own balances" is less real in the modern world than in the world of the nineteenth century. The economies of lending and borrowing regions adapt themselves less flexibly today and readjust less readily so as to produce the movements of real goods and services that must be the counterpart of large inward or outward movements of investment funds. Furthermore, factors noted earlier, such as the slowing down of population growth in the lending countries and the passing of a situation in which opening up a new country paid for itself quickly by meeting a rapidly rising demand for more foodstuffs, mean that investment will have to be directed more carefully in the future. Capital exports will have to be more consciously correlated with the export of goods from lending to borrowing regions, and especially with the possibility of reversing that flow later on when repayments are to be made.

Loans and investments to be financially sound must not only help to improve the borrowing region's general productivity, but must also increase its ability to export goods that will be accepted abroad.[4] Obviously, this makes the soundness of international investments depend on conditions outside the borrowing regions as well as inside.

[4] Of course, the investment may help to make the borrowing region's balance of payments more positive in some other way, as by enabling it to manufacture goods formerly imported. Direct investments in the form of branch factories, for example, may do this.

"One of the clearest lessons to be learnt from the experience of the past few years is that before resumption of international capital movements on anything like the predepression scale can safely be permitted, there must occur a substantial reduction of trade barriers, even compared to their 1929 levels, and that the creditor countries in particular must recognize the inconsistency and the futility of demanding full payment of what is owing to them if they are simultaneously following a trade policy which makes such payment unreasonably burdensome if not impossible." [5]

Secondly, certain new types of investment may usefully become more important in the future than in the past. This applies particularly to medium-term credits for financing trade in capital goods, and to so-called direct investments. Medium-term credits are tending to take the place of publicly issued securities to a certain degree in the building up of the less-industrialized countries. In conditions of currency instability this lessens the risk of strain on the lending country's currency and helps it to maintain a high level of employment by assuring it that the export of funds will be immediately correlated with increased export of goods. The credit risk attached to medium-term lending is usually smaller, also, than the risk attached to securities sold on the public market. Measures have been taken by the state in a number of countries to make more ample provision for medium-term credits in the export trade and to insure private merchants against political and other risks that they might not be willing to assume. In Great Britain, for example, the operations of the Export Credit Guarantee Department of the Board of Trade make it, in effect, a state-conducted international

[5] Jacob Viner, memorandum in the volume on *The Improvement of Commercial Relations between Nations,* published by the Joint Committee, Carnegie Endowment-International Chamber of Commerce (Paris, 1936), p. 78.

investment enterprise.[6] There are dangers, both economic and political, from having investments directed by the export promotion departments of national governments. An international attempt to create non-national credit agencies of this type would be well worth undertaking.

Direct investment, consisting of branch factories or commercial facilities operated directly, and "equity" investment in general, have important advantages over international loans that bear a fixed rate of interest in the conditions of the modern world. The service payments on such investments are less likely to raise exchange difficulties, for their yield is likely to fall in times of depression, thus automatically decreasing the burden of external payments that has to be carried by the economies of borrowing countries. Direct investments also have the advantage of being undertaken, in most cases, by those who have a specialized knowledge of some branch of industry, and this knowledge goes along with the investment, making it more productive.

Thirdly, state control over movements of capital seems likely to be much more important in the future than in the past, even aside from the exchange control systems now operating in many countries. The monetary aspect of new investment in relation to over-all stability has already been touched upon, and this will help to assure governmental concern with investment flows. There is much more reason for governments to concern themselves with influencing the total amount of domestic and foreign investment, however, than with the use made of it in detail. The former is bound up with economic stability. The latter is a question of efficient management of separate enterprises.

As governments become greater factors in the man-

[6] This institution is described in detail in the Royal Institute study cited earlier, pp. 87-94, 107.

agement of capital movements, the political importance and the political dangers of international investment increase. There is no way to meet this situation except through the medium of a world political and economic organization that can gradually make public control mean something other than nationalistic control. There would be advantage in encouraging the development of certain specialized institutional forms for handling the international investment problems of coming years. The great need is for means of accumulating "denationalized" or "anonymous" capital which has been detached from the political ambitions and rival policies of national states. International "mixed" development corporations represent one possibility. Perhaps an international long-term investment bank for financing world public utilities, such as canals and aviation lines, and for collecting funds to be invested in regional developments under international auspices, can be made a practical project in the future. Plans worked out under the League of Nations some years ago for an international mortgage credit company and an international agricultural credit bank, though the depression prevented them from being executed, show the way to another kind of development that is needed. From the point of view of promoting world economic welfare there is much to be gained by these and other devices for separating investment as much as possible from nationalistic politics.

It is worth noting in connection with the political implications of world investment funds that the large capital-exporting countries are relatively few and that they are all found among the so-called democracies. When the depression put an end to large-scale lending the following countries were net creditors—that is, they had net receipts on interest and dividend accounts according to the League of Nations balance of payment studies for 1929:

United Kingdom, United States of America, France, Netherlands, Switzerland, Belgium, Irish Free State, Sweden.[7]

Knowledge and the Productive Arts

Knowledge, together with the productive arts based upon it, is the most potent of all the resources we have for improving the economic lot of mankind. It is a most peculiar resource in that it can be added to one region without subtracting it from any other. Indeed, the more widespread knowledge becomes the more rapidly it grows, for it increases by being applied under new circumstances and by the cross-fertilization of ideas passing back and forth among many minds. Its potency as a factor of production has been shown in recent decades by the phenomenal rise in the industrial output first of Japan and then of the Soviet Union. Both countries have imported some capital, to be sure, but in relatively small quantities. Their main borrowings from abroad have been imports of knowledge and technique.

There are some costs of transition connected with the international transfer of knowledge and its industrial applications. When new methods are introduced into a "backward" region the social life of the community may be gravely disturbed. Fundamental readjustments are required in such a country as China, and even more so in primitive communities of Africa, when the strange methods of the outside world make themselves known. Incomplete knowledge, or borrowing from the outside world only part of what it has learned by experience, is most dangerous of all. Thus, if modern methods of factory organization are to be introduced into countries like Java

[7] League of Nations, *Balances of Payments,* 1933, p. 39. Perhaps Spain should be included. No 1929 figures are available, but in 1931 there were small net receipts to Spain on interest and dividend accounts.

and India they need to be accompanied at the same time by modern methods of protecting the health and safety of industrial workers. As another example, modern methods of sanitation and medical care running ahead of the practice of birth control may bring disastrous social consequences by causing a sudden upsurge in population.

The "export" of technical knowledge, like the export of capital, also calls for eventual readjustment in the country from which it goes. Trade currents must shift as countries formerly unable to produce manufactured goods learn how to make certain things for themselves, and even to make them more efficiently than their teachers. Sometimes a country is tempted to take a short-run view of its interests by trying to maintain a monopoly of new industrial developments in which it has pioneered. The more enlightened view is that a continual interchange of inventions and discoveries is much more important to every country than any temporary gain of this sort, and if one country tries to withhold its knowledge others will do likewise.

Despite some costs and readjustments made necessary by the spread of knowledge over the earth, there can be no doubt about its economic desirability. There is the best kind of a case for positive planning on a world-wide basis in a definite effort to level up the distribution of this resource throughout the world. Of course, knowledge spreads rapidly across boundaries at the present time. It is carried by trade, by investment, by cultural contacts. The internationalism of science is notorious. Technical publications carry new ideas and new processes to faraway places. Governments have sometimes taken part in a deliberate encouragement to the international spread of knowledge. The government of Japan sent students and technical commissions abroad to study the industrial methods of the West. The Soviet Union has hired large numbers of foreign experts to train its engineers and workers. Governments like those of Iran and China send students abroad as part of their program of national development. Sometimes such arrangements have been internationally made and financed. The United States returned to China the indemnity payment due it after the Boxer incident, and the money was used for sending Chinese students to the United States. There is now an inter-American treaty for promoting the exchange of students and teachers among the countries of North and South America. The League of Nations has sent technical advisory committees to various countries. For example, China has been aided by advice on education, health, and other subjects. The International Labour Organisation has loaned its experts to South American countries and others engaged in drafting labor codes.

There is room for a great increase in activities of this kind, and also for the devotion of large sums of internationally-raised capital to the promotion of education in less advanced countries. The economic gain to be realized by the spread of knowledge over the earth is very great, and the stimulus for private enterprise to act on the problem is not so strong as the public interest requires. Even in advanced countries, careful economists have long argued that there is under-investment in the means of making knowledge available to the less privileged groups of society.[8] This applies even more strongly to regions like

[8] "There is no extravagance more prejudicial to the growth of national wealth than that wasteful negligence which allows genius that happens to be born of lowly parentage to expend itself in lowly work. No change would conduce so much to a rapid increase of material wealth as an improvement in our schools, and especially those of the middle grades, provided it be combined with an extensive system of scholarships, which will enable the clever son of a working man to rise gradually from school to school till he has the best theoretical and practical education which the age can give." (Alfred Marshall, *Principles of Economics,* London: Macmillan, 8th edition, 1922, p. 212.)

". . . There is strong reason to believe that, if a moderate amount of re-

China, Java, India, and other places on the earth where masses of human talent are wasted year after year for lack of opportunity to get full development. Just as the whole community gains from a public education program that enables every child to make the most of his capacities, so the world community would gain immeasurably if the level of opportunity to get knowledge could be moved upward by joint international effort.

When one goes beyond material production and considers human values directly promoted by educational opportunities, the case for devoting large sums to the deliberate international spread of knowledge and to efforts at world-wide equalization of opportunities to get knowledge is even stronger. A program of deliberately fostered cultural exchange, if carried on by concerted international efforts and not left to nationalistic propaganda ministries, would also have a decided political value as a means of establishing peaceful coöperation in the world community.

An International Development Program

A glance at the index of machinery available per person in different countries of the world (Chapter IV) shows that there are vast areas where the capacity of the people to contribute to their own economic welfare and to the productivity of the world could be vastly increased if they had better equipment. Even more fundamental, educational opportunity is needed, and that requires capital funds as well as trained personnel. At the same time, the world hears complaints of under-activity in the capital

---

sources were transferred from the relatively rich to the relatively poor, and were invested in poor persons with a single-eyed regard to rendering the poor in general as efficient as possible, the rate of return yielded by these resources in extra product, due to increased capacity, would much exceed the normal rate of interest on capital invested in machinery and plant." (A. C. Pigou, *The Economics of Welfare,* London: Macmillan, 4th edition, 1932, pp. 746-7.)

goods industries (one of the most stubborn recovery problems in the United States, for example), and there are worries in many countries lest lack of employment for young intellectuals lead to further political and social unrest. The capital goods industries are also those most affected by armament orders in countries where military demands now keep the economic machinery turning, and they are the ones where the most difficult problems will arise if the world succeeds in getting past its present war fever and tries to turn once more towards peace economy.

Putting all these elements together, we have the framework for a constructive move which might be undertaken towards economic welfare and peace: a great international development program for the improvement of equipment and knowledge in regions most lacking these things, by means of loaned funds and capital goods and trained men from the countries that have them in abundance. To be sure, no such plan could be executed where wars are raging or where international tension is acute. But a beginning might be made in places less affected by political turmoil—indeed, something on this order seems to be getting under way in the Americas—and concrete plans might be worked out for use elsewhere when conditions permit. The very existence of international development plans and the process of drawing them up might help to bring real appeasement by offering a concrete and attractive alternative to armament races and to the risky gains of aggression.

Constructive possibilities for coöperative international development of an entire region, with benefits both to the people of the region and to the world economy as a whole, are nowhere more evident than in the Orient. Asia, not counting the U.S.S.R., contains 53 per cent of the world's population. In China, India, and the East Indies, just as in Japan, there is no reason why industrial methods should not approach Western standards of efficiency in production, given capital, organization, and, above all, education. Unused human talent with capacity to learn is certainly there. The very good records made by Chinese students who have studied at technical institutes in the United States illustrate that fact.[9] In abstract economic terms the problem is to use resources more effectively by uniting capital and knowledge with the human resources of the Far East and the Middle East. More concretely, this means bringing roads and schools and technical institutes and machinery to China and India and Borneo, so that a skilled, self-reliant generation can grow up equipped with modern tools for meeting their own needs and for exchanging with other peoples.

Let us take China as a specific example. The only hope for giving a constructive turn to the present disastrous war is to end it by a negotiated peace, the terms of which will leave China independent but at the same time will help to solve the economic problems of Japan, aggravated as they now are by the redirection of the whole Japanese economy towards war production. Such a negotiated peace would have to center around a grandiose project for the coöperative economic development of China under international auspices. This would be quite different from the economic development of a conquered China by a victorious Japan or from the competitive scramble for concessions and spheres of influence that took place in the old days. The whole scheme should be guided by the wishes of the Chinese government so far as its internal applications in China are concerned. Developments should be carefully planned not only from the standpoint of making transitions as easy as possible in China itself, but also from the standpoint of the industrial and trade readjust-

[9] Information from President Karl T. Compton, Massachusetts Institute of Technology.

ments in the outside world that must occur as increased Chinese productivity finds its place in the world economy.

Discussion of great capital investments for the industrialization of China has been going on in the United States and other Western countries largely in terms of the outlet which this would provide for under-employed capacity to produce machines and equipment.[10] This is certainly an important immediate consideration. Equally important is the possibility of using the economic provisions of a constructive peace settlement to ease the shock of readjustment for great sectors of industry all over the world that have been built up on the basis of armament demand. But an attitude that puts too much emphasis on making the East a dumping ground for unused productive capacity of Western countries in order to provide employment for their industries would be in danger of giving too little attention to long-range benefits. The development of China and of other countries of the Far East and Middle East would make the world economy permanently more productive. Permanent gains of this sort come from raising the productivity of human labor, and while they can be hastened by large-scale capital investment they depend even more on supplying the peoples of the East with resources in knowledge and skill and organization. In other words education *must* go along with capital investment.

Economic development is bound to come somehow to the countries of the Orient, as to other areas of the world. If left to unguided "natural forces" and to the play of nationalistic imperialisms this development will be accompanied by a long series of wars and revolutions and by repeated sudden upsets imposed upon economic life elsewhere. Here is the challenge for an international

[10] See for example "Discussion of a Plan for an American Loan to Industrialize China," by Philip J. Jaffe, in *Amerasia*, September 1938.

program of positive coöperation to bring the Orient into the world economy in a manner that benefits all people, making the development a promise rather than a menace to the prosperity of the rest of the world. "The closing of the economic gap between the East and the West is indeed one of the greatest problems of the present time." [11]

[11] Harold Butler, formerly director of the I.L.O., *Problems of Industry in the East* (I.L.O., 1938, *Studies and Reports,* Series B, No. 29), p. 70.

CHAPTER EIGHTEEN

MIGRATION OF MEN AND TRANSFER OF TERRITORY

Human Migration

THE migrations that took place during the nineteenth and early twentieth centuries will go down in history as the greatest of all time. They far overshadow in numbers the earlier movements of Huns and Goths and Vandals, and it is likely that future centuries will see nothing comparable. Inter-continental migration throughout the world between 1800 and 1924 has been estimated at approximately 60,000,000. The following countries received over 500,000 immigrants:[1]

Country	*Period*	*Gross Immigration*[2]
United States	1821–1924	33,188,000
Argentina	1857–1924	5,486,000
Canada	1821–1924	4,520,000
Brazil	1821–1924	3,855,000
British West Indies	1836–1924	1,477,000
Cuba	1901–1924	766,000

[1] Imre Ferenczi, "Migrations, Modern," *Encyclopedia of the Social Sciences.*

[2] There was a considerable reverse current at the same time. Thus, it is estimated that against a reported immigration of 37,762,000 into the United States from 1820 to 1930 there must be offset a return flow of about 11,500,000 to allow for persons who returned to their native countries or who emigrated for other reasons, leaving a net immigration of about 26,000,000. Similarly, 2,563,000 persons left Argentina from 1857 to 1924—nearly half of those who entered.

Consult *International Migrations* (New York: National Bureau of Economic Research, 1929), "Immigration into the United States," by Walter F. Willcox, Vol. II, p. 89, and "International Migration Statistics," by Imre Ferenczi, Vol. I, p. 202.

Over one million emigrants left from each of the following countries for overseas territories between 1846 and 1924, according to official statistics: [8]

Country	*Gross Emigration*
United Kingdom	16,974,000
Italy	9,474,000
Austria-Hungary	4,878,000
Germany	4,533,000
Spain	4,314,000
Russia	2,253,000
Portugal	1,633,000
Sweden	1,145,000

These figures indicate the enormous fluidity of population movements during the past century. Today the situation is greatly changed. Restrictions on immigration in the most important countries and difficulties of settlement elsewhere have reduced the former vast flow of migrants to a mere trickle. What is the relation of international human migration to the best use of the world's resources, and what account should be taken of it in framing constructive economic policies?

First of all, migration is not a remedy for short-run cyclical crises. The difficulties of settlement on new lands are greater in time of depression, jobs are scarce regardless of the ratio of population to resources, and new adjustments of all sorts are harder. In fact, migratory movements of a voluntary character actually seem to reverse their characteristic long-run directions of flow in time of depression.

As a long-run adjustment, the economic justification for human migration must rest upon the new relation between men and resources which it brings about. Man is at one and the same time a "factor of production" and the

[8] Same as note 1.

consumer for whom all production takes place. When men move from a region of abundant labor to a region of scarce labor (in relation to other resources) the world distribution of resources *may* be altered in a way favorable to increasing the average productivity of human effort. Shifting consumers from a region where the pressure of population on resources is more intense to a region where it is less intense *may* tend to raise the average level of economic welfare in the world. The word "may" is used instead of "will" in these statements because of two important qualifications. In the first place, it cannot be taken for granted that emigration out of a densely populated region will always lower the ratio of population to resources in that region. If birth control is not practiced, and if population growth is held in check mainly by a high death rate due to pressure on the bare essentials of existence, as in India, outward migration may simply bring a slight fall in the death rate and leave the population as large as before. This would probably not occur in industrial countries where the standard of living has started to rise and the birth rate to fall. It is possible that remittances sent home by those who have gone abroad might increase the population growth in a country of emigration. In the second place, there are important economic and social costs of transition connected with the migration of people, and social and political repercussions of many sorts are involved. These dare not be neglected in discussing migration policy today. They are more important here than for any other problems we have had occasion to investigate.

Few countries of the world can now be considered to be below the "optimum" population in the sense that an increase in numbers would raise the per capita real income of the country for those already there. At least, the major immigration countries of the past, like the United

States, do not themselves believe that their welfare would be promoted by a great increase in population. This situation may change in the next few decades as the population trend reverses itself and starts downward in many European countries and countries of European settlement. For the moment, however, any mass movement of population out of the more congested regions—it would have to be a mass movement to affect the economic welfare of those countries significantly—would probably depress standards of living in other areas where higher levels of income have been attained. The world average of welfare might be raised, but only at the expense of the countries that would have to receive more people. This, as we observed in Chapter V, would not be a sound basis on which to rest a program of world economic welfare which depends upon the voluntary coöperation of different countries.

Social costs of transition connected with large-scale transfer of population into countries already fairly well settled would be much higher than for the international movement of capital or goods or techniques. Experience in the United States shows that the children of immigrants, standing as they do between two cultures—that of their parents which has lost its moral authority, and that of the new environment into which they have not yet been absorbed—show more symptoms of social maladjustment than the parents themselves, and these first-generation native-born contribute more than their share to the social problems of American cities. Large blocks of voters whose traditions and language difficulties make them an easy prey for machine politicians and for demagogues who play on national and religious prejudices lessen the chance for successful working of political democracy. The mixed nationality of workers in large-scale industries has added to the difficulties of labor organization and retarded the development of successful collective bargaining. Mass migrations from the densely populated countries of the East into countries now settled by Europeans would be certain to set going a great racial conflict. In view of these and other costs of readjustment, we must recognize that even from the most cosmopolitan world point of view any wholesale international migrations under present conditions would probably detract more from the welfare of the world than they would add to it.

The fact is that it is no longer possible to count on relieving the economic and social problems of the more densely settled countries by large-scale migrations to great unused areas of the world. Successful settlement of the areas that are left calls as much for capital, expert engineering knowledge, and careful long-range planning with respect to the availability of markets as it does for mere numbers of people. Even apart from political restrictions, migration is not so simple today as it once was. Modern men, accustomed to life in cities, are not willing to go into the wilderness and to build with their bare hands and a few primitive tools. The changed agricultural situation brought about by improvements in production and the slowing down of population growth in European countries means that the world output of staple crops no longer needs such rapid development as before, and the opening up of less settled regions today calls for a more complicated readjustment of trade currents in order to provide economic opportunities.[4]

The possibilities of mass migration as an instrument of economic adjustment are distinctly limited in the modern world. International population movements in the immediate future will, for the most part, have to be carefully

[4] See on these points *Limits of Land Settlement,* edited by Isaiah Bowman, a report to the Tenth International Studies Conference. (New York: Council on Foreign Relations, 1937.)

prepared and guided. Unrestricted freedom of resettlement as in the old days cannot now be justified. However, this is not to make a case for doing nothing at all about the extremely rigid and purely nationalistic barriers to population shifts that exist today. A careful program of detailed and concerted efforts at international coöperation on migration problems can accomplish a considerable amount of good. It can improve the general productivity of the earth, and it may help to some slight extent to relieve pressures in the more crowded areas. The surveys and international conferences already instituted by the International Labour Organisation point the way. Attention will have to be paid to such matters as the training and aptitudes needed for successful settlement in each particular area, the availability of qualified migrants in the emigration countries, the marketing prospects for the products which will provide an economic base for the new settlement in years ahead, the amount of capital required, and the particular kinds of equipment that must be provided. Concerted efforts of this sort are made more than ever necessary today by the problem of political refugees.

Under present conditions there are other and better ways than mass migration for bringing greater equality in the ratio of population to resources in different parts of the world. Natural resources are not by any means the only element in a country's ability to maintain a large population in comfort. Capital funds, making possible good industrial equipment, and intangible resources in knowledge and skill which raise the general level of productivity can be brought *to* the population more easily than the population can be moved to regions where these resources are already present. Needless to say, barriers that prevent the movement of raw materials and finished products must be reduced as part of the process of solving the problem of over-populated countries in this way.

Changes in net reproduction rates offer the long-run solution for problems raised by an extremely high ratio of population to resources in particular areas. A deliberate campaign to hasten long-run adjustment in over-populated countries by spreading knowledge of birth control would be much more productive from the standpoint of the world's economic welfare, and would be more likely to prevent conflict, than would wholesale migration. International efforts to spread the knowledge of birth control techniques should be undertaken, especially in the colonial countries of the Orient where over-population is a pressing problem. There should be no question of forcing peoples to limit the size of their families against their own wishes. This would be neither desirable nor necessary, as experience shows that families voluntarily become smaller when improvements in health conditions give a longer prospect of life for each new-born child, at the same time that industrialization and urbanization bring possibilities of improvement in living standards. The question is rather one of making knowledge freely available. It is definitely anti-social in the modern world for the rulers of low-standard populations—political rulers or religious rulers—to keep this knowledge from them.

Furthermore, the international community must assert an interest in the "cannon fodder" population policies of countries where the government's concern with military power overrides its concern for economic welfare. The world can rightly insist that no government which deliberately encourages population growth by propaganda, taxation of bachelors, and rewards for large families, or which prevents its people from having free access to birth control information, is in a position to plead "population pressure" in justification for any of its claims.

Freedom of movement for migrants in the future can

once more become a realizable ideal on certain conditions. The first is that considerable movements of capital and technical knowledge take place towards the most heavily populated countries, and that these countries develop industrially along modern lines. This will reduce those differences in standards of living which depend on man and his methods rather than on nature's gifts to the locality where he lives. The second condition is greater equality in rates of reproduction as between those countries where population growth has slowed down in response to modern conditions of life, including a desire for higher living standards, and those countries where such influences have not yet become effective.

Transfer of Territory: Colonies

Natural resources cannot be moved about from place to place, but the political sovereignty over them can be changed. When political boundaries are not economic walls, a transfer of territory from one sovereignty to another has no practical effect on the economic welfare of the people on either side, except that the new sovereign may have better or worse laws than the old, and this may increase or decrease the economic productivity of the territory transferred. If the people of New York ceded a piece of territory to the people of New Jersey it would be quite false to conclude that because the private property rights on the territory in question were valued at some millions of dollars the people of New York would be losing that much and those of New Jersey gaining that much by the transfer. New Jersey would gain some tax revenue, but it would also have higher administrative expenses. Where political boundaries are economic walls, however, so that sovereignty over territory is necessary in order to trade with the people that live in it, or to make investments there, or to migrate into it, then control over territory does have importance for economic welfare. Under these conditions, as we saw in Chapter VI, the quest for greater economic opportunity may lead to territorial conflict.

The motive for conquest will be lessened by anything that reduces the economic importance of political boundaries. That, in the final analysis, is the only road to equitable adjustment for territorial claims based on a desire for better economic opportunities. To seek adjustments merely by shifting territory from one sovereignty to another, leaving it the exclusive economic preserve of State B instead of State A, treats the interests of the rest of the world as badly as before and does little to remove the seeds of recurring conflict. The real problem for economic welfare and for peace is to make political boundaries less significant economically—that is, less significant as barriers to the best social use of resources.

Colonial territories present a special problem. The colonial question is important today mainly because of the political passions that it arouses, not because of the economic importance of the territories in dispute. It is popularly supposed that colonies provide an important share of the world's raw materials, but the special League of Nations Committee for the study of the problem of raw materials reached the conclusion that:

> . . . most raw materials are produced wholly, or to a great extent, in sovereign countries . . . A calculation, which necessarily can only be a rough one, seems to indicate that, including production both for domestic consumption and for export, the total present production of all commercially important raw materials in all colonial territories is no more than about 3% of world production, a substantially smaller percentage than is the proportion (12½%) of the population of these territories to world population. Nor is the share of colonial territories in international trade much more important. In 1936, these territories provided 9.7% of world ex-

ports and took 8.1% of world imports. Of course, dominions and other self-governing territories have not been included in these calculations.[5]

Germany's former colonies, about which most of the colonial controversy centers, are particularly unimportant as sources of raw materials or as potential markets or as outlets for European population. In 1914, when Germany had all its colonies, they supplied less than one per cent of Germany's imports of raw materials. There were fewer Germans employed in the colonies than in Paris. There were less than half as many Germans living in the colonies as in the borough of the Bronx, which, of the four principal boroughs of New York City, is the one with the fewest Germans. In the twenty years before 1914, the *total turnover* of the trade between Germany and its colonies (profits, of course, would be only a fraction of this) was 972 million marks. Colonial expenses during the same period were 1,002 million marks.[6]

Now, it is probably true that the extremely unimpressive record of the German colonies up to 1914 understates results that could be achieved today by intensive work as part of a deliberate effort to lessen dependence on outside resources. Furthermore, colonial areas in general may become more productive in the future than they have been in the past if new techniques in medicine, air-conditioning and the like, help to make the tropics more suitable for industrial activities. This is a very long view ahead, however, and simultaneous improvements in technology are equally likely to maintain the relative economic advantages of the self-governing areas in temper-

[5] *Report of the Committee for the Study of the Problem of Raw Materials* (Geneva, 1937, II.B.7), p. 10.

[6] Grover Clark, *The Balance Sheet of Imperialism* (New York: Columbia University Press, 1936), pp. 10-11.

ate zones. More important, if the present wave of exclusive economic nationalism continues to dominate the world, the *relative* importance of colonies will be greater in the future. The economic aspects of colonial issues cannot be neglected entirely, especially in a world of economic nationalism. Despite all these considerations, however, it still remains true that colonial questions today have relatively little to do with a quest for economic welfare. They are mainly questions of pride, prestige, "honor," and the like, complicated by the economics of military power and military strategy. The main point is that "access to raw materials," "access to markets," and relief of "population pressure" depend much more upon opportunity for productive interchange among self-governing areas than upon anything that is done or is not done about colonies.

Regardless of the rather small quantitative importance of colonial economic issues, however, there is certainly no just reason why certain national groups should be favored above others and should be permitted to exploit colonial resources to the exclusion of others. That the unequal distribution of colonies does not involve economic injustice to the extent that the propagandists imply is no reason for failing to recognize the injustice that does exist. The accident of history by which certain nations achieved the means and the will to conquest before others and emerged with the major part of the colonial spoils has to be set right for the sake of political peace and economic fairness. It is clear that we need a constructive settlement of colonial issues. The question is, in what direction shall it be sought?

One proposal is that there shall be a more "equitable" sharing of colonies among the Great Powers, by a redistribution on the same principle which has governed their distribution up to the present time:

"The good old rule . . . the simple plan,
That they should take, who have the power,
And they should keep who can."

In other words, this proposal is that states which can back their demands by threats of military force should be given colonies for the sake of appeasement.

A better proposal, on economic grounds, would be to redistribute colonies on the principle of giving more to those national groups that have shown the best ability to administer intelligently the resources now under their rule. On this principle the writer would award a considerable share of the world's colonies to such countries as Denmark, Sweden and Norway, and would increase the present share of Holland.

The best proposal of all, ideally, would be to internationalize all non-self-governing areas, putting them under international administration responsible to an agency representing the world community rather than any single national government. That is, under the ideal plan colonies would be treated as part of a common world heritage, to be developed under conditions of equal access to their resources for all nations, with careful attention to the welfare of their inhabitants, and with the ultimate end of local self-government and full membership in the family of nations. Rational solutions of this sort, of course, are blocked at present, as are rational solutions of so many other problems in international economics and politics, by the unwillingness of peoples to coöperate in a permanent world organization with sufficient authority and prestige.

At the present time, however, is it too much to suggest that if the great colonial powers expect to appeal to the world's sense of morality in rallying public opinion against threats of aggression they could immeasurably strengthen their own position by announcing an intention to abandon policies of economic exclusiveness in colonial areas? The best guarantee of good faith in the attitude of trusteeship which is often put forward as a reason for not ceding colonies would be a voluntary offer from the colonial possessors to give all their non-self-governing territories the status of League of Nations mandates, with corresponding obligations for regular report to an international body and for practicing equality of economic opportunity.

CHAPTER NINETEEN

ECONOMIC GROUPS IN INTERNATIONAL ORGANIZATION

ECONOMIC problems can never be "solved" once and for all. The very essence of economic problems is change, readjustment to new conditions. Hence, the international coöperation required for a constructive handling of world economic problems cannot be sporadic. It must be permanent, regular, organized. If it is not, then problems that are really world-wide in many of their ramifications slip back into the sphere of purely national control, where the efforts of governments to do something about them are almost sure to be partial, restrictive, and mutually antagonistic.

Economic progress and peace in the modern world will depend in the future upon much more regular and extensive international coöperation than has been seen in the past. It is hard to escape the conclusion that we are already at the stage in technical development where something very much like a world federal government has become a crying need. The fact that allusions to this need are still greeted automatically with calls of "Utopian" from the hard-headed—and with good reason, considering the strength of nationalist sentiment—is the best basis for a pessimistic view of the prospects before the next few generations of mankind. Under the circumstances, is it better for students of these problems to seek a reputation for "practical" wisdom by abandoning the attempt to think rationally and constructively about the future of international society, or to persevere in exploring ways by which men might make beginnings if they wish to adapt their institutions to the modern world? The latter view seems preferable, even though in the mood of today it will be falsely interpreted as "optimistic" and "naïve." The really optimistic and naïve are those who, in effect, urge that the traditional nationalistic ways of dealing with problems of the world economy be continued in the unconscious hope that "something will turn up" to save us all from the consequences that must normally follow—namely, from repeated economic debacles and the holocaust of war.

Various groups have been urging that a new world economic conference be called, on the theory that by getting together around a table ways might be found to relieve international tensions. This is overly simple. There is no magic in the conference method as such. In fact, there is danger in calling a dramatic, spectacular gathering unless it has something definite to accomplish which can be accomplished with reasonable dispatch. The disappointment of a conference which produced nothing tangible might leave the situation worse than before. It would, therefore, probably not be wise at present to try to hold a conference to deal directly with questions on which agreement is problematical or with questions involving complex technical aspects. The substantive problems of international economics—monetary arrangements, trade barriers, coördination of anti-depression policies, migration, raw material controls, international investments, and so on—are better and more safely handled under the circumstances of today by quieter methods working over a longer time.

Yet at some propitious moment in the future—supposing that one can be found (and if it cannot we are indeed in a hopeless plight)—there are certain tasks that a world economic conference might be able to accomplish.

The element of the spectacular is not only the chief danger of such a conference, but its great asset as well. There are certain forward steps in organized economic coöperation that need to be taken and that very likely must be taken, if at all, suddenly and dramatically. Is the peace conference after a great war the only possible setting for such steps? Perhaps a world economic conference could perform important services as a "constituent assembly." That is, its agenda might be planned, not so much to register startling immediate results on problems that by their very nature have to be worked out gradually, but to mark the beginning of a new effort of positive economic coöperation to proceed steadily over the years ahead. Specifically, when a conference becomes feasible its agenda might be set up with the following purposes in view:

(1) To give new impulse to international economic coöperation by adopting certain principles as a rallying point for the future—a purely symbolic act. This would be in the form of a pact (or a resolution, or a preamble) proclaiming a unifying social purpose: that the signers intend to work together for simultaneous improvement of living standards throughout the world, and that they undertake to seek actively to promote peaceful economic exchange so that all peoples, great and small, may benefit by more effective access to the resources of the world. High-sounding principles are sometimes a substitute for action, but sometimes they are a useful prelude to a positive and dynamic program. In the present state of the world there would be great value in such a declaration.

(2) To improve the institutional machinery of international economic coöperation. There needs to be greater recognition of the fact that the world economy consists of factories, farms, consumer and producer groups, individuals, not merely of national states. World agencies of economic coöperation should be so constituted as to be in

more direct touch than they are now with these elementary units. In particular, an autonomous International Economic Organization, with representation of economic groups as well as governments, should be established within the framework of a reorganized League of Nations, to extend the admirable economic work now being done by the League along lines that would be at least somewhat more "federal."[1] This means providing for other than strictly government delegates on the permanent controlling body (as in the International Labour Organisation), and granting authority for positive action by the International Economic Organization on a limited range of problems without depending always on execution by national governments. A world economic conference might frame the terms of a treaty which, when ratified by a specified number of states, would be the constitution of such a permanent International Economic Organization.

(3) To launch concrete measures of positive economic coöperation which would be started by the conference and then carried through under the guidance of the new

[1] The principle of federalism (in contrast with the principle of confederation involved in a league of sovereign states) is the principle that distinguished the Constitution of the United States after 1789 from the Articles of Confederation which were in force from 1781 to 1789 during the so-called "critical period" of United States history. James Madison explained the fundamental decision of the American constitutional convention as follows:

"It was generally agreed that the objects of the Union could not be secured by any system founded on the principle of a confederation of sovereign States. A *voluntary* observance of the Federal law by all the members could never be hoped for. A *compulsive* one could evidently never be reduced to practice, and if it could, involved equal calamities to the innocent and the guilty, the necessity of a military force, both obnoxious and dangerous, and, in general, a scene resembling much more a civil war than the administration of a regular government. *Hence was embraced the alternative of a government which, instead of operating on the States, should operate without their intervention on the individuals composing them;* and hence the change in the principle and proportion of representation." ("Letters," Ed. 1865, I, 344. Italics not in original.)

International Economic Organization. By way of example:

(a) A "world development program" should be launched. It should be a carefully studied effort to improve the productivity of less advanced areas of the world by methods that would at the same time provide an outlet for the capital goods industries of the advanced countries and lessen the shock of readjustment that is inevitable as outlying areas increase their industrial activity. The program might include, as suggested earlier, provision of capital equipment, technical training and advice under international auspices to such areas of the world as South America, southeastern Asia, portions of Africa—areas not now in acute conflict. Later it might be extended to conflict areas, especially to China, where it could conceivably form the basis of a constructive peace settlement. Such a settlement would be typified by the diversion of Japanese heavy industries from making bombs to destroy Chinese towns to making bridges and school buildings which could be supplied as Japan's contribution "in kind" to an international development loan. An international development program will have to be part of any successful effort to stop the present arms race, for the economic problem of providing substitute activity for over-developed armaments industries (especially the heavy, capital goods lines) cannot otherwise be met.

(b) Some kind of world public supervision over international monopolies and international commodity control schemes should be set up. We have today in commodities like tin, rubber, nickel, copper, sugar, coffee, and many others, world problems of monopoly or world problems of coördinating various attempts at regulation. There is a pressing need for continuous international coöperation on these questions.

The action proposed here could be taken by a world

economic conference with or without the attendance, or the agreement, of those "totalitarian" states that today refuse to participate in such economic work as that carried on by the League and the I.L.O. Of course, it would be preferable to have their coöperation. If they go along, at least part of the way, so much the better. If they do not, then the kind of program suggested could be started without them, leaving the door open for their adherence on reasonable conditions at any time. The existence of a concrete and widely dramatized new effort at peaceful adjustment through economic coöperation would set up a positive alternative to war that might perhaps help to dissuade the aggressively inclined, and in any event would improve the moral (and the economic) position of the defenders of lawful procedure in world affairs.

The International Economic Organization proposed above might be thought of as a permanent world economic conference, or as an international planning commission designed to facilitate coöperation between countries. Of course, "machinery" without the will to use it would be futile, but it is untrue to say that where some will for common action exists the type of institutional structure for organizing and expressing it is unimportant. Methods of acting have their effect on the will to act and on the kind of action that can be taken. Can one imagine the forty-eight states of the United States building a unified system of motor highways by the method of interstate compacts, in the absence of the coördinating machinery provided by the federal government? Or could free commerce among the states be maintained by sentiment alone without "machinery" for common action?

The kind of economic organization suggested would not break radically with existing traditions—especially in view of the two decades of experience with the International Labour Organisation—but it would represent a slight step in a direction that might be called "economic federalism": first, in its basis of representation, and second, in its authorization to deal directly on some problems with economic units other than governments. The structure of such an organization might include: (1) a regular annual conference; (2) a basis of representation at the conference which would give half the voting power to delegates of governments, half to non-government delegates representing economic groups such as consumers, workers, employers or managers, agriculture, trade and finance; (3) a small governing body to perform the work of the conference between sessions and to supervise tasks of administration; (4) a permanent secretariat; (5) power to draw up economic legislation in the form of treaties which would become effective upon ratification by governments; (6) power to legislate directly on certain specified topics, such as the regulation of international cartels and commodity control schemes, without the necessity for subsequent ratification by governments.

The principle of functional representation has been applied with considerable success in the International Labour Organisation over the last twenty years. Constituted at the same time as the League of Nations by a section of the Treaty of Versailles, the I.L.O. deals with the international aspects of such questions as factory legislation, conditions of employment at sea, wages and hours, and in general with social and industrial problems affecting the welfare of workers. It consists of an International Labour Conference, which meets annually as the supreme authority of the organization, a Governing Body that acts as an executive committee between conferences, and a permanent Secretariat. Each member state is entitled to two government delegates and two non-government delegates, one representing workers, and the other employers. The employer and worker delegates are actually named by the governments, who undertake, however, to nominate them "in agreement with the industrial organizations, if such organizations exist, which are most representative of employers or work people, as the case may be, in their respective countries." Thus, the official delegation of the United States at the International Labour Conference of 1938 included Secretary of Labor Frances Perkins and Miss Frieda Miller of the New York State Department of Labor, representing the government; Mr. Robert Watt, formerly Secretary of the Massachusetts State Federation of Labor, representing workers; and Mr. H. I. Harriman, a past president of the United States Chamber of Commerce, representing employers. An organization along similar lines for dealing with the broader economic questions of international commerce, international investments, international commodity controls, and the best use of the world's resources in general, would have to represent other economic groups besides workers and employers. The workers' and employers' delegates in the broader International Economic Organization might be nominated by the I.L.O., thus helping to insure harmonious coöperation between the two organizations, and representatives of consumers, trade and finance, and agriculture might be chosen by the various governments.

The proposal to include delegates from economic groups is not based on any supposed superiority of functional representation over territorial representation for general purposes of representative government. Indeed, for general government within the confines of a single nation functional representation would raise grave dangers of disintegrating the state by emphasizing divisive interests that are already in sharp conflict rather than the general interests that unite the community. The world community, on the other hand, suffers most of all from the tendency to exaggerate the divergent interests of territorial groups organized into national states, and to underemphasize the common interests that cut across national boundaries. In this situation functional representation would help to offset the divisive effects of nationalism and to help people to remember the fundamental truth that the world's economy is made up of farms, factories, mines, workers, savers, consumers—not just nations. In the experience of the I.L.O., representation of employers and workers as such has shown itself "particularly adapted to overcome the difficulties in the field of world action due to divergencies of national points of view. The economic groups of workers and employers form units transcending national lines. They look at problems not so much from the point of view of one or another country but from the point of view of the economic interests which are inherent in modern industrial life. While this procedure has difficulties and limitations of its own, it is undoubtedly the most promising method for developing an international point of view and common international standards." [2]

There is another reason just as fundamental and important for bringing representatives of economic groups directly into world economic conferences. If they participate year after year in the formation of policies an important process of mutual education will take place. The British employers' delegate at many I.L.O. meetings is quoted as saying that though he had to vote as he was instructed his mind expanded by being at the Conference, and after every session he took a new set of values back to England with him.[3]

Why have post-war efforts to achieve international

[2] Lewis L. Lorwin, "The I.L.O. and World Economic Policy," *International Labour Review,* Vol. 33, 1936, p. 460.

[3] Miss Margaret Bondfield, former Minister of Labour in Great Britain, in a speech to the 1938 annual meeting of the National I.L.O. Committee of the United States.

coöperation for economic welfare so often ended in dismal failure? Is not one important part of the answer to be found in the fact that governments always have to reckon with the pressure of domestic economic groups at home, but that these groups are rarely brought into direct contact with other groups abroad and have little opportunity to educate each other out of their respective insularities? Government delegates and technical experts from Australia, Argentina, Belgium, and the United States go to international meetings under the auspices of the economic committees of the League and come away with an increased appreciation of each other's problems. But only occasionally, and then usually as individuals and not as representatives of their groups, do American manufacturers and Australian wool-growers, Belgian industrialists and Argentinian cattle-raisers, the representatives of trading and consuming and laboring groups in all these countries, share the broadening influence that comes from confronting the other party's problems and points of view. They continue to think of economic matters in national terms and to press for national solutions. The national solutions in each country conflict with those being urged by similar groups in other countries. Where problems are international, efforts of each cancel out the efforts of the others, and the result is general waste and bad feeling. Would it not be better to bring directly into international conferences on economic policy the representatives of the organized economic pressure groups which set the limits beyond which governments dare not go?

In addition to a start towards federalism in representation, beginnings might also be made in the new International Economic Organization towards federalism in administration—that is, towards direct contact of world agencies with economic enterprises and direct dealing with problems in a certain specified range without having to act through national governments as intermediaries. For example, the International Economic Organization could be given authority to require reports from international cartels and commodity control schemes, like those in copper, aluminum, steel, tin, rubber, sugar, tea. It might eventually charter public corporations for the construction of international public works or for the administration of international public utilities—canals, radio facilities, aviation lines, and the like. Still further in the future, some provision might be worked out for the international incorporation of business enterprises that are owned in several different countries and which do an international business.[4] International "mixed" enterprises in which the voting stock would be held partly by private firms and partly by governments might also be chartered under the same authority as a means of carrying out development programs.

Perhaps outside the field of the economic organization itself, but closely related, there might some day be such advances in world federalism as the direct international administration of polar regions and of colonial areas. In the process of regulating cartels and control schemes, supervising international development projects and international corporations, and administering a "world domain" of polar and colonial territory, it might eventually be possible to develop a direct source of revenue for the needs of world government, thus lessen-

[4] The charters of such international corporations should make plain that they would not be entitled to the "diplomatic protection" of any separate national government, but only to the protection of the International Economic Organization itself. Small states fearing political-economic penetration could make it a policy to grant concessions only to such international companies. Eugene Staley, "Une proposition de sociétés anonymes internationales," *Revue Economique Internationale,* September, 1938, pp. 499-515. Also *War and the Private Investor* (New York: Doubleday, Doran, 1935), Ch. 19.

ing its dependence on national states and increasing its federal nature. These are speculations, however, that go beyond the more immediate problems of the moment.

An international economic organization like that suggested has been proposed in the past, particularly by representatives of labor. A memorandum submitted to the World Economic Conference at Geneva in 1927 is worth quoting. It was presented on behalf of the General Council of the British Trades Union Congress, the National Executive Committee of the Labour Party, and the Executive Committee of the Parliamentary Labour Party.[5] Excerpts follow:

> International combinations, the monopoly of certain important products, the private trade in armaments, the floating of loans for anti-social purposes, the evils rising from certain types of concessions, the investment of capital in undeveloped but populous countries to exploit the relatively inexhaustible supply of cheap and unorganized labour—these and other developments which have in the past created friction and hostility are disturbing factors in a world which has everything to gain from peaceful and harmonious progress.
>
> *Broadly speaking, the economic growth of the world has outstripped the growth of political and social institutions, and unless economic activities and rivalries are controlled in the interests of the peoples of the world, stable peace will be impossible.*[6]
>
> We are convinced that the rapid developments of recent years call for close and continuous examination by an international authority, and in the interests of the world demand international action, if the economic causes of ill-will and hostility in the world are to be prevented or allayed. Moreover, we believe that it is essential to peace to enlarge the field of cooperative effort by the nations in the task of solving the common economic problems. The more the attention of States and their peoples is directed towards the constructive tasks which lie before them in developing, utilising

[5] League of Nations, *Report and Proceedings of the World Economic Conference held at Geneva, May 4th to 23rd, 1927* (C. 356, M. 129, 1927. II.) (C.E.I. 46), pp. 231-2.

[6] Italics in original.

and apportioning natural resources for the welfare of the world's population, in extending intercourse and trade, and in promoting closer cultural relations, in ridding the world of such social evils as disease, the less will be the chance of misunderstanding and hostility. It is as important to extend the matters of common interest amongst nations as to minimise the causes of conflict.

We therefore make proposals for the establishment of a permanent international economic organisation, under the League of Nations, which would cooperate with other sections of the League and would ultimately embrace wider activities than those outlined here.

The memorandum then proceeds to a number of proposals, including activities that should be undertaken by the League of Nations for the regulation of international trusts, monopolies, cartels, and kindred organizations, the establishment of an international code and a tribunal to handle problems arising from the growing importance of state trading, measures to regulate the exploitation of economically backward areas, reduction of protective customs barriers and extension of the most-favored-nation principle of non-discrimination. Under the head of "Permanent League Economic Organisation" the memorandum continues:

If the world economic problems causing international friction are to be solved, continuous consideration and appropriate action are necessary. It is therefore proposed that the Economic Section of the League of Nations should be developed on lines broadly analogous to those of the International Labour Organisation. An economic Council, representative of States, producers (including employers and workers) and consumers should be established. It should consider the surveys and reports made from time to time by the Economic Secretariat. It should formulate policy in international economic conventions or by means of recommendations. It should, of course, work in close cooperation with the International Labour Organisation and other organs of the League.

A declaration along similar lines was also made to the 1927 Conference by a group of representatives of workers' organizations including MM. Diamand (Poland), Eggert (Germany), Johansson (Sweden), Jouhaux (France), Mertens (Belgium), Nielsen (Denmark), Oudegeest (Netherlands), Pugh (Great Britain), Tayerle (Czechoslovakia), Weber (Switzerland), and Mme. E. Freundlich (Austria).[7]

[7] *Ibid.*, pp. 233-4.

CHAPTER TWENTY

THE UNITED STATES IN WORLD ECONOMY

The Best Use of American Resources

THE permanent significance of the world economy for the United States, as for other countries, lies in the means which world-wide exchange offers for raising productive efficiency in the use of national resources, and hence for increasing the country's ability to support a high standard of living. Wide market areas and wide supply areas for materials permit greater technical efficiency in production. No country is better situated than the United States to take full advantage of the productive advantages offered by modern technology. Division of labor between the United States and other regions makes it possible for Americans to specialize, up to a point set by transport costs, trade barriers, and other factors, on those tasks which best suit the aptitudes of the people and the resources of the country. In return for supplying other lands with some of its specialties, the United States is itself supplied with things that it either cannot produce or cannot produce so cheaply as it can get them abroad.

The growth of barriers to trade and general world instability in recent years has lessened the opportunity of the United States to make the best use of its resources by specialization and exchange. This is reflected in the decline of the percentage which exports bear to total production of movable goods:

UNITED STATES EXPORTS IN COMPARISON WITH
TOTAL PRODUCTION OF MOVABLE GOODS[1]

Year	*Per cent of production exported*	*Year*	*Per cent of production exported*
1909	9.6	1927	9.9
1914	10.2	1929	9.8
1919	16.0	1931	7.4
1921	12.8	1933	6.6
1923	8.9	1935	6.8
1925	10.1		

When American labor can be employed at tasks like designing and making machinery or at mechanized agriculture it is better employed than when it is engaged in laborious, unskilled, hand operations like raising sugar beets. Then if sugar is obtained from abroad on a swap for machinery or wheat the effectiveness of American labor has been improved just as definitely as by some new invention, and the capacity of the American people to consume both machine products and sugar has been raised. Artificial encouragement of employment for labor in the sugar beet industry by excluding sugar imports is no adequate substitute for a loss of employment in machinery and wheat industries caused by the stifling of exports, because it is less efficient employment. The interest of the people of the United States is to encourage conditions in the world economy under which they can make the best use of their resources through world-wide economic relations.

The United States has a vast free trade area within its own boundaries, and its resources are so varied that it

[1] U. S. Department of Commerce, Bureau of Foreign and Domestic Commerce, *Summary of United States Trade with World, 1937* (Trade Information Bulletin 839, 1938), p. 39. The latest year for which complete production data are available is 1935. The proportion of goods exported in 1937, based on a rough estimate of total production for that year, is 7.5 per cent.

could stand a descent into "autarchy" or self-sufficiency better than other countries. What the United States would lose if an enemy blockade cut it off from exchange with the world, or if a will to economic isolation did the same thing, would be two things. First, it would have the transition costs of a difficult readjustment. We have mentioned Secretary of Agriculture Wallace's estimate that 40 to 100 million acres of crop land would have to be taken out of cultivation. Half of the market for American cotton, unsatisfactory enough to the producer in any event, would be gone. Hog-corn producers would lose 17 per cent of their present market for lard, on the basis of 1937 figures, but that does not take into account the markets they have lost already by reason of economic nationalism over the world, and particularly because of foreign efforts to prepare for war by self-sufficiency in foodstuffs. Lard exports fell from 54 per cent of American production in 1923 to 48 per cent in 1929, to 35 per cent in 1933, to 17 per cent in 1937. Producers of sewing machines, refined copper, lubricating oils and greases, dried fruits, gum turpentine, tobacco leaf, and other products would have to adjust to a loss of a third to a half of their present markets if the United States turned away from the world economy. Here are some other lines in which a considerable fraction of the industry is employed in making goods for sale abroad, with figures on the percentage of production exported:[2]

Industrial machinery in general	13.3 per cent
Power-driven metal-working machinery	20.0 per cent
Office appliances	23.2 per cent
Printing and bookbinding machinery	26.2 per cent
Automobiles	10.1 per cent
Aircraft	26.7 per cent

[2] *Ibid.*, pp. 39-41. Most figures here and above are for 1937, but some, notably those on machinery of various kinds, are available only for 1935.

To bring about a transfer of productive power from industries such as these into the home production of some of the things now imported would mean no little disturbance to American economic life, meshed as it is with that of other countries in countless places. Talk of the advantages or disadvantages of "entanglement" in world economy has to start from the fact that the United States is "entangled" now, and that the transition costs of pulling out would be great.

Second, these transition costs incurred by insulating the United States from world economy would be for the sake of achieving a permanently less efficient employment of American resources. Even with this handicap, the American people might be able to maintain a tolerable standard of life. Perhaps in time, with the aid of technical progress, they might be able to surpass the present standard. But why should they be satisfied with anything less than the utmost that technology and resources, wisely applied, can give in leisure and comforts?

There are many purely domestic measures that enter into a program of wise resource utilization for the United States: improved labor training and vocational placement, better methods of commodity distribution, stimulation of technical research and new inventions, betterments in financial organization, city and regional planning, education of consumers in "buymanship," large-scale power developments, and so on. These are outside the field of this book. In its international aspects the problem of raising consumption standards in the United States by better resource utilization is at bottom a problem of promoting an ever more efficient and smoothly operating division of labor between the United States and the rest of the world economy. With all its vast resources, the United States, like every country, has some types that are relatively more abundant than others. The best use of its material and human resources can be made by expanding the output of all those products that call for large proportions of its most abundant resources, exchanging part of the expanded output for imports that embody large proportions of resources relatively more scarce in the United States than elsewhere.

Let us make a hasty survey of American resources from this point of view. Human resources relatively more abundant in the United States than in the rest of the world include engineering skills, mechanical inventiveness, organizing ability of many types, labor backed by a high degree of education, initiative, and technical training. On the other hand, the United States has smaller proportions of cheap, low-grade labor than other countries, particularly as compared with the countries of Asia that are now beginning to participate in world exchange. The United States also has a scarcity of certain kinds of craftsmanship, especially those required for turning out the finest hand-made goods or goods individually designed. These skills are much more abundant in Europe where the artisan traditions survive. Capital resources, including new savings available for investment and equipment already in use, are very abundant in the United States. Land adapted for mechanized farming is abundant. So are mineral resources of many types. Other minerals are lacking, or are present only in small deposits or at low concentrations that cannot be worked economically under present methods, though they might be valuable in a national emergency. Temperate climate, with many varieties of rainfall conditions, is abundant, but tropical climate is lacking and semi-tropical is scarce.

Under these conditions the policy of the United States should be to favor the expansion of those types of manufacturing which require large amounts of engineering skill, mechanical ingenuity, technical education, and capital investment. In agriculture, the products to be encouraged should be those adapted to mechanization, to broad lands, to skilled methods of production. Using the output of these well-adapted branches of machine-industry and agriculture to provide the means of payment for international purchases, it should be the definite policy of the United States to shift gradually to an import basis for factory products that are less adapted to a high degree of mechanization, especially those that require brute labor power or the quickly learned skills of machine "operatives" who simply repeat motions. Likewise in agriculture, the United States should look with disfavor on the grubbing labor required to grow sugar beets and should get out of that industry as soon as it can, to take advantage for its consumers of the startling technical advances made in the yield of sugar cane in Java and Cuba. It should prefer to encourage machine-handled wheat and corn, and by helping to reconstruct international trade—which means encouraging imports as well as exports—it can do something positive to aid these better-adapted branches of its agriculture that now suffer from the restrictive trade policies of the United States and other countries.

The United States excels in standardized automobiles, but rightly leaves expensive custom-made models to the artisans of Europe. In the cotton-textile industry "mule" spindles represent capacity to produce high grades of yarn by processes in which labor craftsmanship counts heavily; "ring" spindles go with low or medium grades of yarn made by techniques that depend more on mechanical and engineering skills and capital. The United States has more than one-fourth of all the "ring" spindles in the world, but less than one per cent of the "mule" spindles. Ninety-nine per cent of the spindles in the United States are of the highly mechanized type, and this is as it should be. Similarly, 68 per cent of the looms in the United States are "automatic," while no other country except Canada has as many as 25 per cent of its looms in this class.[3] The United States should deliberately encourage an international division of labor which allows it to import those kinds of yarn and cloth best adapted to the skills and equipment of other countries, while making those best adapted to its own conditions. The practical means for such a "positive planning" policy, of course, is to lower the trade barriers erected by "restrictive planning" measures in the past, at the same time giving encouragement—through technical research, labor training and placement, and the like—to the expansion of the better-adapted lines.

From the point of view of making the best use of the opportunities offered by world economic exchange, we might think of all American industries as divided into three groups, as follows:

Group A: Industries capable of export. In this group are branches of production especially well adapted to the natural resources, skills, capital, and traditions of the United States or some part of the United States, whose products can be shipped, and which are capable of expanding output without too sharp an increase in costs per unit. These industries are able to pay high American wages and still keep their costs low enough, by reason of natural advantages and efficient operation, to meet foreign competition on its own grounds.

Group B: Purely domestic or local industries. This group includes: (1) industries able to produce economically for a part of the United States demand but not to expand (for example, by reason of limited amounts of the right kind of land or labor or mineral deposits),

[3] *The World Textile Industry, Economic and Social Problems* (I. L. O., 1937, Studies and Reports, Series B, No. 27), pp. 49-52.

and (2) industries whose production must take place at or near the point of use. This latter sub-group would include housing, building materials and construction of most kinds, transportation and communication services, medical and hospital services, professional services, educational services, automobile service and repair—indeed, all the "service" trades in general.

Group C: "Protected" industries that cannot compete with imports. This does not include all industries that have lobbied for and obtained tariff protection (many industries quite able to compete have done that), but only those which are ill adapted to the country in the sense that they are not able to pay American wages and still keep their costs per unit of output low enough to meet competition from abroad.

The policy of economic nationalism is to sacrifice the industries in Group A for the sake of those in Group C—for when imports are restricted exports are also restricted. This is not the way to raise real wages, or to improve the real income of consumers. Wise resource utilization calls for an international economic policy that makes it possible to encourage additional employment of labor and other resources in Groups A and B, shifting gradually out of industries in Group C. This possibility depends, of course, upon creating a more stable world situation, economically and politically, and increasing world trade. Domestic policy should facilitate productive resource shifts of this kind as they become possible, seeking to keep transition costs low without blocking economic changes that represent improved use of resources.

Finally, the notion that insulation from the world would contribute to economic stability in the United States is false. The boom and crash of 1929 and the recession of 1937–8 were certainly two economic events that gave the rest of the world more cause to complain of unstable influences from the United States than *vice versa*. There is no reason to think that greater economic nationalism would be associated with a sudden access of wisdom and rationality in internal planning. Withdrawal from the world economy by the United States would intensify political conflict all over the world by sharpening the contest for control of the remaining markets and raw material sources. That in itself, by psychological reactions even in the absence of all trade contacts, would not fail to turn policy within the United States from welfare economy decidedly towards power economy. If the instability of the world economy as a whole causes trouble in America—and it certainly does, along with internal influences—the remedy is to be sought in a broad program of intelligent world coöperation. The United States can do more to influence world events in that regard than any other nation.

The Economic Power of the United States

In the long run, the effect of American international economic policy upon the prospects for a peaceful or a warlike world may be even more important for the American people than the considerations of economic welfare discussed above. Secretary of State Cordell Hull has rightly presented his program for lowering trade barriers not only as a means of promoting economic prosperity but as a necessary part of the foundation for durable peace. In view of what has already been said in Chapter VI about the way in which nationalistic restrictions build up economic pressures that may lead to war, it is unnecessary to stop for long on this point. The amount of reality behind such complaints as those about "lack of access to raw materials" and "population pressure" depends much more upon the international economic policies of the United States than upon all the colonies in the world. If the United States engages actively in world trade, promotes the welfare of its own people and of other people by lowering trade barriers, takes part in the development of less advanced regions by a wise policy of capital investment in coöperation with the regions affected, exerts its influence for monetary stability and world-wide measures to control the business cycle, and coöperates also for the political organization of peace, there is a chance that satisfied and dissatisfied powers alike may be able to find a common basis for easing present tensions. But if the United States should turn its back on the world economy, refuse to proceed farther along the path of positive economic coöperation, and try instead the path of economic nationalism, then the germs of war will find more economic discontent all over the world in which to grow. Once more the word will go out that access to the resources of the world is not to be had by peaceful trade, but only by conquest.

Curiously enough, the citizens of the United States as a whole do not appreciate how important their country really is in the world economy. Thinking unconsciously in terms of the young frontier community of their grandfathers, many of them fail to see that the United States, by its own decisions, can sway the course of world development today. Its positive aid in building an economic foundation for peace would go far to assure success. Its refusal to coöperate would block the path of world coöperation. This applies in the political as well as in the economic sphere, for economic weight these days confers political weight.

Consider, for example, the problem of the economic prosperity, the ability to make improvements and to pay debts, and the general social and political stability of countries that depend on raw material exports. The

United States *alone* normally uses well over half the world output of rubber, asbestos, platinum, silk and vanadium, and buys all or a large part of its supply from outside its own borders. Rubber comes principally from the East Indies, asbestos from Canada, platinum from Canada, silk from Japan, vanadium from Peru. All those countries are linked thereby to the United States. Other materials of which the United States consumes from a fifth to more than half of the entire world output and buys most of its supply abroad are tin (East Indies), sisal (Mexico), nickel (Canada), chromite (Cuba, Rhodesia, Turkey), antimony (China), coffee (Brazil), jute (India), manila hemp (Philippines), manganese (U.S.S.R., Brazil), sugar (Cuba), and tungsten (China). The United States is normally the largest consumer in the world of every important metal, and of most other raw materials. The economic relations of raw material producers with the United States naturally affect, also, the prosperity of industrial regions, through the purchases of finished goods by raw material producers and through investments in raw material countries.

Or consider the problem of applying economic sanctions against an aggressor. The United States is not only the largest consumer of raw materials, but the largest producer as well. In that highly strategic group of commodities, petroleum and its products, the domestic output of the United States is well over half the output of the whole world. It has a larger and better-rounded supply of commodities important in war than any other country. No program of economic pressure could possibly be successful without its coöperation. In most long-drawn wars between great powers the United States would be in a position, even without entering the war itself, to swing the balance one way or the other by giving or withholding its economic support.

By reason of its sheer economic weight the United States cannot help exerting a great positive or negative influence on the course of world economic and political coöperation. When the League of Nations set up a world index of manufacturing activity based on the 1925–29 period it had to allot a weight of *45 per cent of the world total* to the United States. The rise of the Soviet Union and Japan in the last decade has lowered that percentage somewhat, but still "the manufacturing output of all the industrial countries of Western Europe is somewhat less than that of the United States alone."[4] A computation was recently made of the raw material resources of the fifteen richest countries, measured by their share in world output of 73 commodities weighted in accordance with the importance of these commodities in international trade. The result placed 32 per cent of the total raw material output for all these countries in the United States alone.[5] The United States holds about 60 per cent of the world's monetary gold stock,[6] drives 81.7 per cent of the world's motor vehicles[7] and currently produces 79 per cent of the new motor vehicles,[8] has 49.69 per cent of the world's telephones,[9] and carries on a volume of international trade far exceeding that of any other coun-

[4] League of Nations, *World Economic Survey, 1936–7,* pp. 199-200.

[5] Herman Kranold, *The International Distribution of Raw Materials* (London: Routledge, 1938), Chapter IV.

[6] While this helps to indicate the economic weight of the United States, the manner in which the enormous American gold stock has accumulated and the problem that it represents might well be cited as evidence of weakness rather than strength in the current economic situation of the world and of the United States. See "Has Gold A Future?" by Frank D. Graham and Charles R. Whittlesey, *Foreign Affairs,* Vol. 17 (April 1939), pp. 578-598.

[7] As of January 1, 1938. Secretary of Commerce Roper, quoted in *New York Times,* August 18, 1938.

[8] 1937 production. *Statistical Yearbook of the League of Nations, 1937–8,* Table 112.

[9] As of January 1, 1937. *Telephone and Telegraph Statistics of the World,* American Telephone and Telegraph Company, April 15, 1938.

try in the world except Great Britain.[10] *If the United States is ready to work for the upbuilding of a peaceful, orderly system of world exchange operated in the interest of economic well-being instead of military power, then by its decision alone a third to a half of the present economic weight of the world has been turned towards that course.* If its actions are indifferent or hostile to the needs of modern international economy, then the balance of world forces is indeed in doubt.

[10] See charts comparing trade of various countries for 1929, 1932, and 1937 in the Report of the Director of the International Labour Office, 1938, pp. 72-3.

CHAPTER TWENTY-ONE

SUMMARY

MEASURED in travel-time, the whole world today is actually smaller than the United States of George Washington's day or Europe in the reign of Napoleon. In terms of communication and trade the size of the world is also a mere fraction of what it used to be. New production techniques have increased the advantages of mass output and hence of wide market areas, especially for the more specialized forms of capital goods. Raw material supply areas have expanded in answer to the extremely varied needs of modern technology, the larger volume of modern consumption, and the more precise adjustment of material to function characteristic of the most recent technical advances. In all these ways our scientists, inventors, and production engineers have been laying the basis of a planetary economy.

While technology has been making for easier and larger movements of goods, capital, persons and knowledge across boundaries, politics in recent years has seemed bent on erecting walls to resist all these tendencies. The conflict of technology and politics has produced strains throughout the entire social fabric. Economics, closely linked to both, is a major battlefield. Stability and peace will reign in the world economy only when the forces on the side of technology and the forces on the side of politics have once more been accommodated to each other.

From the point of view of raising living standards in

the world, it is desirable that the forces of technology should triumph, and that we should have a system of world-wide economic exchange rather than a collection of more or less closed national economies. World-wide exchange of the resources most abundant in each region, either directly through movements of capital and knowledge or indirectly through trade in goods, is capable of making every region more productive than it otherwise could be, thus raising the real income level of every people. This conclusion rests on unalterable facts about the world distribution of resources and upon general principles of social economy in the use of resources. It is true for capitalism or socialism or for any other system of economic organization. Good social economy, however, demands careful attention to the "costs of progress" which arise as better trading relations and industrialization of undeveloped areas improve the use of the world's resources. There should be every effort to make transition costs as small as possible, without blocking the path towards better economic welfare. It is unsound to argue that because there are difficulties in adjusting to a larger world economy we should turn back towards a national localism, for we have come a long way already, and abandoning the world economy now would cost at least as much in social upsets and political friction as to develop it further.

Does the tendency of technology to expand or the tendency of politics to contract the volume of international economic relations offer the better prospect for stable peace? Here again the verdict must be for working with rather than against the forces of technology. Merely extending the area of economic contact will not automatically insure peace; in fact, it raises many political problems. But it does not follow that the cause of peace will be served by blocking economic contacts. Quite the contrary. Barriers to economic intercourse between nations make economic opportunity depend on possession of territory and lay the basis for imperialistic wars of conquest. They make "population pressure," "access to raw materials," and "access to markets" fighting slogans in international politics. One of the first principles for progress towards political peace as well as towards economic welfare must be: Lessen the economic significance of political boundaries.

The world economy of the immediate future will have to be a "mixed" system in two senses. In most countries the principle of free enterprise and the principle of conscious control over economic life (by governments or by large organizations) will have to function side by side. At the same time, the mixture of these two principles will be different in different countries, and there will be a practical problem on the international plane of working out methods for mutually beneficial relations between economic systems of divergent types. The key to the problem of making laissez faire and planning work side by side with a minimum of friction and a maximum of benefit for economic welfare is this: make laissez faire competitive rather than monopolistic, and make planning positive rather than restrictive. Positive planning on problems that have international aspects is hampered today by the lack of organized, permanent international coöperation. One of the main reasons why so much economic planning of recent years has been restrictive is that the demand for governmental economic action has run ahead of the development of world government, so that economic action has had to be national, even on world problems.

This is an era of totalitarian war. In default of any system of joint community defense that can be relied upon internationally, each country is forced to prepare separately for its own defense, and its economic policies are forced into channels that undermine the whole basis of peaceful "welfare" economy. Policies dictated by the quest for military power, whether for attack or to resist attack, make efficient functioning of a world economy impossible. Thus, constructive economic action cannot go far today until something is done to lessen the acute need for war preparedness that now dominates the thoughts of statesmen. The economic transition from power economy to peaceful welfare economy—the problem of "economic demobilization"—will require careful attention and considerable amounts of international coöperation for its successful solution, once the political prerequisites have been met. It will be necessary to facilitate the finding of peacetime outlets for the industries now engaged directly or indirectly in making war equipment.

In seeking a practical basis for constructive action in the world economy of today, coöperation with the "dictatorships" is not precluded by their "totalitarian" economies. The real difficulty comes from their political policies, which threaten aggression and violence against the rest of the world. The only effective way to meet this threat is through a policy which combines two elements: (1) willingness to go very far indeed to coöperate economically on a peaceful basis, in return for positive assurances that threats and force will not be used in the future and that elementary rights of man will be respected; (2) determination to meet aggression with a collective defense effective enough to leave the aggressor little chance of success. Even in the absence of coöperation from the dictatorships the other countries of the world should band together to begin practicing among themselves as many of the principles of economic progress as may be possible in view of the threat to their security and the necessity of preparedness. Membership in the economic "club" thus formed should be open to all, regardless of economic system, on conditions which give assurance that aggressive political designs have been renounced.

Monetary stability in the future will have to be a managed stability. International coöperation on monetary problems should aim at counteracting the business cycle and creating the conditions under which a steady economic expansion can take place. Positive coöperation of this sort would go far towards eliminating the conflict between internal stability of a currency in terms of domestic purchasing power and external stability in its ratio to other currencies.

The bulk of international trade is still carried on by private enterprises, and the most important means at the moment for getting better performance of the important social function of trade is to remove the obstacles, political and economic, which hinder its flow. The great task of public policy is to create a framework of economic and political stability.

Trade between regions on widely different standards of living does not tend to pull down the general wage level or the labor standards of a high-standard country, but rapidly increasing labor efficiency in low-standard countries does make transitions necessary in the industrial structures of other countries. The problem must be met positively by measures, such as those promoted by the International Labour Organisation, which help to make modern labor standards follow rapidly where modern methods are being introduced and which encourage simultaneous readjustment of the industries affected in other countries. The rôle to be played by commodity control schemes is a problem of increasing importance in international trade. The main object of constructive statesmanship should be to see that such controls are operated in the social interest rather than in the interest of particular groups, which means that they must not be managed solely by or for producers.

In the future, as in the past, the world's productivity can be greatly increased by international movements of capital, but the investments of the future will, naturally, have to be of a somewhat different character and will have to take different directions from those of the past. The spread of knowledge and techniques into those regions where modern methods are not yet in use likewise offers great possibilities for improving the well-being of all countries, though it does create problems of transition that must be given attention. Wholesale migration offers little hope for constructive adjustment of economic problems today, and neither does transfer of territory from one political sovereignty to another offer any real way out of present difficulties—though both in the field of migration and in the field of colonial policy there are some things that could be done to improve the situation. Mobility of goods and capital and knowledge across political boundaries must be made to substitute for mass migration and for conquest.

International economic problems can never be "solved" once and for all. Continuous, organized coöperation, rather than one great burst of activity at a spectacular world conference is the need. Nevertheless, there are some things that might usefully be considered for the agenda of a future world economic conference, when a propitious moment comes: a symbolic act setting forth certain principles as a rallying point for economic coöperation in the future; the creation of a permanent International Economic Organization in which economic groups as well as governments would be represented; the launching of a development program designed to carry modern capital equipment and technical knowledge into parts of Asia, South America, and Africa.

Disintegration of the world economy would deprive the United States of opportunities for making the most effective use of its own resources in ways that would raise the living standards of its people. Similarly, a policy of economic nationalism by the United States would lessen its own productivity and that of the world, and would promote conflict and war all over the world by giving support to the view that with peaceful trade blocked military conquest is the only path to economic opportunity. The enormous economic power of the United States—representing something over a third of the present economic weight of the world—will make its actions or its refusals to act vital in determining whether the world economy can take a peaceful and productive course.

INDEX